Values in Sex Education

Sex education is rarely out of the news. Despite this, there exist surprisingly few studies of the principles, policies and practices of sex education. This book provides such an examination, focusing on the values to which children are exposed in sex education.

Sex education inevitably involves the transmission of values, regardless of whether this is intended by teachers. Throughout the book, academic and professional literature on both values and sex education is reviewed and discussed. The authors look at the implicit liberal values which underpin programmes of sex education and at the challenges presented by the diversity of values in contemporary societies. The book also considers:

- Why values are central to sex education.
- Children's voices and children's values.
- Religious and family values.
- Achievable aims for school sex education.
- How to help young people to reflect critically on the influences to which they are exposed and on their own developing sexual values.
- How to build values into practical approaches to sex education at both primary and secondary levels.

This timely book will help all those involved in sex education to steer a path between controversial and often opposing views and will be essential reading for students on PGCE and BEd courses. It will also be a valuable resource for teachers and professionals involved in teaching sex education such as teachers of personal and social education, form tutors, school nurses, health workers and academics.

Mark Halstead is Professor of Moral Education at the University of Plymouth. **Michael Reiss** is Professor of Science Education at the Institute of Education, University of London and is inaugural editor of the journal Sex Education.

Values in Sex Education

From principles to practice

J. Mark Halstead and
Michael J. Reiss

RoutledgeFalmer
Taylor & Francis Group

LONDON AND NEW YORK

First published 2003
by RoutledgeFalmer
11 New Fetter Lane, London EC4P 4EE

Simultaneously published in the USA and Canada
by RoutledgeFalmer
29 West 35th Street, New York, NY 10001

RoutledgeFalmer is an imprint of the Taylor & Francis Group

© 2003 J. Mark Halstead and Michael J. Reiss

Typeset in Palatino and Gill by BC Typesetting, Bristol
Printed and bound in Great Britain by
Biddles Ltd, Guildford and King's Lynn

British Library Cataloguing in Publication Data
A catalogue record for this book is available from the British Library

Library of Congress Cataloging in Publication Data
A catalog record has been requested

ISBN 0–415–23257–0 (pbk)
ISBN 0–415–23256–2 (hbk)

To Anne Outram Halstead and Jenny Chapman

Contents

PART 4

Figures

Acknowledgements

We would like to thank Sue Waite for her assistance with the research described in Chapter 3, Dr J. L. Chapman for helping to prepare the index, Alex Palmer for technical support, and our editors Alison Foyle and Jude Exley for their patience and support throughout the writing and production of the volume.

The authors are grateful for permission to reproduce the following material:

Figure 9.1: Cartoon entitled 'Condom on the Patio' reproduced by kind permission of the artist, Ros Asquith.

Figure 11.1: Taken from *Sexuality and Mental Handicap: An Educator's Resource Book* by Hilary Dixon (Cambridge: LDA, 1988) and reproduced by kind permission of the author.

Figure 12.1: Cartoon entitled 'Good Timing' taken from *Pure Posy* by Posy Simmonds (London: Methuen, 1989) and reprinted by permission of PFD on behalf of Posy Simmonds.

Part I

Chapter 1

Why values are central to sex education

Values in sex education

The central argument of this book is that values permeate every aspect of sex education in schools. It is impossible to plan or put into practice any programme of sex education without reference to values, though sometimes the values may not be brought to consciousness and made the subject of reflection. The selection of aims for sex education involves explicit or implicit value judgements, and so does the selection of content and method. The decision to provide sex education in the first place is based on the assumption that it will be valuable for children. We shall argue further that sex education involves the transmission of values, whether or not this is conscious and intentional on the teacher's part, and whether or not the values are actually accepted by the students.

In some respects, sex education is just like other subjects on the curriculum: it involves the transmission of information; it contributes to the development of personal autonomy; and it seeks to promote the interests of both the individual and the broader society. In other respects, however, sex education is quite different. It is about human relationships, and therefore includes a central moral dimension. It is about the private, intimate life of the learner and is intended to contribute to his or her personal development and sense of well-being or fulfilment. It generally involves intense emotions, to do not only with intimacy, pleasure and affection but often also with anxiety, guilt and embarrassment. In all of these respects, values are involved. We can decide what information merits transmission, what the interests of the individual and of society are, or how to reassure young people, only by making value judgements. Of course, young people recognise this, almost intuitively. As we shall see later, if students are asked what they want to learn in a sex education course, questions of values figure very highly on their lists.

Most serious books on sex education nowadays acknowledge the importance of values, though many give the topic of values in sex education comparatively brief attention before moving on to what they present as more pressing matters (e.g. Scott *et al.* 1994: 15; Ray and Went 1995: ch. 4; Harrison 2000: ch. 3). However, since the early 1990s a few contributions have appeared with a major focus on the relationship of values to sex education (Lenderyou and Porter 1994; Morris 1994; Reiss 1997a), and rather more on the educational implications of the sexual beliefs and values of religious and ethnic groups (Sarwar 1989; Brown 1993; Thomson 1993; Catholic Education Services n.d.; D'Oyen 1996; Reiss and Mabud 1998; Blake and Katrak 2002). What is still needed – and what the present book seeks to provide – is a serious investigation of the place of values in sex education, combined with an attempt to explore the implications of these values for planning and practice.

We shall argue throughout this book that it is only when we have a clear and detailed grasp of the principles that should guide sex education that we can move to effective planning and practice. As a first step, we shall argue in the remainder of this chapter that:

- the term 'values' refers to the principles by which we judge things to be good, right, desirable or worthy of respect
- an analysis of the concept of sex education reveals that values are at its core
- even if it were in some sense desirable, it would be impossible in practice to devise a value-free form of sex education
- the process of values development begins in earliest childhood and goes on throughout life whether or not the school does anything about it, but the school is uniquely placed to influence the process by providing suitable opportunities for discussion, reflection and increasing understanding
- because of the above, planners and teachers have a duty to reflect seriously on the explicit and implicit values which underpin their work, in order to ensure that they are reasonable, justifiable and in the best interests of the young people they teach.

The final section of this chapter looks more closely at the role of the school in values education in the area of sexuality, and argues that schools have three distinct duties: to uphold the values of the broader society, especially where these have emerged through open debate and the democratic search for shared values; to fill in gaps in children's knowledge and understanding, including their understanding of core values; and to encourage children to pick a rational path through the variety of influences that impinge on their experience and to construct their own developing value framework through a process of critical reflection.

What are values?

Although several surveys of values have been carried out since the early 1980s (for teenage values, see Francis and Kay 1995; for British values, see Abrams *et al.* 1985; for European values, see Barker *et al.* 1992), there is still much disagreement about the term 'values'. People disagree, for example, over whether values have universal validity, or apply only within particular cultures or traditions; whether values must be shared or are simply a matter of personal preference; whether there is a difference between private and public values; and whether there are any overarching principles by which conflicts between values may be resolved.

Warnock (1996) defines values as shared preferences; she writes, 'What we value is what we either like or dislike . . . The crucial word in this definition is *we*. In speaking of values, there is a presumption that humans . . . *share* the preferences so designated' (1996: 46, original emphases). However, this definition is open to criticism on three grounds. First, 'values' seems to refer to something more fundamental than 'preferences', as many writers have recognised; Shaver and Strong (1976), for example, define them as 'our standards and principles for judging . . . things to be good, worthwhile or desirable' (1976: 15). Second, the extent to which values have to be shared is open to debate. Certainly it makes sense to talk of 'personal values', and Raths *et al.* (1966) emphasise this personal dimension in their definition of values: 'beliefs, attitudes or feelings that an individual is proud of [and] is willing to publicly affirm' (1966: 28). On the other hand, no community can exist without some shared values, and no community activity (such as teaching or running a school) is possible either. As we shall see in Chapter 2, the biggest problem facing sex educators today is the sheer diversity of sexual values that exist in our society. Third, Warnock's definition confuses 'values' with 'valuing something'. I may value chocolate, but this does not make it one of my values. It is true that to talk of the *value* of something (as in the phrase 'value-added') has always been to talk of its worth, and that when we *value* something we are making a high estimate of its worth. However, the term *values* (in the plural) now seems to be used to refer to the criteria by which we make such value judgements, that is to the principles on which the value judgements are based.

For the purposes of the present volume we have adapted the following definition from Halstead and Taylor (2000). Values are *principles and fundamental convictions which act as general guides to behaviour; enduring beliefs about what is worthwhile; ideals for which one strives; broad standards by which particular beliefs and actions are judged to be good, right, desirable or worthy of respect.* Examples of values are love, fairness, equality, freedom, justice, happiness, security, peace of mind, truth. Values can therefore be distinguished from related and sometimes overlapping terms like 'virtues' (which are personal qualities or dispositions like truthfulness, generosity, courage, loyalty or kindness) and, to a certain extent, though there is some overlap, from 'attitudes' (which are acquired tendencies or predispositions to make judgements and behave in a predictable manner, such as openness, tolerance, respect, acceptance and freedom from prejudice).

This definition occupies the middle ground in the debate about whether values are subjective or objective. At one extreme is the view of values as a set of subjective criteria for making judgements. This may be linked to a postmodern, relativist view that no set of values can be shown to be objectively better than another. This view has sometimes been claimed to provide a useful way of resolving disputes over values in culturally plural societies: 'You have your values and I have mine'. At the other extreme is the view of values as absolute, that is, as applying everywhere and at all times. On this view, certain human actions are always right or always wrong, irrespective of circumstance. Between the two extremes is the view that certain values, such as human rights or equal opportunities, have some kind of objectivised quality, perhaps because 'some social arrangements and patterns of behaviour promote well-being more than others' (Beck 1990: 3). These values may therefore be explored in a systematic and objective fashion, though it is also acknowledged that they are socially constructed and that the extent to which they are recognised may vary over time and from one group or society to another.

It is important to note that there are different types of values. There are clearly significant distinctions between moral values, intellectual values, aesthetic values and what Dunlop (1996: 69) calls 'hedonic' values (i.e. the values of pleasurable and painful sensations). Moral values are so dominant in our thinking about sexual matters that sometimes the terms 'values' and 'moral values' are used interchangeably. But perhaps the other types of values also have some relevance to sex education. The provision of accurate, relevant information in sex education (rather than, say, propaganda) illustrates the intellectual value of truth. Archard (2000) points out that sex may sometimes be regarded as bad not just for moral reasons but because it is 'ugly, unbecoming and repellent' (2000: 20), which presumably belongs in the domain of aesthetic values. Jones (1989) puts forward as one aim for sex education 'helping people to achieve as much sexual satisfaction and pleasure as possible' (1989: 57), which illustrates hedonic values. However, values are more frequently categorised on the basis of the ideology which gives rise to them (e.g. liberal, Catholic, democratic or humanist values) or on the basis of the different disciplines or departments of life to which they belong (political, economic, spiritual, moral, social, cultural, artistic, scientific, religious, environmental or health-related values). In Part 2, where we discuss certain values in detail in relation to sex education, we use a mixture of these categories.

What is sex education?

Sex education is more than the study of human sexuality in a biology or social science course. The aim of the study of human sexuality is for students to come to know more about sex, whereas the aim of sex education extends beyond this, and includes encouraging certain kinds of skills, attitudes, dispositions, behaviour and critical reflection on personal experience. Another way of expressing this is to say that sex education must in some way be educational, and education is an inescapably value-laden activity. If we think of 'education' as the initiation of children into a programme of worthwhile activities, then, as we have seen, values provide the criteria by which we judge something to be worthwhile. If we think of 'education' as primarily concerned with the balanced development of the whole person, then it is clear that the choices that any person makes in relation to behaviour and lifestyle are shaped by values. If this is true of education, it applies all the more to sex education, for the aims, content, methods and success of sex education are all determined by values. Sex education can never be, as Jones (1989: 57) suggests it is, a matter of 'disinterested enquiry': we all have a vested interest in sex.

One way of clarifying the concept of sex education would be to ask what the characteristics of a sexually educated person would be (see Collyer 1995: 9–12). A few examples will suffice at this stage. First, a sexually educated person will have certain information – for example, how to achieve pregnancy and how to avoid it. But it is clear that deciding which information to give students (e.g. prioritising the avoidance of pregnancy over the preparation of students for the pleasures and responsibilities of parenthood) involves a value judgement. The value judgement made here may have as much to do with socio-economic values as with personal well-being. Second, a sexually educated person will have certain personal qualities – for example, appropriate self-assertiveness in resisting peer pressure and in saying 'no' to unwanted sexual experience. Behind the encouragement of personal qualities like these lie the liberal values of autonomy, equality, fairness and personal security. Third, a sexually educated person will have certain attitudes – for example, respect for people whose views differ from his or her own on controversial issues such as abortion, contraception, same-sex relationships, celibacy and divorce. Once again, these attitudes are underpinned by the liberal values of tolerance, freedom, equality and respect. Fourth, a sexually educated person will have certain skills – for example, the skill of responsible sexual decision-making. Since sexual desire usually focuses on another person, responsible sexual decision-making involves taking account of that person's needs and wishes as well as our own. It involves evaluating conflicting desires and choosing between them, respecting and being sensitive to the sexual vulnerability of others, reflecting on what we owe to others and on what we can expect from them. All of these skills are firmly grounded in moral values.

In brief, values permeate the whole process of sex education. The question therefore arises why anyone should want to try to provide value-free sex education. There are two possible answers to this question:

- because the diversity that exists in contemporary society makes a consensus on values impossible, especially in a controversial domain like sexuality (see Archard 2000: ch. 5)
- because some of the aims of sex education, notably the reduction of teenage pregnancy and the reduction of risk-taking behaviours such as exposure to disease, are so important that anything which gets in the way of the 'safer-sex' message (such as moral guidance or advice) should be discarded as more of a hindrance than a help.

The issue of values diversity is a major topic and will be discussed in detail in Chapter 2, but let us consider a number of points in response to the second statement. First, it is clear from what has already been said in this chapter that the decision to prioritise the reduction of risk-taking behaviour is itself a value judgement. Second, both the reduction in teenage pregnancy and the avoidance of infection involve values including responsibility and respect for others. For example, students need to know why it would be wrong to have unprotected sexual intercourse with someone without revealing that one was suffering from a sexually transmitted infection. Not to teach such issues as moral matters is to sell both students and society short. Third, it is not helping students to make moral decisions, but undue moralising is likely to put students off (see Warnock 1979: 89). By moralising we mean preaching, or trying to 'improve' the morals of students prescriptively by imposing specific moral values on them (as opposed to helping them to reflect on moral values and think through the implications of these values for their own lives). Fourth, where sex educators decide to adopt a 'non-judgemental' approach (though clearly they cannot be non-judgemental about rape or sexual abuse), they are making a value judgement that it is wise in certain circumstances to avoid alienating particular individuals or families through criticising particular behaviour or lifestyles. Thus non-judgemental, explicit, raunchy, non-moralising comics like *Smack in the Eye* and *Hang on, Just a Sec* may be justifiably used to develop AIDS awareness and promote condom use, but their use is not really value-free or incompatible with more overt moral education. Non-judgementalism does not imply the absence of values, and indeed, it would be dangerous if taken that way. The danger is highlighted in Nick Fisher's (1994) popular sex guide, *Your Pocket Guide to Sex*, which sets out its approach to morals under the heading 'Human Beings are Sexual Animals':

It's all perfectly natural. As in all areas of human activity, people want to make rules about sexuality. The truth is, there are no rules.

(Fisher 1994: 4)

Taken at face value and out of context, such a statement could be used to justify all kinds of sexual exploitation and abuse.

Values development in sex education

Inevitably there is a close link between the values which underpin the conceptualisation, planning and implementation of sex education and the values which are taught to students in sex education (see Halstead and Taylor 1996). Theoretically it is possible to argue that although the whole process of of sex education is value-laden, values should not be included as part of the content of sex education (see Archard 2000: ch. 7). But it is impossible in practice to keep values out of the learning process. Students in schools not only learn what they are taught, but also pick things up through the varied processes of the hidden curriculum. And if sex education is as saturated in values as we have suggested, there is nothing we can do to stop students from picking up some of these values, albeit unconsciously. This being so, we believe that sex educators have a moral responsibility to recognise the way they are influencing children's developing values and bring this influence to consciousness. This in turn enables careful reflection on the influence they are having on these developing values, in order to ensure that this influence is reasonable, justifiable and in the best interests of the children they teach.

Reluctantly or enthusiastically, therefore, one is forced to conclude that moral education (and values education more broadly) is inextricably bound up with sex education, just as it is with education in general. The key questions now are what sort of values schools should teach in sex education, and what approach they should adopt. This is not something that can be decided in a one-hour workshop (see Lenderyou and Porter 1994: 31); on the contrary, it requires detailed reflection on the nature and justifiability of the values schools may choose to teach. Part 2 of this book provides a framework for such reflection. But first we need to agree on the general approach that schools should adopt to values education. Though the process of values development begins in earliest childhood and goes on throughout life, the school is uniquely placed to influence the process by providing opportunities for discussion, reflection and increasing understanding. We argue here that schools have three distinct (and not always compatible) roles.

The first is to 'reflect the values of society, and the kind of society we want to be' (Department for Education and Employment (DfEE) 1999: 10). The school adds its voice to the other voices telling children what to think about sex. In this sense, the voice of the school goes into the child's consciousness alongside all the other influences which together form the raw material from which the individual child constructs his or her own sexual values. The influence of the school perhaps helps to counterbalance any extreme opinions and values which the child has picked up elsewhere. Its influence as a source of sexual values may not be as powerful as other influences, because it may lack their emotional impact, but the school has a responsibility to ensure that the influence it exerts is balanced, in part because it represents the official view of society. The more this influence is the result of reflection, open debate, and the democratic search for shared values, the more justifiable it is in seeking to shape children's developing values.

The second role is to fill in gaps in students' knowledge and understanding, including knowledge of the importance of values. As has already been said, school-based sex education can never have more than a limited impact on the developing sexual values of young people, because these values will have started to develop before the children begin attending school and will have developed quite fully before formal sex education begins, and throughout their school life children will continue to be influenced by other factors, including family, peers and the media. But schools have the strong advantage of being able to assess students' existing knowledge and understanding from a position of neutral expertise, and to adapt their provision in the light of emerging needs.

The third role of the school, and perhaps the most important, is to encourage children to choose a rational path through the variety of influences that impinge on their experience. Children need help to make sense of the diversity of sexual values which they have picked up from a variety of sources, and gradually, through a process of critical reflection, they will begin to shape, construct and develop their own values. The process involves sifting, evaluating, synthesising, appraising and judging, and schools are uniquely placed to develop these essential skills.

However, if teachers are to help students to become critically reflective adults capable of developing their own sexual values, this implies not only that the teachers themselves must have a clear sense of what it is to be critically reflective in the domain of sexual values, but also that they must have a good knowledge of different kinds of sexual values (and their implications for practice), experience of critical discussions of such values and the ability to relate such values to the differing needs and experiences of children *before* starting to plan any programme of sex education in practice. It is precisely the opportunity to reflect seriously and in depth on a range of different kinds of sexual values that we seek to provide in Part 2 of the present volume.

Setting the agenda

Implicit in the content of this chapter is an agenda for thinking about sex education. It would be a mistake to move into the detailed planning of a practical programme of sex education in terms of method, process, content and evaluation before identifying a clear framework, and an important part of the framework involves being clear about the aims of the activity. As we have already seen, aims imply values. Values may be implicit, but in a diverse society which demands accountability there is a need to bring them to consciousness. This is the first step in the process of reflection and justification. The starting point for this is a critical examination and discussion of the key values that underpin sexual behaviour and attitudes in contemporary society.

Before even this can take place, however, there are two preliminary issues which need to be clarified. First, we require some indication of what children need in the area of sex education, and this involves being clear about the basis on which we are judging children's needs. Different disciplines (such as psychology, sociology, biology, politics, philosophy and law) have different ways of talking about children's needs, but it is clear that the concept of 'needing something' implies both that one has not got that thing and that to obtain it would be to achieve something that is regarded as desirable – by children, parents, politicians, teachers or society at large (see Dearden 1966; Hirst and Peters 1970: 32–6). The concept of desirability brings us back to the question of values again, for to regard something as desirable is to make a positive value judgement about it, and we make such judgements on the basis of our values. But any discussion of children's needs would be unsatisfactory if it did not pay attention to children's current knowledge and understanding, their perceptions of what is practical and relevant to their own lives, their views about what they want to learn, and their existing frameworks of values (and the sources of those values – since, as we have seen, schools can never have more than a limited impact on the developing sexual values of children and young people). These considerations are not necessarily paramount (because education must aim to expand children's current levels of understanding), but it would be absurd to construct a programme of sex education which paid no attention to what children themselves have to say.

Second, we need to explore an issue that threatens to undermine the whole argument that has been constructed so far. The main reason why people are reluctant to adopt an openly values-based approach to sex education is the current lack of consensus over values. All disagreements about practice in sex education can be traced back to incompatible and conflicting values. Many people feel that the sheer diversity of values, and especially sexual values, in contemporary society makes it impossible to identify a set of values which is generally accepted as an appropriate basis for a programme of sex education. They therefore argue that it may be best to get on with vital issues such as contraception and the avoidance of infection in as value-free a way as possible.

The agenda implied in this list of requirements for the effective planning of sex education is made explicit in the remainder of the volume. In Chapter 2, we examine the impact of values diversity on the identification of values as the foundation of sex education. In Chapter 3 we listen to children's voices as they talk about their own sexual values and attitudes, the influences on their thinking about sex and their own perceptions of their current understanding and needs for further provision. These two chapters draw heavily on the findings of a research project on Values and Sex Education carried out at the University of Plymouth. Part 2 is designed to support sex educators as they explore and reflect on the values which are most frequently mentioned as relevant to sex education: liberal values generally (Chapter 4); personal well-being (Chapter 5); religious values (Chapter 6); family values (Chapter 7); and love (Chapter 8). In Part 3 we turn to the factors involved in developing a school policy for sex education, and examine how values influence both the selection of aims and the identification of an appropriate framework for sex education. Finally, Part 4 explores a range of approaches to practice that are based on a clear understanding of and commitment to core values.

Summary

1   The central argument of the book is that values permeate sex education and that sex education is essentially a form of values education. Even if it were in some sense desirable to do so, it would be impossible in practice to devise a value-free form of sex education.

2   The term 'values' refers to the principles by which we judge things to be good, right, desirable or worthy of respect. Though there are many types of values (and many ways of categorising values), moral values are the most important in relation to sex education.

3   Schools are uniquely placed to influence the process of values development by providing opportunities for discussion, reflection and increasing understanding. In particular, their role is to uphold the values of the broader society, especially where these have emerged through open debate and the democratic search

for shared values; to fill in gaps in children's knowledge and understanding, including their understanding of core values; and to encourage children to pick a rational path through the variety of influences that impinge on their experience and so construct their own developing value framework through a process of critical reflection.

4   Because of the above, planners and teachers have a duty to reflect carefully on the explicit and implicit values which underpin their work, in order to ensure that these are reasonable, justifiable and in the best interests of the children they teach.

Issues for discussion

1   (a) Where do your own values come from? (Think of the role of your family, your friends, the media, religion, school, politics and other factors.)

(b) Have your own values changed over time?

(c) How far are your own values implicit and taken for granted, and how far are they the result of careful reflection?

2   Do you think of values as having universal validity, or do they only apply within particular cultures or traditions?

3   Can schools avoid teaching values? If not, what sort of values should they teach, and how should they teach them?

4   Think of one film you have seen and one novel you have read. What sexual values do they assume, and how are the values illustrated by the behaviour of the characters?

5   What values (either explicit or implicit) underpin any programme of sex education with which you are familiar?

6   Do men and women generally have different sexual values?

7   Make a list of your own sexual values. Now write another list for someone you know well who has a quite different personality from your own. How much common ground is there between the two of you?

Further reading

For books on the place of values in education generally, see:

- Halstead, J. M. and Taylor, M. J. (eds) (1996) *Values in Education and Education in Values,* London: Falmer Press.
- Halstead, J. M. and Taylor, M. J. (2000) *The Development of Values, Attitudes and Personal Qualities: A Review of Recent Research,* Slough: NFER (National Foundation for Educational Research).
- Haydon, G. (1997) *Teaching about Values: A New Approach,* London: Cassell.

For books on values in sexual relationships, see:

- Scruton, R. (1986) *Sexual Desire: A Philosophical Investigation,* London: Weidenfeld and Nicolson.
- Wilson, J. (1995) *Love between Equals,* London: Macmillan.

For books on values in sex education, see:

- Archard, D. (2000) *Sex Education (Impact Series no. 7),* London: Philosophy of Education Society of Great Britain.
- Blake, S. and Katrak, Z. (2002) *Faith, Values and Sex and Relationships Education,* London: National Children's Bureau.
- Lenderyou, G. and Porter, M. (eds) (1994) *Sex Education, Values and Morality,* London: Health Education Authority.
- Morris, R. W. (1994) *Values in Sexuality Education: A Philosophical Study,* Lanham, MD: University Press of America.

Finally, two special issues of journals contain useful articles:

- Moral Values and Sex Education, special issue of *Journal of Moral Education* 26 (3) (September 1997) edited by M. J. Reiss.
- Sexuality and Spirituality, special issue of *International Journal of Children's Spirituality* 6 (2) (August 2001) edited by J. M. Halstead.

Chapter 2

Diversity and change in sexual attitudes and values

Lack of consensus on sexual values

The widespread support for school-based sex education among parents and others in the UK (Health Education Authority 1995) and elsewhere masks considerable disagreement about the nature, aims, content and methods of sex education. It is not just that some people have religious beliefs about sex and others do not (though, as we point out in Chapter 6, religion is a major influence on many people's thinking about sex). Nor is it simply that people occupy different positions on a continuum which has restrictive sexual ideologies at one extreme and permissive sexual ideologies at the other (see McKay 1997). When it comes to opinions about sex, people all too often inhabit different worlds, speak different languages, hold incompatible and widely divergent views. The situation is further complicated by differences compounded by gender, social class, culture and other factors, and by the existence of numerous pressure groups, each with a different agenda, and often each talking at cross-purposes with the others, vying for influence in sex education policy.

In view of this, it is not surprising that sex education has become one of the most contentious areas of the curriculum, with disagreements surfacing at the most fundamental level. For some people, sex education is primarily about safer sex, and the effectiveness of a sex education programme may be judged in terms of the extent to which it leads to increased condom use (Harvey 1993). For others, it is about empowering young people by increasing their freedom to make competent choices about their own sexual behaviour (Archard 2000: 45), or helping young people to understand 'the importance of marriage for family life, stable and loving relationships, respect, love and care' (DfEE 2000a: 5), or helping people to satisfy their sexual needs (Harris 1971: 9), or increasing understanding and acceptance of 'differences in sexual norms and practices' (Sex Education Forum 1992), or enjoining 'chastity and virginity before marriage and fidelity within marriage' (Mabud 1998: 124, 131), or developing a greater sense of style, satisfaction or fun in sexual relations

(Wilson 1965: 145; Jones 1989: 57), or encouraging 'a confident search for a partner for life, respect for whom demands the control of one's short term desires' (Riches 1998: 49). A fuller, more considered discussion of the aims of sex education is provided in Chapter 9. But even a relatively uncontroversial aim for sex education, like encouraging responsible sexual behaviour (Reiss 1995: 377f), may be subject to quite different interpretations: for one person it might be a matter of wearing a condom, for another it might include not being in the same room as a member of the opposite sex without a chaperone.

It is our belief that practically all disagreements about aims and practices in sex education can be traced back to conflicting values. In 1994, for example, there was extensive media coverage when it came to light that during a sex education lesson in a Leeds primary school for children aged 9 to 11 a school nurse had answered questions about oral sex and 'Mars bar parties' and had involved the children in role-playing an extra-marital love triangle (Meikle 1994). But behind the arguments about content and method lay serious disagreements over the values which should underpin sex education lessons. The nurse concerned, and the parents, teachers and governors who supported her, stressed the values of openness, honesty and frankness in answering children's questions (Burstall 1994), whereas those who complained about her approach, including some parents and politicians, placed more value on the preservation of children's innocence (White 1994). The same year, a pocket sex guide for the 16–25 age group (Fisher 1994), commissioned by the Health Education Authority, was withdrawn on the orders of the then Health Minister Brian Mawhinney because he thought it was 'smutty' and 'distasteful'. Once again there was a fundamental clash of values between those who thought that the book's unpatronising language would give it 'street-cred' among its target readership and those who saw it as pornographic and subversive (see Connolly 1994). In a US court case (Brown v. Hot, Sexy and Safer Productions, Inc. 1996), two male students claimed they had been humiliated and intimidated by the explicit nature of a safer-sex assembly presentation at their school involving suggestive skits, simulated masturbation and 'lewd language' (Zirkel 1996). What all of these examples show is that people come to the topic of sex education with widely divergent expectations based on differing and apparently incompatible frameworks of values.

Teachers thus find themselves on the horns of a dilemma. On the one hand, if the arguments in Chapter 1 are correct, sex education is centrally and inescapably a value-laden activity, and it is the role of schools to influence and, to some extent, reflect the values of society. The National Curriculum emphasises the importance of recognising 'a broad set of common values and purposes that underpin the school curriculum and the work of schools' (Qualifications and Curriculum Authority (QCA)

1999: 10). On the other hand, there is a greater diversity of sexual values in contemporary society than ever before, and this diversity means that there is little agreement over the values that should underpin sex education. However convinced teachers of sex education are of the profound importance of the topic for schools, they therefore face uncertainty about what values should underpin the planning of sex education and what values, if any, should be taught to children. Undoubtedly this is the main reason for the comparative neglect of the topic of values in sex education that was mentioned in Chapter 1.

In this chapter we explore the dilemma more fully and seek for ways of resolving it. In the next two sections we review the two main causes of the increased diversity of sexual values. The first is the combination of technological and social change which has ushered in new sexual attitudes and patterns of behaviour among many (but not all) groups and individuals in the western world since the early 1950s. The second is the impact of cultural, political and religious diversity. In the following section, we examine a number of unsatisfactory responses to the dilemma about values: abandoning sex education altogether; attempting a 'value-free' form of sex education; adopting a monocultural framework of values; and emphasising only neutral, 'enabling' values rather than more substantive moral ones. In the final section, we attempt to turn the dilemma on its head by arguing that diversity may be seen as a strength rather than a problem, in that it forces us to explore alternatives, to reflect, to evaluate. It also forces us to recognise that what we need most is a set of justifiable, defensible values arrived at through rational debate and democratic discussion. We also need to recognise the importance of respecting minorities who do not share the common values. This chapter provides the basis for the systematic examination of values relevant to sex education in Part 2.

Changes in sexual attitudes and values since the early 1950s

There is strong evidence to support the claim that sexual values, attitudes and behaviours have changed more and become more diverse in the United Kingdom and other western countries in the last half-century than they did in the previous five hundred. The development and increased availability of the birth control pill has been described as 'the defining event' of the second half of the twentieth century (Gelles 1995). By breaking the natural link between sexual activity and reproduction, the contraceptive pill had a dramatic impact on everyday life: reproduction became for many people a matter of choice and family planning, and the sexual revolution of the 1960s, with its emphasis on recreational and promiscuous sex, was ushered in. The combination of these two facts has had two opposing consequences. On the one hand, since the post-war baby boom, families have tended to become smaller, with many people postponing having a family and a growing number of women reaching the age of 40 without having conceived. On the other hand, young people have tended to become sexually active earlier than in previous generations, and there has been a corresponding growth in the number of teenage pregnancies and in pregnancies outside marriage (and in social acceptance of these). Cherlin (1996) links this tendency to the 'deregulation of intimate unions', including the blurring of the legal and social boundaries between marriage and cohabitation (1996: 498f). Thomson (1997) draws attention to the expansion of the period of adolescence that has occurred as a result of the earlier onset of puberty and the delay of the economic independence required for long-term commitments such as marriage and parenting (1997: 258). Teenage pregnancy in turn has led to a conservative backlash of blame and demonisation (Selman and Glendinning 1996).

Four other crucial factors have affected this overall picture of contemporary sexual attitudes and behaviour. The first is the general if uneven decline in the influence of religion on sexual behaviour. The second is the legalisation of abortion in the UK and other western countries, and the dramatic subsequent rise in the number of abortions. The third is the rapid spread of HIV and AIDS in many countries of the world since the late 1980s, which has had a powerful impact on many people's lives, has led to significant changes in both public health policy and sex education, and has brought about lasting changes in sexual behaviour and attitudes to 'unprotected sex'. Fourth, massive advances have been made in reproductive technology, and expected future developments in biotechnology have the potential to transform many aspects of human sexuality (see Goldman and Bradley 2001: 200–2).

Alongside the flight from marriage and the growth in the number (and acceptance) of single-parent families and other non-traditional families, there have been changing expectations of marriage and partnership. Under the influence of feminism, gender roles have become less clear-cut as many women have attained a degree of economic independence, and the traditional breadwinner–homemaker bargain between men and women is in rapid decline. The greater emphasis on equality within marriage or cohabitation may have led more couples to expect companionship, respect, emotional support, individual fulfilment and long-term sexual satisfaction from their relationships. More marriages have been breaking down in divorce (and even more partnerships breaking up) when these highly personalised expectations have not been achieved or maintained. Most forms of legal discrimination against children born outside wedlock have been abandoned in most western countries. Gay and lesbian sexuality has become much more visible and much more widely accepted; undoubtedly the gradual decline of discrimination, prejudice and injustice directed against homosexuals has been helped by positive representations of homosexuality in the media and by a range of equal opportunities policies. Similarly, transsexuals are gradually gaining wider recognition. On the other hand, there is a growing sense of outrage at child sexual abuse and domestic violence, and a growing bewilderment when such abuse and violence are perpetrated by children themselves (Masson 1995).

A further feature of the changing sexual values and attitudes in western societies has been the growing openness about sexuality, particularly in the media. The failed prosecution of Penguin Books in 1961 for publishing D. H. Lawrence's novel *Lady Chatterley's Lover* proved a major turning point in the freedom of the press to publish material with a strongly sexual content, and in the decades since 1961, novels, magazines, television, films, the tabloid press, the music industry and advertisements have all seen an increase in their sexual content and in the degree of sexual explicitness they permit. For example, a study of *Cosmopolitan* magazine over a twelve-year period found that virtually all the articles dealt directly or indirectly with sex and that many of the visual images were sexually provocative (McMahon 1990). There are many consequences of this greater openness about sexuality in the media:

- Sex has been demystified, the romanticisation of sexuality is in decline and sex has become more closely linked with entertainment.
- Sex is increasingly viewed as an important part of human life ('Are you getting enough?') and as an important component of self-identity ('Do you think I'm sexy?').
- Pornography has become more widely available, particularly on videos and on the Internet, and more acceptable in many circles (as well as more accessible to children). Sex, we are told, is the top search word on the Internet (Goldman and Bradley 2001: 203).
- Culture more generally has been sexualised: sex is depicted, talked about and alluded to everywhere; it sells commodities and is itself treated as a commodity (Archard 2000: 10).
- There is an increased sophistication in the sexual knowledge of children and young people, with television in particular making accessible to children the secrets that adults used to keep to themselves. While Postman's claims about the 'disappearance of childhood' (1983) may be exaggerated, it is true that children nowadays are encouraged to present themselves as sexual beings at an ever younger (and thus arguably more vulnerable) age.

These changes have affected the attitudes and behaviour of many, but not all, individuals in the west, and this is a major cause of the increased diversity of sexual values. Several social theorists have tried to characterise the dominant sexual mores of contemporary society taking into account the changes described above, but with only limited success. In his book *The Transformation of Intimacy*, for example, Giddens states:

> 'Sexuality' today has been discovered, opened up and made accessible to the development of varying lifestyles. It is something that each of us 'has', or cultivates, no longer a natural condition which an individual accepts as a preordained state of affairs.
>
> (Giddens 1992: 15)

Sexuality, he argues, has become 'plastic' – in other words, a 'malleable feature of self, a prime connecting point between body, self-identity and social norms' (Giddens 1992: 15), through which a kind of personal autonomy marked out by the 'radical democratisation' of personal life can be achieved (1992: 188ff). Sexual relationships have largely freed themselves from external social expectations and constraints, and are entered into for their own sake and continued only in so far as they are 'thought by both parties to deliver enough satisfactions for each individual to stay in [them]' (1992: 58). This kind of 'pure relationship' involves 'confluent love', a love which is distinguished by mutual intimacy and the full equality of the partners (1992: 61ff). In such relationships, he argues, traditional norms and moral codes are irrelevant:

> No limits are set upon sexual activity, save for those entailed by the generalising of the principle of autonomy and by the negotiated norms of the pure relationship. Sexual emancipation consists in integrating plastic sexuality with the reflexive project of self.
>
> (Giddens 1992: 194)

Three factors, however, militate against this rather neat reassessment of sexual values, which Giddens would like to suggest is both 'deep-lying' and 'irreversible' (1992: 28):

- Relationships are rarely as 'pure' (in Giddens' sense of 'free from external constraints') as he makes out. For example, when a relationship no longer delivers enough satisfactions for the individuals concerned to stay within it, all too often the separating parties bring children (and sometimes aged parents or other relatives) with them into their new sexual relationships and the responsibility to care for such dependants introduces an element of external moral constraint into the relationship.

- As has already been pointed out, the speed and character of the changes described in this section have been such that they have not carried everyone with them, perhaps not even the majority. Many people retain the traditional values which Giddens discards, and though television (and the media more generally) is a great leveller, some people have managed to maintain a critical approach to the values which it espouses and promotes.
- The increasing political, cultural, ethnic and religious diversity in the west has had a further diversifying influence on sexual values. As Weeks (1995) points out,

> The contemporary sexual world appears as irrevocably pluralistic, divided into a host of sovereign units, and a multiplicity of sites of authority . . . There is no longer a hegemonic discourse telling how we should behave.
>
> (Weeks 1995: 27)

We discuss this factor more fully in the next section.

Political, cultural and religious diversity

Some of the strongest opposition to school sex education has come from right-wing thinkers who claim that contemporary sex education subverts the law, or that it damages family values, or that it encourages behaviour which results in outcomes (including teenage pregnancy and sexually transmitted infections) that are a drain on the public purse (Whitehead 1994; Whelan 1995; Riches 1998). In the USA, but not so much in the UK, political conservatives have tended to support abstinence-based sex education programmes such as *Sex Respect* and *True Love Waits*, which have had a significant impact since the mid-1980s (Landry *et al.* 1999). Liberal critics, who place more emphasis on encouraging free, informed and responsible choice about sexual matters, sometimes dismiss the promotion of abstinence as a form of 'unethical manipulation' (Massey 1990: 138), but Lickona (1991) attempts to justify the approach by emphasising the need for young people to internalise values such as self-control and protection against damaging emotions such as loss, guilt, betrayal and the feeling of being used (1991: 354f). The liberal perspective is explored more fully in Chapter 4.

One particular political pressure group that has had significant success in recent years in arguing the justice of its cause (often with the support of liberals) has been the gay and lesbian movement, which has campaigned in the name of homosexual equality for the equalisation of the age of consent, the recognition of same-sex partnerships, protection against job discrimination on the grounds of sexual orientation and more generally for the acceptance of homosexuality as a worthy alternative life-style. So successful has this campaign been, and so prolific the writing by its protagonists, that the term 'diversity' in the context of sex education is now sometimes used exclusively in the sense of 'diversity of sexual orientation' (Atkinson 2002). The educational implications of this campaign fall into two related categories: meeting the specific needs of gay and lesbian pupils (for example, by ensuring that library books and textbooks provide honest and non-stereotyped representations of homosexuality and that issues relevant to the lives of gay and lesbian pupils are addressed where appropriate across the curriculum) and developing appropriate attitudes towards homosexuality among all pupils (for example, by challenging homophobia, and providing balanced and accurate information and a positive school ethos).

Cultural values (such as beliefs about marriage and family life, romantic love or the importance of sexual pleasure) may be linked to social class, ethnic origin, religious belief and other factors. There is much research still to be done on the relationship between social class and sexual values, but the relationship between religious belief and sexual values has been studied much more fully. As we point out in Chapter 6, different religions uphold widely differing sexual values, and there is rarely consensus on values even within a single religious tradition (to say nothing of consistency between teaching and practice). The growth of ethnic diversity in western societies since the early 1950s has also increased the diversity of sexual values and behaviours, as well as the possibility of misunderstanding and lack of trust. In some cases this has led groups to exercise their right to withdraw their children from sex education classes (see Mabud 1998: 121, 130).

Often the diversity which has been the topic of this section results in serious disagreement and conflict between different sectors of society – between conservatives and liberals, between members of religious faiths and those who have no religious beliefs, between those who support the rights of gays and lesbians and those whose religion dismisses homosexuality as an abomination. These clashes make it all the more important to respond with careful critical reflection and democratic discussion to any claims that are put forward in support of any particular approach to the planning of sex education. In the next section we examine a number of unsatisfactory responses to the problem of the diversity of sexual values.

Unsatisfactory responses to change and diversity

At the end of the introductory section to this chapter we highlighted a dilemma faced by sex educators: that values are an unavoidable part of sex education, but at the same time there is such a diversity of sexual values in contemporary western societies that a consensus seems hard to achieve. In this section we examine four unsatisfactory ways of resolving this dilemma.

Abandoning school-based sex education

After its extensive debate on sex education in 1994, the Muslim Parliament of Great Britain passed a resolution to the effect that Muslim children 'would be better off without the sex education presently offered in state schools'. Pressure groups promoting conservative family values have sometimes reached the same conclusion, arguing that sex education is in much safer hands if it is left up to parents. It is also sometimes argued that young children have a natural innocence which may be prematurely lost as a result of lessons designed to raise their sexual awareness (see Collyer 1995: 27–9).

However, even if one accepts the debatable point that children should be protected from exposure to values different from those of their parents, there is no point in abandoning school-based sex education unless it can be shown not only that parents can make adequate alternative provision, but also that this would indeed protect children from contact with unacceptable values. In fact, both of these are problematic. First, though parents are normally the most natural and most important sex educators of their children, they generally lack the specialist resources and training of the school and may not always be in the best position to appreciate the influences to which their children are subject as they grow older. Second, withdrawing children from sex education classes does not in itself protect them from exposure to values unacceptable to their parents, for formal sex education classes probably contribute only a small amount of the learning about sexual values that goes on in school. As we shall see in Chapter 3, even very young children pick up a lot of information about sex from their peers – in the playground, through sharing magazines, and through the hidden curriculum generally, though the learning may be haphazard and inaccurate. Television and other media are also a major source of sexual knowledge and values which parents cannot easily control. In any case, the answer is not necessarily to attempt an even tighter control of everything the children see and hear. As Collyer (1995: 28) points out, the quality of innocence should not be confused with ignorance. The sexual abuse of children is more likely to thrive where they are kept in ignorance about sexual matters. Formal sex education responds to these challenges not by trying to protect children from the influence of peers or television but by developing their ability to reflect critically on the sexual values to which they are exposed in the broader society and to deconstruct the sexual messages of television and advertising. Indeed, developing the capacity for such critical reflection is what education is centrally about.

Developing 'value-free' sex education

As we have seen in Chapter 1, this view seeks to restrict sex education to imparting knowledge to children about reproduction and related matters. The approach assumes that 'facts' are separable from 'values' and that whereas sexual 'facts' should be taught by the school nurse or biology teacher, sexual 'values' are the responsibility of the parents, or the place of worship, or of the children themselves (if 'values' are viewed as personal matters which should not be 'imposed' by anyone: see Warnock 1979: 89).

There are two main problems with this approach. First, as we have seen, it is impossible to impart knowledge without at least an implicit values framework. But if the values are unacknowledged (and thus left at the implicit level) and there is no systematic discussion of the values involved, then children are more likely to develop their values in a haphazard manner. Indeed, it is not uncommon for the values which pupils develop in school to be different from those the school intends (see Halstead 1996a). Second, if children are not given direct guidance and help in school but are left to pick up their values as and when they can, this may leave them open to manipulation at the hands of those less concerned for their well-being than the school is. This vulnerability among pupils suggests that it should be a high priority for the values of the school to be explored and articulated, rather than left within the hidden curriculum, so that teachers may have confidence in offering guidance to pupils. Research suggests that many student teachers currently consider themselves inadequately prepared to teach values, and lack confidence in this area (Arnot 1996). Yet in the early 1980s, Lee (1983) warned of the dangers of the 'ostrich position', which involves a refusal to take on contentious issues or to discuss the conflicting and confusing emotions and values that sexual matters generate.

Teaching monocultural sex education

The attempt to teach sex education in a monocultural way, regardless of the diversity of sexual values that exists in our society, takes two main forms. The first is the abstinence-based programmes mentioned earlier in the chapter (see also Chapter 9). The second is programmes based on a particular substantive framework of cultural values, such as those that claim to be 'in accordance with the teachings of the church'. The problem comes with such programmes if they are taught in a closed way which does not respect the future autonomy of the child. In this case, sex education would be in danger of becoming indoctrinatory. We believe that parents have the right to choose a religious education for their children, and that faith schools have the right to teach and guide children in line with their own distinctive beliefs and values. But the children must nonetheless be free to choose whether or not to make those beliefs and values their own, and freedom to choose implies a knowledge of alternatives. In any case, if they are to live as effective citizens of a diverse society, they need to know something of the values of those outside their own faith. There is little point in hiding from children the reality of differing sexual values in society, especially in an age where they are given so much sexual information through the media.

Emphasising 'enabling' values

Some sex educators argue that schools should promote 'enabling' rather than 'prescriptive' values in sex education (Lenderyou 1995: 54ff; Ray and Went 1995: 27; Thomson 1997: 265ff), where 'enabling' suggests positive, inclusive values like tolerance, equal opportunities and respect for difference that empower children to make full use of their individual freedom and choice. This approach thus tends towards a philosophy of neutrality and relativism, recognising as equally valid a wide diversity of sexual beliefs, values, practices and identities.

The approach is initially seductive, especially when it is presented as the only alternative to a closed, monocultural approach, because it seeks to avoid controversy and confrontation in a pluralist society. But is it really possible to teach sex education in this way? First, we must note that the neutrality would not extend to rape, child abuse or the exploitation of others. There are certain fundamental values on which our society is based, such as human rights, equality and respect for persons (see Chapter 4), which would be undermined if a neutral or tolerant attitude were adopted to such actions. Second, there are certain qualities of character which are highly valued in our society which teachers are not expected to be neutral about. It is not a matter of indifference to most parents whether their children grow up caring or uncaring, responsible or irresponsible, sexist or non-sexist. Such personal qualities are very relevant to sexual attitudes and behaviour. Third, the wisdom of encouraging children to make all moral choices for themselves, particularly in the sexual domain, before they have developed the maturity of judgement and breadth of knowledge, understanding and insight to do so with confidence, is certainly open to question. Many people believe that children need moral guidance, confidence and a stable base for their own lives if they are to grow into mature and responsible adults, and this is unlikely to be achieved through an exclusive stress on 'enabling' values.

The search for defensible values

Any adequate response to the dilemma facing sex educators must follow a careful path between a value-free approach, a monocultural approach and an approach based purely on 'enabling' values. In this final section, we argue that some of the lessons learned from multicultural education since the mid-1970s are relevant to sex education, and that what was presented as an impasse in previous sections can actually be viewed as an advantage. This is because the diversity of sexual values in contemporary society forces us to explore alternatives, to engage in rational debate and demo-cratic discussion, to reflect, to evaluate, and to be open to new (but not unlimited) possibilities.

There are three different categories of values in the sexual domain, which raise different issues. The first is a set of fundamental sexual values that can justifiably be insisted on as universal principles, such as the unacceptability of rape, child abuse or exploitation. These sexual values are shared by virtually everyone, and are often embedded in law. They are based on core liberal values such as freedom, human rights, equality and respect for persons. The second is a much larger set which we may call 'common values'. In a monocultural society these may be simply taken for granted as applicable to all, but in a multicultural society they can be arrived at only through a process of reflection and discussion in the light of the democratic values which are actually shared by all citizens. These values may not command a full consensus, but represent a working agreement which satisfies most people most of the time (see Lenderyou 1995: 51). Thus Catholics might not share the general view that contraception is morally acceptable and that masturbation is normal and harmless, but they would not seek to impose their beliefs and values on the broader society. A working framework of justifiable and defensible common values must be identified and articulated if effective programmes of sex education are to be produced in a multicultural society. The third category consists of controversial values, where there is a fundamental and irreconcilable disagreement between groups. This occurs, for example, on the issue of the moral acceptability of homosexual acts. Of course, there is debate about what belongs in the second and what in the third category, and judgements about this may change with changing circumstances.

The response of sex education to the first and third categories is clear. Sex educators in the common school (i.e. a school which is open to all students irrespective of religion, ethnicity, gender or social class, and which seeks to provide a common educational entitlement to all students: see McLaughlin 1995) must uphold the universal sexual values of category one. They must adopt a neutral stance to the diversity of values in cate-gory three (so long as these are not in conflict with the universal values), encouraging individuals to develop an attitude of tolerance, respect and understanding towards people who have category three values different from their own. But the second category is more complicated. It is important because without it the first category does not provide a framework of values that is substantial enough to underpin a programme of sex education, but as already pointed out, it can be identified only through reflection and democratic discussion. The values must be demonstrably rational and defensible, and must command reasonably widespread support. We argue both that sex educators themselves must reflect critically on this category of values, and that part of sex education involves helping pupils to do the same. We believe that so long as teachers remain neutral about fundamental disagreements and respectful of diversity, the first two categories together provide a strong foundation for a values-based approach to sex education.

In Part 2 we provide a systematic examination of some of the main kinds of justifiable, defensible common values that might provide the basis for sex education. In Chapter 4 we look at liberal values, to see if a fuller range of sexual values can be derived from a general liberal position (in addition to the universal principles that are embedded in law). Of particular relevance here are personal autonomy, the avoidance of harm, honesty, respect for others, personal responsibility and non-exploitation in sexual relationships. In Chapter 5, we examine the values of happiness, pleasure and well-being. In Chapter 6, we consider the role of religion in shaping sexual values and behaviour. In Chapter 7, we explore family values and in Chapter 8 the value of love in personal and sexual relationships.

Before we proceed to Part 2, however, there are a couple of final points. First, it is important that the needs and interests of those children who belong to minority groups that do not accept the common framework of values are not neglected. While, in the west, some Muslims and other minority faiths will be happy to accept the threefold categorisation of values set out above and to take part in the democratic discussions of common values, others will find the whole structure alien. For them, the basis of fundamental sexual values lies in 'the idea of accountability to God' (Islamic Academy 1991: 4), and children should be taught the need for obedience to divinely ordained rules relating to sexual behaviour. The only areas where there is room for discussion and debate is cultural matters like family honour and arranged marriages. We believe that so long as they do not conflict with any universal values, these beliefs must be respected. In practice, such respect involves not putting children from minority faiths in the position where they are expected to act contrary to their own deeply held beliefs, and not contradicting the beliefs and values which they have internalised as part of their religious or cultural identity. Of course, the children need to be taught about the beliefs,

values and practices of other groups, and about the need for respect, tolerance, understanding and acceptance, but schools have no mandate to
undermine or ridicule the values of minority faiths. Respecting minority
values in sex education might include checking materials used to ensure
that they would not be considered immodest, indecent or sinful, and
ensuring that minority perspectives on contraception, abortion and other
controversial issues are presented alongside the dominant values of
society (see Halstead 1997).

In addition to listening to minority voices, however, it is important to
listen to children. In the past, children's needs, wishes and values have
been largely defined by the experts in child development. However,
Thomson (1997) warns of the danger of 'leaving the experiences and
voices of young people out of the debate over values in sex education', so
that 'the debate becomes a battle between different adult groups over
their preferred vision' (1997: 267). In recent years there has been a greater
willingness to listen directly to children, and we believe that this is an
important part of the process of critical reflection. We turn to this topic in
the next chapter.

Summary

1   If sex education is inescapably a value-laden activity, the wide-
    spread disagreements that exist over sexual values create a
    dilemma for teachers: without a fair level of agreement on under-
    lying values it is difficult for them to carry out their work
    effectively.

2   Dramatic changes have occurred in sexual attitudes and values
    since the early 1950s as a result of increasingly effective contra-
    ception, the growth of reproductive technology, the decline in
    the influence of religion on sexual values, changing attitudes to
    marriage and cohabitation, the growing sexualisation of culture
    and many other factors. However, many people still retain more
    traditional sexual values.

3   Increasing political, cultural, ethnic and religious diversity has
    had a further diversifying influence on sexual values.

4   It is unsatisfactory to respond to the dilemma facing teachers by
    abandoning school-based sex education altogether, by develop-
    ing 'value-free' sex education, by attempting to teach sex
    education from a monocultural perspective or by emphasising
    'enabling' values at the expense of more substantive ones.

5 We argue that some sexual values are so fundamental that they must be insisted on as universal principles. Others, which we call 'common values' can only be arrived at through a process of reflection and discussion. A third category is made up of values on which there is irreconcilable disagreement. In the last case, teachers must be neutral and respectful of diversity, but the first two categories together form a strong foundation for a values-based approach to sex education.

Issues for discussion

1 Is there a generation gap in sexual attitudes and values? To provide support for your response, try to discuss sexual values with someone of a different generation from yourself.
2 Should sex education protect children's innocence? What are the implications of this?
3 Are there limits to what should be tolerated in sexual attitudes and behaviour? How are the limits to be defined?
4 Does pornography subvert sexual values, or is it a useful outlet for sexual fantasy? How do you respond if you find that students have been watching pornographic videos or accessing pornographic websites?
5 How far is neutrality an appropriate response for a teacher in a class where there is a diversity of sexual values and attitudes? What alternatives to neutrality are there?
6 Is it possible to meet the needs of all students through a common programme of sex education?

Further reading

For investigations into the contemporary state of sexual values, see:

• Giddens, A. (1992) *The Transformation of Intimacy: Sexuality, Love and Eroticism in Modern Societies*, Cambridge: Polity Press.
• Weeks, J. (1995) *Invented Moralities: Sexual Values in an Age of Uncertainty*, Cambridge: Polity Press.

For a variety of perspectives on the impact of culture and values diversity on education, see:

- Leicester, M., Modgil, C. and Modgil, S. (eds) (2000) *Education, Culture and Values* (Vols I–VI), London: Falmer Press. In addition to many articles on values in education generally, these volumes contain a few articles on values in sex education.

For examples of the diversity of sexual values in an educational context, see:

- Reiss, M. J. and Mabud, S. A. (eds) (1998) *Sex Education and Religion,* Cambridge: Islamic Academy.
- Thomson, R. (ed.) (1993) *Religion, Ethnicity and Sex Education: Exploring the Issues – A Resource for Teachers and Others Working with Young People,* London: National Children's Bureau.

For ways of responding to the diversity of sexual values, see:

- Halstead, J. M. (2000a) 'Developing a values framework for sex education in a pluralist society', in M. Leicester, C. Modgil and S. Modgil (eds) *Moral Education and Pluralism,* London: Falmer Press.
- McKay, A. (1997) 'Accommodating ideological pluralism in sexuality education', *Journal of Moral Education* 26: 285–300.
- Thomson, R. (1997) 'Diversity, values and social change: renegotiating a consensus on sex education', *Journal of Moral Education* 26: 257–71.

Chapter 3

Children's voices and children's values

Why it is important to listen to children

At the end of the previous chapter we wrote of the need to listen to children's voices as they talk about their own sexual values and attitudes, the influences on their thinking about sex, and their perceptions of their own developmental needs in relation to sex education. There is a growing trend in some areas of educational research to value children's perspectives and to support their right to be heard (John 1996; Alderson 2000; Bosacki and Ota 2000), but this trend has not been a major feature of research into sex education until recently. We argue that there are in fact many reasons why we should pay attention to what children say about sex and sex education:

- Children can clarify what they want to learn in sex education (and when and how they want to be taught it). Of course this is not the only factor sex educators should take into account in their planning, but, if nothing else, pupils' motivation will increase dramatically if planning does take account of their self-determined needs and wishes.
- It is difficult to ensure that sex education is 'tailored not only to the age but also to the understanding of pupils' (Department for Education (DfE) 1994) without some insight into children's existing attitudes, values and conceptual schema.
- If children tell us about the sexual understanding and values they have already picked up, this helps us to predict how they will experience and interpret the sex education they are given
- If teachers are to help children to reflect critically, it is helpful to have some knowledge of the values, attitudes and understanding that they have started to pick up in the course of their everyday lives, and of the main influences on those developing values.
- Other sources of information about children's sexual values (such as teenage magazines) are mediated through adults and therefore defined in adult terms or in line with adult values. Sometimes this is inevitable

and in the children's best interests; for example, when Rogers and Rogers (1999) ask 'What is good and bad sex for children?', the concepts used may be too difficult for children to handle clearly. But on other occasions when adults speak on behalf of children, the freshness of the children's perspective may be lost.

- In any case, children have a right to be heard, and listening to them is an important way of showing them respect.

Research into children's values is always difficult, and when it is combined with a controversial topic like sex education, it is hard to imagine a more complex and sensitive area for research than children's developing sexual values and attitudes. No doubt this explains the dearth of research in the area. The only research project of which we are aware which involved listening to children talking about their own sexual values and attitudes was funded by the University of Plymouth and carried out by one of us in the late 1990s among 9 and 10 year olds in primary schools in the south-west of England (Halstead and Waite 2001a, 2001b). This research is the main focus of this chapter. The topic of values and attitudes was specifically excluded from Goldman and Goldman's major study of the sexual thinking of children aged 5–15 in Australia, North America, England and Sweden (1982: 20–2, 57) and they described it as a 'difficult and unresolved issue' (Goldman and Goldman 1988: 236–40). Other smaller studies with primary school children have tended to focus mainly on identifying what the children already know about sex, so that any gaps can be filled (for example, Collyer 1995). Research carried out by Bourne (1995) in the London Borough of Enfield sought to 'establish what primary pupils understand about the concepts underlying the sexual transmission of diseases, in order to inform sex education in the primary school' (1995: 3), but it did move into the domain of values when the children were asked to draw and write about 'how people use their bodies to show people they love them' (1995: 10–13).

Sexuality research at secondary level tends to fall into three categories:

- Studies that focus on developing gender awareness and power relations between young men and women (see, for example, Francis 1997; Kehily and Nayak 1997; Baxter 2002).
- Studies of young people's values generally, including their sexual values (for a large-scale survey of teenage values in Britain, see Francis and Kay 1995; for a qualitative examination of teenage girls' values in the USA, see Orenstein 1995).
- Studies of young people's experiences of sex education (see, for example, MORI 1991; Woodcock et al. 1992; Lees 1994; Measor et al. 2000). Among the most important findings that these different studies share are that girls and boys talk about sexuality in different ways and that

both sexes (but especially the girls) considered there to be inadequate coverage of feelings and emotions. For example, Measor *et al.* report students as saying that 'there was no chance to talk about the feelings' and 'they tell us about the danger, never the love and enjoyment' (2000: 123, 126).

Not all research into children's attitudes involves listening to children. For example, we came across one book which in spite of its title *Talking with Children* was based entirely on the views and experiences of adults (Kitzinger and Kitzinger 1989). But even where data are gathered from children, they may not be free to decide for themselves what they want to talk about, or how to express their ideas. Surveys utilising question-naires usually force children to respond to an agenda of questions pre-determined by adults. Often the atmosphere in a classroom inhibits children from expressing their views on sex freely and openly, or in language they feel comfortable with. 'Listening to children' implies a particular research methodology which allows children to speak openly about things that are on their mind and to expect a sympathetic and respectful response. The next section considers how the principle of respecting children affects the details of research planning and research methodology.

Listening to children: research methodology

The research which is the focus of the remainder of this chapter took place in the late 1990s in two primary schools in socially disadvantaged loca-tions in the south-west of England, one a large city school and the other a smaller school on the outskirts of a generally more prosperous town. It involved Year 5 pupils (aged 9–10) who had not been taught sex educa-tion in school (see Halstead and Waite 2001a, 2001b). The research had the following aims:

- to explore children's ways of thinking about sexuality and relationships
- to identify the values and attitudes implicit in these ways of thinking
- to explore how meanings and values are negotiated and constructed through family relationships, through interactions with peers, through the influence of the media and other external sources, and through discussion and reflection
- to consider the extent to which the taken-for-granted values which lie behind the sex education which children are offered in their final year of primary school (i.e. at the ages of 10–11) are in line with their devel-oping sexual values and attitudes.

The methodology adopted included a number of features designed to demonstrate respect for the children whose opinions, attitudes and values were being explored. First, an ethical code was devised and discussed with the children. This clarified issues of confidentiality and anonymity, the obtaining of permission to carry out the research, the right of the children to confide in their class teacher about any issue that was raised, their right to withdraw from the research at any time, and the responsibilities of the researchers if revelations of abuse occurred. Detailed advance planning of the activities and research techniques was a further way of reassuring the children (and their parents) about the research, so that they knew precisely what information was wanted and why the research was being carried out. The children's permissions were also obtained for their oral contributions to be taped and later transcribed.

Second, the children were seen in discussion groups of six to eight pupils, with each meeting lasting about 45 minutes. This was thought to be less threatening than individual interviews, and enabled the children to take a greater lead in the discussions with less input from the researcher. In any case, we were interested in relationships and interactions and observing how meanings were negotiated between children. In the first school, one all-male, one all-female and one mixed group were chosen at random from the register. However, the mixed group appeared to be less comfortable for the children, and they were unable to discuss issues as freely. At the second school therefore the teacher allocated four single-sex groups (two all-male and two all-female). The groupings remained constant throughout the visits to help build up a relationship of trust with and between the pupils. As the data show, sometimes the boys' and girls' groups expressed very similar opinions, sometimes they appeared to be living on different planets (the gender differences are discussed more fully in Halstead and Waite 2001a).

Third, the children were invited to talk, write or draw pictures in response to a variety of stimuli, including video extracts from soap operas and problems from teenage magazines focusing on relationships and puberty. The children were comfortable with these, because they were familiar and were often in any case the topics of spontaneous playground discussion. The discussions also covered the children's personal interests and experiences, the people most important to them, what they thought their own future lives would be like, and what, when and by whom they thought they should be told about sexual matters.

Fourth, the researchers were aware of the danger of unintentionally influencing the children's responses, and so they kept their own input into the discussions to a minimum, though they did occasionally intervene to enable less vocal members of the group to contribute. Where stimulus questions were used, the children controlled the extent to which each was discussed. The focus of power was thus, so far as possible, with the children.

Fifth, the researchers took pains to distinguish their role from that of the class teacher. For example, when children asked the researchers' opinions about issues, the question was bounced back to the group, and other children then often offered opinions. They clearly did not regard the researchers as equivalent to their teachers; they made several remarks about the dire consequences of talking about sex to teachers, but they seemed to exhibit considerable enthusiasm and freedom of expression, and few signs of embarrassment, in the presence of the researchers.

As a result of repeated listening to the interviews and re-reading the transcriptions and written responses, a number of common strands within the interviews were identified, including many of particular relevance to the theme of this book: the value the children placed on love and family life; their awareness of their own and other people's emotions; their attitudes to sexual relationships and parenthood; the influence of the family, the media and the hidden curriculum; peer influence and the joint construction of values; and the children's views on sex education (Halstead and Waite 2001a, 2001b). We now turn to examine the most important of these.

Research findings I: children's sexual values and attitudes

The importance of love

Love features extensively in the children's writings and discussions. Writing about relationships, one child states:

Girl: I think relationships are about love and trust. If you really love someone you don't hurt their feelings or keep breaking up with them. You must be open to each other about your feelings. You don't rush your relationships else you might get upset.

The children may still be struggling to make sense of the love between two adults, but love itself is seen as a powerful motivating force which can change lives. For example, in a discussion of the impact of drink and drugs on relationships, some of the girls maintain that love can help people to give up drink or drugs. Behind the more joking responses of the boys, there is still the same belief in love as the most important value in relationships. In a discussion about the importance of good looks, the boys themselves raise the topic of love:

Boy: Looks don't matter, it's what's inside.
Boy: All that'll be inside is sort of love trying to burst out.
Boy: No, what S. means is what's under their clothes [*giggling*].
Boy: No, it's what's under their skin.
Boy: I forgot to wear a vest today, Miss.
Boy: Don't be stupid. It's what's bursting out, what's inside. Like some-
        one could have a face like this [*pulls grotesque face*] and someone
        might love them and we might think they're stupid but inside
        they're a really nice person.
Boy: They could be not [*giggling*].

There is clearly a need for more research into what 'love' means to children and into what they think makes relationships special, but both boys
and girls seem to take love in some sense as fundamental to their own
worldview. This value attached to love by pre-adolescents adds weight to
the point raised by older students (as mentioned by Measor *et al.* 2000:
123–6) that love and the emotions generally are neglected in sex education
(see Chapter 8).

Awareness of emotions in self and others

Emotional literacy is often seen as a key element in children's development (Park 1999), and this may be defined in terms of (a) a growing
awareness of one's own feelings, (b) a growing awareness of the emotional responses of others, and (c) the ability to use these developing
understandings as a foundation for relationships with others (see Steiner
and Paul 1997). Both the girls and the boys in Halstead and Waite's
study demonstrate in different ways a growing awareness of their own
feelings. Some of the boys were aware of their own vulnerability and
insecurity:

Boy: It ain't hard to say I don't want to go out with you. It's hard to ask
        her out and that.
Boy: Yeah, that's what I find hard.
Boy: Are they gonna say no or are they going to go off laughing and
        that?
Boy: No one likes me.
Boy: I've got a girlfriend but she doesn't like me.

The girls, on the other hand, sometimes show a higher level of confidence
and self-esteem:

Girl: If I had a boyfriend, if he sort of like hurt me, I would call it off
        straightaway, 'cos there was this boy in the other class – he's not

my boyfriend or anything – but he pushed me in the arm today for no reason. If I had a boyfriend who was anything like that, I wouldn't really like it.

Girl: Miss, if he went like that [*threatening gesture*], I would call it off.

Generally, the girls show a greater awareness of the feelings of others than the boys. This can be seen when they talk about the special bond between mother and baby and in their awareness of the 'wonder' of babies. The build-up to adolescence is often seen as a time when boys may deny their softer emotional feelings in an attempt to appear more grown up, but even in the middle of a series of jokes the boys sometimes make a point which shows their awareness of emotions. The following comments occur as part of an extended and mainly light-hearted exchange of ideas in a boys' group on the topic of girls' looks:

Boy: There's two things: good-looking, and if they're kind or something.
Interviewer: What's more important out of those?
Boy: If they're kind.

Importance of families

Families feature extensively in the children's discussions. For the girls, their own developing sexuality is set within a context which reflects back to their own families as they consider examples of desirable and undesirable relationships and map out their future within a clear framework of what they consider necessary for a stable family life. They appear to believe that giving birth confers special privileges, though they are also very aware of the difficulties that early pregnancy can cause. Some of the boys have also thought about parenthood, though generally they make fewer connections between their own family upbringing and their visions for their future.

A few children complain of overprotective fathers:

Girl: My dad, if he had a boy, he wouldn't be like it, but because it's a girl, he's so protective over girls. Because he's so protective, he won't let us go near boys, so whenever we're in school I got to stay away from boys, but I don't . . . My dad said if he catches me going anywhere near a boy he'll absolutely kill me, but I do anyway at school.

Most, however, seem to take for granted the unconditional support of parents and mutual love between parents and children. For example, in

Figure 3.1 Picture by Kylie: 'People most important to me'

their discussion of early pregnancy, the girls generally believe that their parents would be supportive:

Girl: If the baby had to be fostered, I would give it to my parents to look after . . .
Girl: I think they would be a bit angry 'cos I had it at an early age, but I think they'd be pleased to have a grandson or daughter.

But feelings of family loyalty rarely spill over into sentimentality among the girls. They are often critical of their mothers for interfering or not taking account of their feelings:

Girl: She may want to listen to her mum, but sometimes you don't have to because it's up to you what you want to do because it's *your* choice.

Although the family is evidently very important for girls, they are also beginning to make up their own mind about issues and becoming aware of the fallibility of the adults around them. Such signs of growth towards independence and autonomy are not so apparent among the boys. When one boy speaks of doing something just to annoy his mother, others reprimand him for it and stress his duty to love her:

Boy: You don't like your mum?
Boy: You should do, you should do.

Strong family bonds are clearly evident in the girls' drawings of 'people most important to me'; family members often have arms around each other or stand close together (see Figure 3.1). The boys, on the other hand, shun such family closeness (see Figure 3.2). They are more likely to depict their 'cool' friends and peers than members of their family (where 'coolness' is defined in terms of wearing sunglasses and trainers with high-status brand names), and one boy includes his 'worst enymy' in the 'people most important to me'.

Writing about their own future lives, both boys and girls mention marriage and having children more frequently than future jobs or careers. The boys' responses are sometimes stereotypical and sexist:

Boy: I'll get married, I prefer one boy and one girl 'cos then a girl can do shopping with their mum and the boy can go off and play football with the dad.

The girls, on the other hand, have generally thought through the reality of marriage and parenthood more fully; they often have names already

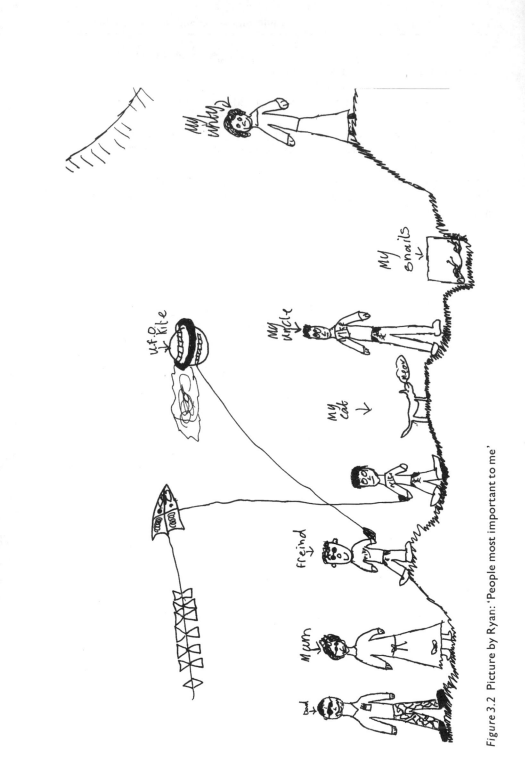

Figure 3.2 Picture by Ryan: 'People most important to me'

chosen for their children, and also have a clearer idea of the kind of behaviour they would consider unacceptable in a partner, such as smoking or taking drugs.

Research findings 2: the sources of children's values

Halstead and Waite's research provides support for the view that apart from programmes of sex education the main sources of children's sexual learning are the family, the media, the hidden curriculum and peers. There may be a fifth source of adult influence, the religious community, but no examples of this were apparent in this particular piece of research. As we shall see, all of these potentially play a part in the development of children's values and attitudes.

Influence of the family

Children appear to share the expectation that their parents will provide them with sexual information:

Boy: If you're a boy you talk to your dad. If you're a, um, er, girlie, you talk to your Mummee.

However, this neat division of labour often does not work in practice (see Allen 1987). Several children speak of the embarrassment in their family when it comes to talking about sex. Some of the children still await the occasion:

Boy: . . . when your parents give you the big talk.

One girl who is desperate to know what condoms are for finds out by listening through the floorboards to her mother and father:

Girl: My dad accidentally let it out one day, 'cos . . . you can hear through the floorboards, can hear my dad talking about them. I zoomed upstairs . . . and my mum and dad were talking about the packets . . . The day after I told him I could hear, and he goes, 'I suppose you want to know the proper reason why then?' He goes, 'When you actually put it on, it stops it going in, the sperm, into the woman's body, 'cos they don't want to have kids.'

Sometimes the children pick up information accidentally by listening in to family discussions, or find things out from older siblings or cousins:

Girl: In the swimming pool my brother and his girlfriend were talking
(I was quite far away, and my step-dad), they were talking, I think
it was about if they were going to do it.

If adults are embarrassed at talking to children about the mechanics of
sexual behaviour, they are likely to find it even harder to talk about
sexual values with them. Some parents clearly find it difficult to move
from instrumental explanations of contraception (''cos they don't want to
have kids') to a discussion of sex in terms of enjoyment, desire or the
expression of love. On the other hand, a caring dimension is implicit in
some families by the modelling of warm and positive relationships within
them, which is evident in the discussions of both boys and girls in this
research. However, embarrassment may lead to a fracture between the
modelling and the discrete bubble in which the 'big talk' is placed. When
the expected 'big talk' is given, it rarely covers more than practical matters
like periods, contraception and 'keeping out of trouble'. Few parents appear
to discuss values in relationships, or the nature of love, or sex appeal or
desire, or the strength of emotions, with their children. There is also little
evidence in this research or elsewhere that parents discuss the myriad of
sexual images on television with their children or help them in any way
to understand or make sense of them.

Influence of the media

The media appear to have both positive and negative influences on
children. The research confirms that much of the children's sexual knowledge and many of their values come from TV, videos and magazines,
though there is an important gender difference: the girls are more interested in the relationship-oriented sexual values of soap operas and teenage magazines, while the boys are more likely to take pride in having
watched 18-certificate films and pornographic videos and magazines:

Boy: My sister found a porn video.
Boy: And a video *Sex Watching*.
Boy: I watched *Predator* for 18 year olds.
Boy: Man and lady having sex, and the man got shot.
Boy: I was watching *Bottom*, and there was Rik Mayall – he's a person in
it, yeah? He tried having it off with this dummy, this blow-up thing
[*giggle, giggle*] 'cos he couldn't get a girlfriend, so he sent for this
package of a dummy, and he opened it up, blows it up and then
had it off with it [*hilarity*]. It had a hole in it as well to do it with
[*laughter*].

Often the boys speak of 'adult' films connecting sex and violence, but they seem unable to distinguish between different genres: documentary films and pornographic videos are interchangeable sources of information about sex. Their familiarity with 'adult' films may provide an explanation for the fact that much of their own discourse is peppered with jokes and references to violence:

Boy: I can't wait for all those Spice Girls to get thrown out of the window by their hair.

Some boys volunteer violent solutions to the problems in teenage magazines:

Boy: She should slap the lady round the face and punch her.

The girls, on the other hand, show much more interest in discussing the relationships, emotions and moral dilemmas illustrated in soaps and teenage magazines. In their discussion of the video clips, the girls express strong views about the 'rights' and 'wrongs' of the characters' actions, and the value of love seems fundamental to their moral judgements:

Girl: If you really love someone, like Lorraine says she loves Grant, well if I was Lorraine and I really loved Grant I would care for Joe but I would also back him up because I loved him, so I would help him get custody of his own child . . .
Girl: There are two things I was going to say about what A. said: I don't think he did just want the baby, I think he really did love her.
Girl: Yeah, but – he did love her, but – until she lied to him . . .

The girls' ability to empathise without becoming sentimental gives them a powerful means to use the fictional dilemmas in the soap operas to begin to formulate their own set of values and aspirations. They articulate values such as loyalty ('sticking by') and honesty ('being straight with') and are aware of the conflicting pressures on individuals, so that their judgements are not black and white.

Influence of the hidden curriculum

The term 'hidden curriculum' refers to the learning that goes on at school which is not part of any planned course of study – in other words, anything that children pick up consciously or otherwise from interaction with teachers or other adults, from the ethos of the school, from teaching styles, from teacher example, from the playground, from the example set by older pupils, or from structures, rules, sanctions, policies and procedures. For example, rules about school uniform (such as the length of school skirts, or the unfastening of blouse buttons in the summer) contain hidden messages about provocativeness, decency and the sexual statements that clothing can give out. Because such learning is unintentional, or at least not fully thought through, it can be haphazard and misleading. The influence of the hidden curriculum is such that it is not uncommon for the sexual values and attitudes which children develop in school to be quite different from those the school intends.

One example of hidden curriculum learning that comes to light in the research is the children's perception of the dire consequences of talking about sex to teachers. One girl expresses total incredulity when the researcher asked if it is easier to ask teachers than parents about sexual matters, while the boys in one school point out that there is a file where such demeanours are logged:

Boy: You say anything to do with sex and they say 'Green file' or something.
Boy: Yeah, shove your name on the list.

On another occasion, a boy describes bringing a book about sex into school only to have it confiscated by the teacher. Either because of sensitivity to teachers' inhibitions or simply because of the fear of being told off, children are often very careful to moderate what they say according to what they think teachers expect them to say. The children's perception that it is naughty to talk freely and openly about sex opens up the possibility for all sorts of negative and unhealthy attitudes towards sex to develop. At the very least, the boys' joking attitude to sex may be linked to the pleasure in doing something perceived to be 'naughty'.

Another example of the hidden curriculum is found in the playground, where the children learn a world of rules and rituals that have little to do with adults. Skipping and clapping songs are a central part of this world, and are passed on from child to child and from group to group. These songs were studied as an extension to the research on children's developing sexual values (Halstead 2000b), and it was found that many of the songs are charged with sexuality and sexual awareness. Indeed, adults can sometimes be shocked by their rude, violent, scurrilous and surprisingly worldly wise nature. They give expression to children's sometimes limited understanding of sexual matters, and make a significant contribution to children's informal sex education. One song common in primary school playgrounds in south-west England (and, indeed, around the world: see Opie and Opie 1985; Cram 1996) is 'Susie', which contains the following verse:

When Susie was a teenager,
   A teenager Susie was:
She went, Oo, Ah, I've lost my bra,
   I've left my knickers in my boyfriend's car.

Others are even more sexually explicit:

We are the sexy girls,
We wear our hair in curls,
We wear our dungarees
Down to our sexy knees.

A boy came up to me
And gave me 50p
To have it off with me
Under the apple tree.

I counted one to three,
He put it into me;
I counted one to ten,
He took it out again.

My mum was so surprised
To see my belly rise;
My dad was full of joy
To see a baby boy.

Halstead (2000b) argues that such songs are part of spontaneous, child-oriented, fun-loving playground counter-culture through which children resist the dominant rational, adult-focused ethos of the school. But the fact that such songs are rarely referred to, or even acknowledged, in the formal curriculum of the school probably conveys several messages to children: that the things children learn from each other are not valued by teachers; that there are areas of children's everyday experience that it may be inappropriate to talk to teachers about; and that teachers do not approve of the sexual language and content of playground songs. In fact, the songs are a good example of children learning from each other.

Influence of peers

Peer influence takes many forms in addition to the sharing of playground songs: sharing magazines and videos, discussing experiences and observations, clarifying expectations of behaviour, sharing jokes or worries, social acceptance and social inclusion, encouragement to conform to certain patterns of behaviour, establishing patterns of domination, arousing curiosity, expressing or seeking sympathy, discussing and refining attitudes and values.

The joint construction of standpoints is clear in both the boys' and girls' groups and perhaps gives glimpses of the process by which the children acquire and develop values through peer influence. Among the girls, most of their peers' opinions are accommodated rather than challenged, for example by prefacing a contribution with 'I agree with . . .' or 'Yeah but . . .' Here, for example, are three girls discussing the extracts from soap operas:

Girl: This is about Alan and Frankie. I think it was wrong to go off with Frankie. I think he knew in the first place she was gonna use him. I don't think it was fair that he went off and left Carole and his children, and he just went off with Frankie and she went off with Tony and everything . . .

Girl: I agree with [that] really because every so often she really wanted him because she wanted to use him, and then all of a sudden when he was going out for one meal, Frankie thought he was going off when she should have believed him. And then she just went with another man again, and then a couple of weeks later, because he had more money, that's why she asked him back: 'I need you more than Carole.'

Girl: It's about Grant and Lorraine. I reckon Grant was wrong to go with Lorraine 'cos I hate Lorraine 'cos she's nasty 'cos she won't give Grant custody of her child. I know she's got a lot of problems on her mind. And I reckon that Grant and Tiffany make a good couple.

What is going on here is the joint construction and refinement of values. The emerging framework of values and moral understanding arises not from an externally imposed system ('. . . and the moral of this story is'), but as an autonomously produced code of shared values which comes into being as a result of discussion and negotiation with peers.

On another occasion, the girls develop their skills of expressing (and perhaps manipulating) sympathy through interaction with peers. This is an exchange about a girl (aged 9!) being 'dumped' by her boyfriend:

Girl: He could change.

Girl: Yesterday, Miss, he said he'd never dump me again, 'cos he dumped me three, um, two times, but yesterday he said he'd never dump me again.

Girl: Yeah, but he will soon [*sad, wistful tone*].

Girl: But you don't know that. He might not.

Girl: Might still be together.

The boys are subject to peer influence in different ways: 92 per cent of the incidences of laughter and giggling in the interviews and group discussions comes from the boys, and all of the sexual slang. Their attitude is generally more flippant than the girls', sometimes bordering on rudeness. The joking may have been something to do with maintaining a macho image. Certainly there is a widespread fear of being thought 'gay'. The facade of bravado, horse play and violent language may, like their claims to know more about sex than they actually do, be an attempt to hide their own insecurities and confusions and maintain their masculine status among their peers (Connell 1987; Morgan 1992: 92). Their behaviour may also be an attempt to embarrass the researchers, and the girls in the group, for similar underlying reasons. On one occasion when the researcher briefly leaves the room, the boys seem to take delight in running through all the 'rude' words they can think of, while the girls try to quieten them down:

Boy: Do you think we should all lay down and have sex? [*giggling*]
Girl: No, this is recording your voice.
Boy: I forgot about that.
Boy: Prick.
Boy: Vagina.
Boy: Thighs, they get bigger.
Boy: What about hugging?
Boy: Shagging, sex . . .
Girl: This is going.
Boy: Oh, I didn't know that. Who's listening to it?
Boy: Nipple.
Boy: Boobs.
Boy: Tits.
Girl: You naughty little boy.

On other occasions, they may simply be trying to impress their peers as they talk about their various sexual exploits: playing with condoms, experimenting with sex lines, watching other boys expose themselves, looking at 'girlie' magazines and watching adult and pornographic videos. Some of the girls, too, are able to dominate their groups and influence the direction of the discussion by harrowing accounts of violence they have witnessed either on television or in real life. They talk about the possibility that they might experience violence at the hands of boyfriends in the future. Interestingly, this sometimes provides them with pragmatic reasons for adopting values such as honesty and loyalty, arguing that these might be the best way to avoid getting beaten up:

Girl: I'd rather tell them up front than use an excuse, because they're gonna find out the excuse anyway. They'll find out what you're doing anyway . . .

Girl: I'd be straight 'cos if you lie they're gonna find out anyway and might harm you.

Girl: Tell the truth.

Girl: He might slap you for not telling him straight.

Girl: Tell him face to face.

Once again, negotiation with peers is the means of clarifying values.

Research findings 3: children's thoughts about sex education

Both boys and girls agree on the need for school-based sex education. Although many of the boys claim they 'know all about it' – and some are willing to expound at length, albeit often inaccurately, on the physical facts of puberty, intercourse, pregnancy, birth, contraception and even gay sex – most are anxious to pick up more information wherever possible (see Tunnicliffe 2000). The girls, on the other hand, consider school-based sex education as a preparation for periods, which they see as imminent, and for sexual activity, which most expect to start around the ages of 16–18. Many of the children have views on when sex education should commence, with the majority favouring an early start (about their own age), but in single-sex groups.

The girls in this sample are happy to talk about what they expect their sexual lives to be like in the future. They seem very well aware of the problems of early pregnancy, which they are able to spell out quite clearly. Interestingly, falling in love is never mentioned by the girls as a prelude to sexual experience, though they discuss feelings extensively on other occasions. However, there is a sense among some of the girls of not being fully in control of their own lives, and they are aware of the possibility that their early sexual encounters might occur 'accidentally', that is without full intention, as a result of drink or fear of being 'dumped' or rebellion against an over-protective father or simply out of curiosity:

Girl: You may want to do it so you know what it's like.

Girl: Some people don't think.

Girl: What if they done it by mistake? Say if they were drunk, that's the problem.

One of the main reasons they put forward for being taught about sex at a comparatively early age is so that they know what is coming and so that they can be more in control of what happens to them (though one girl also suggests there are limits to what they should be taught at their present age):

Girl: I think in case just by accident you get into it, you need to know it.
Girl: Sometimes, I know I'm only 11, I feel like I was going to do it. I'm not being horrible or anything. It keeps coming into my mind, but I know I'm not going to.
Girl: We should know most things but not things too serious like for us to get into, because we might get into it too quick.

Statements like these are not made by the boys, whose sexual references, as we have seen, are more in the here and now and focused more on the immediate entertainment value of sex.

Implications of the research

Validity of findings

Before any implications can be drawn, we must first consider how typical the children in the research sample are. This question is particularly important because the children in the case study do not seem to display the degree of sexual innocence which many adults assume should be characteristic of children of this age. Three points may be made in response to this question. First, although the sample is restricted to the south-west of England and thus does not reflect the ethnic diversity found in other parts of the country, there is nothing in the sampling techniques to suggest that the children are not otherwise typical of the wider population of children in England. In fact, the findings are consistent with other studies of the developing sexual attitudes and values of younger children (Tunnicliffe 2000), older children (Measor *et al.* 2000) and young adults in England (Ford 1991).

Second, it is true that widely differing sexual values and attitudes may be picked up at home by pre-adolescent children and that a broader sample might have reflected this diversity more clearly. As already mentioned, none of the children interviewed make any reference to God or to religion, though a bigger sample might have included children for whom religious beliefs about sexuality are important. However, it is also true that almost all children of this age are exposed to the same sexual influences through television and other media, and in this sense, the sample is typical of the wider population of children. In fact, as we have seen, television is a major source of sexual knowledge and values for most children (Ward 1995).

Third, it is clear that children are often wary of talking about sex to adults generally, perhaps because of the fear of being told off, but in this case the researchers tried to create conditions in which the children felt free to talk openly about sex. What they said might thus be a truer reflection of their sexual knowledge and values than other accounts of children's values.

Children's sexuality

The research clearly shows that children are sexual beings (see Rogers and Rogers 1999). They are deeply interested in sexual matters, the more so because of the conflicting messages emanating from adults: on the one hand, children cannot escape from sexual images being thrust at them from all of the media (including, for example, magazines designed for their own consumption), but on the other, many adults appear to be rather secretive and disapproving about sex. These double standards add to children's natural inquisitiveness, with the result that sex occupies a central place in much of their thinking and many of their conversations, activities and games. Sex education cannot ignore the growing sexual awareness and sexualisation of children.

Sex education

It is not seriously open to question (except, perhaps, by some minority religious groups: see Chapter 6) that there is a need for children to be given more information about sex, and for their misconceptions to be corrected. But we believe that their biggest need is for support and guidance with their developing sexual values and attitudes. The research has shown that by the age of 9 or 10 they are beginning to pick up a range of sexual values from the family, the media, the hidden curriculum and peers, but they all too often have no one apart from equally inexperienced peers with whom to discuss them. Both boys and girls need help in learning how to engage in a critical evaluation of these informal influences on their values and attitudes. In particular, the boys need help to develop a positive self-image based not on macho posturing but on a sense of having an important and responsible role to play within the family and the broader society, and to learn to respect others and treat them fairly whatever their beliefs, ethnic background or sexual orientation. They also need help to develop appropriate critical responses if they see adult videos and magazines and to reflect critically on the links they make between violence and sex. The girls' needs may lie more in the direction of developing their existing assertiveness and autonomy, learning to take further control over the direction of their lives. In each case, sex education can help them to construct a coherent set of values for themselves out of the diversity of perspectives they have come across. It would be helpful if sex education were to include education of the emotions and offer all children opportunities to reflect on the nature of love, including sexual love, intimacy and desire. It may also include an exploration of the part played by sex in personal development, and of the range of options open to individuals. It should provide children with opportunities to reflect on personal values such as responsibility, respect, loyalty, sensitivity to others, forgiveness, personal integrity and commitment, especially in the context of relationships and the family.

Sometimes an indirect approach is more helpful in dealing with these issues, rather than direct teaching which children may experience as embarrassing, confrontational or out of touch with reality, and several school subjects may contribute to this. Children can learn about different kinds of relationships and different frameworks of values, for example, through reading fiction, poetry, drama and biography. Indeed, the study of the underlying values of any piece of literature is widely recognised as an important aspect of literary criticism. In role-play and other drama activities children may be encouraged to enter into different characters and explore their behaviour and motivation from the inside. Religious education may have a different but equally important part to play in sex education. In the common school this would not, of course, involve imposing religious rules about sex on children or encouraging them to develop a commitment to any particular religious framework of sexual values; most children would rebel against this anyway. But religious education could help to give children an understanding of what a coherent worldview looks like, and how such a worldview incorporates certain attitudes to sex alongside other human values and experiences. This might be of practical help to children as they struggle to make sense of the varied influences and values to which they are generally exposed as their sexual knowledge expands. It might also, more simply, help them to understand others.

Alongside the contribution that different subjects can make to sex education, schools need to pay attention to the hidden curriculum of sex education. Unless the messages of the hidden curriculum are brought to consciousness, they cannot be the subject of discussion, reflection and reappraisal. For example, if teachers are embarrassed talking about sex, or if they imply that sex is 'dirty', pupils will consciously or otherwise pick up such messages. As we have seen, pupils will learn much from the ethos of the school, from what is permitted and not permitted in the school rules and from the example set by teachers, and teachers need to be aware of the messages which they are passing on to pupils in this way (see Halstead and Taylor 2000).

The research suggests that not all schools are currently making as helpful a contribution as they might towards children's developing sexual values. To some extent this is a result of external constraints. School sex education in some countries is placed in a protective bubble because of the legal requirement that parents must be free to withdraw their children from it, and this militates against a seamless portrayal of love and sexual relationships across the curriculum. The sex education policies of individual schools (which are again required by legislation in some countries) may be written by governors some of whom will hold outdated notions of childhood innocence and therefore restrict the broader curriculum base that may be more appropriate to adopt. However, there are still many ways in which the contribution that teachers make towards children's sexual values can be enriched. One is a greater willingness to respect children and listen to them. Another involves paying more attention to the processes involved in children's learning and development. Another is for schools to ensure that children encounter different models of sexuality through the curriculum, reflecting the many standpoints that exist in society, and to encourage children to discuss these and to construct their own worldview.

All of these have clear implications for teacher training, both initial and in-service. Teachers and others with responsibility for education will not be able to help children to reflect critically on their developing sexual values if they have not themselves engaged in the same process. It is with this in mind that we turn in Part 2 to a critical discussion of some of the main sets of values that underpin contemporary thinking about sex and sex education.

Summary

1   The chapter is based on a research project on values and sex education carried out at the University of Plymouth. The project involved pupils aged 9–10 and was designed to explore how children think about sex and relationships, the values and attitudes implicit in their ways of thinking, and the sources of these values. The methodology emphasised the need for children to be free to express their opinions openly in their own terms.

2   Boys and girls spoke freely about sex. The boys appeared more interested in the physical aspects of human sexuality, made more jokes, and often linked sex and violence, while the girls were more interested in relationships and parenthood. Love and families were important features of children's worldviews, and they showed a growing awareness of their own feelings and the feelings of others.

3   The four main influences on their values and attitudes were the family, the media, the hidden curriculum of the school, and particularly peers. Boys and girls seemed to be susceptible to different influences, with the result that their values and attitudes were significantly divergent.
4   The children had clear views on what form sex education should take and when it should be taught, and a definite preference for single-sex groupings, and the girls in particular had a clear vision of how their sexual lives might develop over the next few years.
5   It is suggested that sex education needs to take account of the increasing sexualisation of children, and must involve much more than the transmission of knowledge.

Issues for discussion

1   Are children becoming more sexually aware than they were in the past? How does this manifest itself, and what implications does it have for sex education?
2   Buy a copy of a magazine targeted at teenage girls. What values does it promote, and how do these values differ from the values underpinning any programme of school-based sex education with which you are familiar?
3   What contribution can sex education make to the development of emotional literacy, and vice versa?
4   What messages about sex are picked up by children through the hidden curriculum of schools with which you are familiar?
5   Can the differing needs of boys and girls be met in the same programme of sex education? Consider the pros and cons of single-sex classes for sex education.

Further reading

For fuller accounts of the methodology of the research discussed in this chapter, together with a fuller discussion of specific issues (gender differences and links between spirituality and sexuality), see:

- Halstead, J. M. and Waite, S. (2001a) '"Living in different worlds": gender differences in the developing sexual values and attitudes of primary school children', *Sex Education* 1: 59–76.
- Halstead, J. M. and Waite, S. (2001b) 'Nurturing the spiritual in children's sexual development', *International Journal of Children's Spirituality* 6: 185–206.

For a large-scale research project into children's sexual thinking, see:

- Goldman, R. and Goldman, J. (1982) *Children's Sexual Thinking*, London: Routledge and Kegan Paul.

For a critical insight into the experiences and values of North American adolescent girls, see:

- Orenstein, P. (1995) *Schoolgirls: Young Women, Self-esteem and the Confidence Gap*, New York: Anchor.

For research into young people's views on sex education, with a particular focus on gender relations, see:

- Measor, L., with Tiffin, C. and Miller, K. (2000) *Young People's Views on Sex Education: Education, Attitudes and Behaviour*, London: RoutledgeFalmer.

There are various articles in the journal *Sex Education* that describe young people's experiences of sex education and development of sexual attitudes around the world, and in *Gender and Education* that examine gender issues in young people's developing understanding of sex.

Part 2

Chapter 4

Liberal values

Liberal values and sex education

It has been argued elsewhere (Halstead 1996b) that the best way to come to understand the educational values of any society is to examine the broader framework of values in that society. We therefore begin Part 2 with a discussion of liberalism, which, we contend, provides the theoretical framework of values that comes closest to reflecting the actual political, legal and economic circumstances that prevail in western societies generally. Liberal values influence both the way we think about sex and the way we think about education, and so it is inevitable that they permeate the theory and practice of sex education.

Most serious writing about sexual values in the western world positions itself in a framework of liberal thinking. In *Sex and Social Justice* (1999), for example, Nussbaum explores concepts such as personhood, autonomy, rights, dignity and self-respect in her discussions of issues including homosexuality, pornography and prostitution. Drawing extensively on Aristotle, Kant and Mill, she argues that the liberal tradition holds rich resources for addressing violations of human dignity on the grounds of sex or sexuality. As we saw in Chapter 2, Giddens argues that the transformation of intimacy that is taking place in contemporary society involves the principle of autonomy and the 'democratisation of personal life' (1992: ch. 10). This implies that the democratic ideals of the liberal state, including the right to free and equal self-development, respect for others, the right to freedom from oppression and values such as trust and accountability, are increasingly becoming features of personal relationships, lifestyles and forms of partnership. Wilson (1995) argues that love and sexual relations are best when they occur between equals and involve an equal sharing of self. Although promising 'a radically different stance' from most writing on the theme of sexual values, Weeks (1995) also emphasises 'democratic principles and values' including freedom of choice, equal opportunities, authenticity and toleration. In the virtues of care, responsibility, respect and knowledge he finds a system of values in relationships 'which make individual autonomy possible while encouraging diversity to flourish' (1995: 11, 73).

Unsurprisingly, dominant conceptions of sex education in the west reflect a similar commitment to liberal values. In an article written in 1971, Harris (1971) suggests that the purpose of sex education is to promote 'rational sexual autonomy', and this has remained a fairly constant theme of philosophers and others discussing sex education ever since (see Jones 1989). Archard (2000) argues that sex education should be based on the liberal principle that 'whatever is freely chosen by those competent to choose so long as it harms no-one else should be allowed' (2000: 45). Giving choice a central role in the legitimation of sexual conduct, he argues, has two consequences for sex education: first, young people need to be given 'enough information [about sex] to make informed, considered choices'; and second, they need to 'be taught to make their own choices' (2000: 37).

We ourselves refer frequently to liberal values in Part 1 of this volume. For example, in Chapter 1 we argue that behind the personal qualities which we would expect a 'sexually educated person' to have (such as appropriate self-assertiveness, responsible sexual decision-making and tolerance of sexual diversity) lie certain liberal values including autonomy, equality, freedom, respect, fairness, personal security, responsibility and freedom of choice. In Chapter 2 we adopt a liberal framework in identifying three categories of values in the sexual domain:

- universal sexual values (such as the unacceptability of rape), based on core liberal values such as freedom, human rights, equality and respect for persons, which must be universally upheld in schools
- common values, arrived at through democratic discussion and reflection, which must be upheld in a critically open way that acknowledges they may change over time
- controversial values, on which the school must adopt a neutral stance, encouraging individuals to develop an attitude of tolerance, respect and understanding towards diverse beliefs and practices.

A dominant theme of both chapters is the liberal view that children must be encouraged to develop the abilities to pick a rational path through the variety of influences that impinge on their experience and to construct their own developing value framework through a process of critical reflection.

In the three remaining sections of this chapter we examine the relationship between liberal values and sex education more closely. In the next section we construct a framework of liberal values, showing how the different values relate to each other and affect people's thinking about education and morality in general. Then we relate this framework to sex education in particular, and outline how liberal values help to clarify the purposes of sex education. Finally we examine challenges to the dominant liberal framework of values, focusing particularly on feminist, religious and communitarian critiques, and we identify other value domains which we think are important for sex education but for which liberalism appears to provide an inadequate basis.

A framework of liberal values

Liberalism is difficult to define, not least because, as Nussbaum points out, it is 'not a single position but a family of positions' (1999: 57). The understanding of liberalism that we adopt here is as broad as possible, but where we need to concentrate on one typical form, we focus on a strand which can be traced from Kant to contemporary philosophers like Rawls, Dworkin, Hart and Raz, leaving more utilitarian forms of liberalism to be covered in Chapter 5. Philosophically, liberalism may be said to have its origin in the conflict between two core values or principles. The first of these is individual liberty – freedom from arbitrary external restraints in the pursuit of one's own interests and desires and in the fulfilment of one's potential. The second is the equal right of all individuals to such liberty, which implies an equality of respect for all individuals within the structures and practices of society and a rejection of arbitrary discrimination against any individuals. These two values, freedom and equality, exist in a state of tension, though some liberals have argued that the first value is more fundamental (Hayek 1960; Berlin 1969) and others the second (Dworkin 1978; Gutmann 1980; Hart 1984). It is partly this tension which gives rise to the need for a third core liberal value, that of consistent rationality, which requires that all decisions and actions are based on logically consistent rational justifications, and which rules out the uncritical acceptance of dogma.

Taken together, these three values provide the basis for a liberal worldview. The principle of personal autonomy – the freedom to work out a course of action for oneself – depends on the core values of freedom and rationality. The principles of state impartiality and individual tolerance and respect combine the core values of rationality and the equal right of all individuals to liberty; thus the liberal state is expected to show official neutrality on religious matters, together with a respect for the equal freedom of conscience of all individuals unless their religious beliefs are harmful to other individuals or against the public interest. The principle of the just resolution of conflict relates equally to freedom, equality and rationality.

On the basis of these values and principles, it is possible to construct liberal theories of politics, of law, of economics, of ethics and of education. For example, in the political domain, liberalism sees democracy as the most rational safeguard against tyranny and the best way of guaranteeing the equal right of citizens to determine for themselves what is in their own best interests, and pluralism as the most rational response to diversity. We have already noted that both Giddens (1992) and Weeks (1995) emphasise the centrality of democratic principles in contemporary sexual values (see also McKay 1997). Liberalism upholds the rule of law, which exists to prevent harm (Mill [1859] 1972) and to maintain order in society by protecting persons and property. Key liberal causes that are often enshrined in law are human rights (including the rights of women, children and minorities), free speech, opposition to censorship and opposition to the enforcement of common moral values through the criminal law (Hart 1963). Liberal values also underpin legislation in the sexual domain, such as the protection of children from corruption and abuse, the preservation of the public interest (through legislation against perversion and unrestricted access to pornography, for example), and the protection of individual rights, including freedom from invasive behaviour.

Liberal economic theory accepts the holding of private property as legitimate, and supports the notion of the free market economy, though the state may intervene to regulate the economy if necessary, to ensure free and fair competition and to prevent harm to others through gross inequalities of wealth and welfare (Gaus 1983: ch. 7). Economic liberalism raises further questions in the sexual domain, including issues of population control, public expenditure and the provision of social welfare; one of the basic assumptions underlying many sex education programmes is that such education can reduce teenage pregnancy and thus alleviate the social and economic problems that have been blamed on teenage sexual activity.

But it is with liberal ethics and liberal education that we are particularly concerned here. It is in liberal moral theory that the different versions of liberalism are most clearly distinguished. A major parting of the ways comes between those like Bentham and Mill who believe that *good* is of prior importance and who therefore justify actions and decisions in terms of their consequences, and those like Kant who believe that *right* is of prior importance and therefore justify actions and decisions in terms of a set of moral duties. The dominant view in the former category is utilitarianism, which maintains that the justice of institutions and individual actions may be measured by their capacity to promote the greatest happiness of the greatest number. Utilitarianism is discussed more fully in Chapter 5, together with its implications for sex education. The dominant view in the latter category is that of social justice, though the way this is achieved in practice is a matter of dispute between libertarians such as Hayek and Nozick who emphasise equality of opportunity within the marketplace and the right of individuals to a fair reward for their talents and labour, and egalitarians like Rawls and Dworkin, who emphasise (among other things) civil and moral rights, social welfare, and meeting the needs of the least advantaged. At a personal level, certain forms of human behaviour are ruled out in principle by reference to the core liberal values; these include prejudice, intolerance, injustice and repression. Other forms of human behaviour are necessary in principle on a liberal view: personal autonomy, self-respect, respect for human dignity and for the freedom and rights of others, justice, truth-telling, promise-keeping, the rational resolution of conflict, acceptance of the general rule of law, responsibility, tolerance of diversity, the avoidance of harm to others and control over one's own life and body. Morality is seen as a rational activity, in which decisions on how to act are reached after careful reflection, paying due attention both to the principles involved and to the likely consequences of the actions taken.

It is personal qualities such as those listed in the previous paragraph which liberal education seeks to develop. Like liberalism, liberal education has a long history and a range of different meanings. Its roots are often traced to ancient Greece, where liberal education involved the development of mind and the pursuit of knowledge for its own sake, and to nineteenth-century thinkers like Mill, Newman and Arnold, with their emphasis on all-round development, the pursuit of excellence and high culture and their continuing belief in the humanising effect of the liberal arts. As noted at the start of this chapter, however, we believe that the central strands of liberal education are best understood in terms of the liberal framework of values outlined above. The vision of education which these values encompass has come to dominate western educational thinking. All the values typically associated with liberal education – including personal autonomy, critical openness, equality of opportunity, rational morality, the celebration of diversity, the avoidance of manipulation and indoctrination, the refusal to side with any particular, definitive conception of the good, democratic values, citizenship and children's rights – are clearly based on the three fundamental liberal values of freedom, equality and rationality. Supporters of liberal education have gone so far as to suggest that it is the only justifiable form of education (Hirst 1974; Crittenden 1999). For them, education *is* liberal education.

Implications for sex education

Sex education, we have suggested, cannot operate with values different from those of the whole educational enterprise. It is essentially a moral activity, concerned with the balanced development of the whole person and with the development of particular attitudes, skills, dispositions and personal qualities. For example, the promotion of 'responsible sexual behaviour' (a motif that we discuss in more detail in Chapter 10) encompasses a number of liberal educational values such as respect for others, honesty and non-exploitation in sexual relationships, while leaving many of the specifics of sexual behaviour up to the individuals concerned. In this section we discuss liberal sexual values under the headings of the three core liberal values: freedom, equality and rationality.

Freedom

A useful distinction is often made between 'freedom to' and 'freedom from' (see Bantock 1965: 99). 'Freedom to', or positive freedom, does not mean the unrestrained indulgence of desires and impulses, but means the freedom to determine the course of one's own life and to pursue a path of individual self-fulfilment. In relation to sex education, this means that children should be encouraged to develop into autonomous adolescents and adults who have control over their own lives and bodies and able to make mature, independent choices about sexual behaviour and sexual values and attitudes. Liberal education has been described as an education which liberates individuals from the restrictions of the present and the particular, so that they can become free choosers of their own beliefs and behaviours (Bailey 1984). Indeed, they may choose sexual values and adopt patterns of sexual behaviour that are quite different from those of their parents. Archard argues that education should 'maximise the opportunities and capacities of individuals to exercise their own free choices' (2000: 37). A prerequisite for maximising choice in this way is an awareness of alternative beliefs and lifestyles, and on this basis the Sex Education Forum has argued that sex education should involve the sharing and exploration of 'a range of moral views and choices' (Thomson 1993: 1).

However, two provisos must be made about the promotion of personal autonomy in sex education. First, as Archard points out, children below a certain age may not be mature enough to make wise choices amid the complexities of contemporary life (2000: 37). It may be more a matter of preparing them for the time when they can make considered choices, and offering them appropriate guidance in the mean time. Second, although it is true that to become sexually autonomous children need certain knowledge (such as the nature of human sexuality, physical development, reproduction, sexual health, contraception, human emotions and relationships) and certain decision-making skills, including being aware of the consequences of one's decisions and actions, these two things in themselves are not enough. Autonomy is a complex and controversial concept (Halstead 1986: ch. 4). It would be a mistake to construe it too narrowly as concerned simply with making a rational judgement between hypothetical possibilities and options. An enriched understanding of autonomy must take account of beliefs, attitudes, motivations and qualities of character, and must involve the wider development of the person, including self-respect, self-esteem, self-worth and dispositions such as personal integrity and the courage to withstand pressure where necessary, whether from peers, the media or other sources, and to persist in the chosen course of action. We examine more fully in Chapter 10 some of the implications for sex education policy of a commitment to the value of personal autonomy.

The other side of freedom is 'freedom from', or negative freedom. Most obviously, children need to be free from abuse and exploitation. Teachers have a responsibility to help children to recognise and avoid exploitation and abuse, so that the vicious circle in which the abused may become the next generation of abusers is broken. UK guidance clarifies the boundaries of teachers' legal and professional roles and responsibilities in relation to child protection (DfEE 1995, 2000a), and also clarifies some of the difficulties experienced by children with special educational needs who may be 'more vulnerable to abuse and exploitation than their peers' (DfEE 2000a: 12). We return to the theme of abuse in Chapters 9 and 11.

Some people have argued that freedom from harm is at the heart of liberal sexual morality. According to the 'harm principle' (Morgan 1996), the basis for judging the acceptability of sexual behaviour lies in whether or not it harms others. Some of the guidance issued by the Department for Education and Employment appears to be based on this principle, including the suggestion that young people need to be prepared for an adult life in which they have 'sufficient information and skills to protect themselves and, where they have one, their partner from unintended/ unwanted conceptions, and sexually transmitted infections including HIV' (DfEE 2000a: 20). However, 'harm to others' is sometimes difficult to define, and surely does not provide a substantial enough basis for evaluating how satisfactory a sexual relationship or activity is.

There are many things that can act as constraints on young people's development of happy and fulfilling sex lives, and since Aristotle, freedom has been seen by many as meaning the absence of such constraints. On this view, sex education can help children to be free:

- from being pressured (by peers, the media or others) into unwanted sexual activity (it is this principle which lies behind attempts to empower young women in particular through assertiveness training, which we discuss further in Chapter 10)
- from undue interference in intimate and family relationships (issues of confidentiality are discussed in Chapter 11; see also DfEE 2000a: 30–3)
- from being conditioned through pressure from the media or other sources into accepting as normal particular sexual attitudes, such as the exploitation or depersonalisation of women (attaining freedom from this kind of pressure requires the development of skills of critical thinking, which we discuss below)

- from the suffocating influence of closed attitudes which discourage questioning and critical thinking
- from prejudice and discrimination (this last point leads us directly to the next section).

Equality

In terms of policy, the liberal principle that no one conception of the good life is to be favoured results in acceptance and respect for a vast range of lifestyles, commitments, priorities, roles and life-plans, and these form a marketplace of ideas within the liberal framework. Equality and respect for a diversity of worldviews are key values in liberal education, not least because disrespect generates friction in society (Beck 1990: 10). These values provide the foundation for educational policies opposing discrimination on irrelevant grounds such as differences of race, gender, ethnicity, nationality, religion, social class or sexual orientation. Some of these are of particular relevance to sex education. Schools need to ensure that students are helped as far as possible to 'develop skills to enable them to understand difference and respect themselves and others and for the purpose also of preventing and removing prejudice' (DfEE 2000a: 4). This includes teaching students about the value of gender equality, the unacceptability of homophobic bullying and the need to respect cultural and religious differences, and ensuring that children with special educational needs and learning difficulties are properly included in sex education.

Equal respect is also an important principle in intimate relationships. Wilson (1995) has convincingly argued that love between equals involves intrinsic friendship and sharing the self and allows no space for possessiveness and power relationships. It also involves loyalty and honesty in relationships – a fact that the children in the case study discussed in Chapter 3 had already begun to appreciate – and respect for one's partner. We discuss these issues more fully in Chapter 8.

Rationality

The development of the rational mind is at the very core of liberal education, and it is achieved by encouraging open, critical thinking and ensuring that students have good reasons for their beliefs and actions (see Siegel 1988). Critical openness involves impartiality and objectivity in assessing the validity of the beliefs of oneself and others, and a willingness to revise beliefs as new evidence comes to light. We have already referred to the role played by critical thinking and an awareness of the consequences of one's actions in rational decision-making in the sexual domain, and to the need for children to develop a critical response to the sexual attitudes and values that they encounter every day in the media and else-

where. However, it would be wrong to construe a commitment to rationality too narrowly, in a way that ignores the emotions and dispositions
and a balanced sense of personhood. As Hirst (1999) points out, there is
much more to a person than the activities of reason.

Rationality also plays a significant role in children's moral development.
Kohlberg (1969) places great emphasis on moral reasoning and argues
that development in moral reasoning proceeds through a series of socio-
moral perspectives. He claims that progress across the stages of moral
development can be enhanced where teaching involves exploring moral
dilemmas. There is widespread acceptance of the view that moral reasoning – having and being able to give reasons for a judgement or an action
– is a central part of moral development, and its cognitive emphasis fits
well with school-based sex education. However, an exclusive focus on
the ability to reason morally ignores other aspects of what it is to be a
morally educated person. As Jones points out, 'in order to make rational
and informed decisions in the sexual sphere a great deal is necessary'
(1989: 60). These requirements include concern and respect for others,
emotional awareness and empathy, practical skills and dispositions to act
in principled and person-oriented ways (Wilson 1990; McLaughlin and
Halstead 2000).

Challenges to liberal values

As we have seen, liberal values permeate much philosophical thinking
about sex and sex education, as well as policy guidelines and practical
approaches to the topic. However, the liberal vision of education as a
means for promoting personal autonomy, critical understanding and
respectful human relationships is not universally shared. Fundamental
challenges to liberal education come, in particular, from Marxism (see
Matthews 1980); radical feminism (see Stone 1990; Graham 1994); postmodernism (see Aronowitz and Giroux 1991; Carr 1995: ch. 9); communi-
tarianism (Mulhall and Swift 1992); and various religious worldviews
(including the Roman Catholic and the Islamic) which claim that liberalism lacks an adequate moral and spiritual foundation. To those committed
to such worldviews, liberal education may appear as just one more chal-
lengeable version of what is good for children. However, in terms of their
perspectives on sexual values and sex education, not all of these ideologies
are incompatible with the liberal values outlined above. It is more helpful
to discuss challenges to liberal sexual values not from an ideological but
from a thematic perspective. Apart from right-wing critics of sex education
(who suggest that schools should promote abstinence – see Chapter 9 –
and traditional family values – see Chapter 7), the main criticisms of the
liberal approach to sex education set out in this chapter fall into four
categories.

First, there is the criticism that liberalism (or at least the Kantian version of liberalism with which we have been concerned in this chapter) adopts too rational an approach to what is essentially a natural, instinctive activity. Nussbaum (1999), slightly tongue-in-cheek, finds similarities between the prostitute and the professor of philosophy, in that they both take money for their interactions with others, both provide skilful performances and both aim to produce satisfaction or pleasure (1999: 283–4). But the aspects of personhood with which the prostitute is concerned are quite different from the more rational preoccupations of the professor, and the pleasure or satisfaction which is the goal of the prostitute's work is again quite different from any pleasure to be had from the study of Aristotle. In short, sex is a natural activity that can be complicated by too much thinking. On this view, the most important sexual values are pleasure and the satisfaction of desire, so long as the associated health risks can be avoided.

The second criticism is that liberal sexual values do not satisfy the defenders of religious sexual moralities. Liberal neutrality with regard to religion may convey the impression to pupils that all religions are equally wrong. As one of us points out elsewhere, there is a danger that sex education could indoctrinate pupils into a primarily agnostic perspective (Reiss 1996: 101). On this view, religious perspectives on sexual values not only should be included in sex education programmes, but also should be taken seriously, treated fairly and not relegated to separate periods of religious studies.

Third, liberal sexual values have often been accused of involving excessive individualism by prioritising personal autonomy and self-fulfilment over obligations and commitments to others, such as children and family. As Nussbaum points out, liberalism does indeed insist on the separateness of one life from another and the equal importance of each life, seen on its own terms, rather than as part of a collective social entity such as a family (1999: 10, 58–67). However, it is clear that in the sexual domain perhaps even more than in other domains, our desires cannot be satisfied independently of the desires of others. For many people (and for many children, as we saw in Chapter 3), the family is the context for intimate relationships, and as such it merits a more central place in sex education than is provided by liberalism.

Fourth, the liberal emphasis on reasonableness, understanding and rational decision-making tends to play down the significance of caring, love and emotional depth in sexual relations. Gilligan's rejection of Kohlberg's approach to moral education based on justice and rational morality in favour of a more care-centred approach illustrates a feminist rejection of a form of liberal rationalism (Gilligan 1982), but the critique is not restricted to feminists. Weeks (1995) too, at the end of his book on sexual values in an age of uncertainty, comes back to love and care as core values which incorporate but also transcend liberal values:

> A truly loving care can be built only on a recognition of the autonomy of the other, the equality of carer and the person cared for, the recipro-cal needs thus addressed, and ultimately on the recognition that the autonomy of oneself is dependent on the autonomy of others. Love as care, in other words, implies an act of imagination, an ability to enter sympathetically into the life of others. But that in turn requires that we love responsibly.
>
> (Weeks 1995: 179)

On this view, it would be an important part of sex education to help pupils to develop an understanding of what love and care are and what possible relationships there are between love and sexual behaviour.

The approaches to thinking about sexual values suggested in these four perspectives may not be totally incompatible with liberal values, but may rather offer different emphases. The four perspectives provide the starting point for the next four chapters, which deal respectively with pleasure, recreation, health and well-being; religious values; family values, and love.

Summary

1 The values of liberal education reflect the broader framework of values in the western world, and permeate the theory and prac-tice of sex education.

2 Core liberal values include personal autonomy, rational decision-making, self-respect, respect for human dignity and for the freedom and rights of others, justice, equality, truth-telling, promise-keeping, the rational resolution of conflict, acceptance of the rule of law, responsibility, tolerance of diversity, self-determination, the avoidance of harm to others and control over one's own life and body. Morality on a liberal view is seen as a rational activity, in which decisions on how best to act are reached after careful reflection, paying due attention both to the principles involved and to the likely consequences.

3   Liberal sex education encourages children to develop into auton-
    omous individuals who are in control over their own lives and
    bodies and able to make responsible, informed decisions about
    their own sexual behaviour. Children have a right to freedom
    from abuse and exploitation and from other influences which act
    as constraints on the development of their potential for sexual
    happiness and fulfilment.
4   The liberal approach has been criticised as putting too much
    emphasis on rationalism and individualism, and paying inade-
    quate attention to religious values, the emotions and the family.
    These issues are dealt with in later chapters.

Issues for discussion

1   How persuasive do you find the claim that liberal values should
    be at the heart of any programme of sex education? Is the devel-
    opment of personal autonomy in sexual matters a wise goal for
    sex education? If liberalism is open to a wide diversity of lifestyles
    and worldviews, how can this help to determine the content of
    school sex education?
2   Is all sexual behaviour acceptable if it does no harm to others?
3   Wilson (1990) attempts to define the characteristics of a 'morally
    educated person'. Try to define the characteristics of a 'sexually
    educated person' (you may find it helpful to refer back to
    Chapter 1). How much overlap would you expect to find between
    the concept of 'morally educated' and the concept of 'sexually
    educated'?
4   Why are some feminists dissatisfied with the liberal framework of
    values? How might a feminist approach to sex education differ
    from a liberal approach?
5   What steps should sex educators take to implement a policy of
    inclusivity in their work?

Further reading

There are many texts on liberal education. Among the best are:

- Bailey, C. (1984) *Beyond the Present and the Particular: A Theory of Liberal Education*, London: Routledge and Kegan Paul.
- Gutmann, A. (1987) *Democratic Education*, Princeton, NJ: Princeton University Press.
- Levinson, M. (2000) *The Demands of Liberal Education*, Oxford: Oxford University Press.
- Peters, R. S. (1966) *Ethics and Education*, London: Allen and Unwin.

There are a number of useful essays on liberal moral education in:

- Halstead, J. M. and McLaughlin, T. H. (eds) (1999) *Education in Morality*, London: Routledge.

See also:

- Wilson, J. (1990) *A New Introduction to Moral Education*, London: Cassell.

For current accounts and critiques of liberal sexual values, see:

- Giddens, A. (1992) *The Transformation of Intimacy: Sexuality, Love and Eroticism in Modern Societies*, Cambridge: Polity Press.
- Nussbaum, M. (1999) *Sex and Social Justice*, New York: Oxford University Press.
- Weeks, J. (1995) *Invented Moralities: Sexual Values in an Age of Uncertainty*, Cambridge: Polity Press.
- Wilson, J. (1995) *Love between Equals: A Philosophical Study of Love and Sexual Relationships*, London: Macmillan.

For an approach to sex education based on liberal values, see:

- Archard, D. (2000) *Sex Education (Impact Series no. 7)*, London: Philosophy of Education Society of Great Britain.

Chapter 5

Pleasure, recreation, health and well-being

Identifying the good life

What does each of us want from life (Deigh 1995)? This fundamental question is sometimes posed as 'What is the good life?' – though this is to presume that we want to lead good lives, however 'good' is understood. In any event, answers to these two questions can be given at various levels of generalities. At the most general, we might say that we want to lead a life that is fulfilling, or a life that enables us to flourish, or a life that makes us happy, or a life that lets us do what we want to do, or a life where we behave as we believe we ought. Each of these answers overlaps, though each has a different slant. A fulfilling life might suggest a life that enables us to feel that we have filled ourselves with what is on offer – I might find it fulfilling to go on holidays to exotic places to enjoy new experiences. A flourishing life perhaps has connotations of us realising our potential – so that athletes flourish by excelling at their sport, and actors on stage. A happy life implies that our pleasure is maximised – perhaps by having deep friendships and other close relationships. And a life that lets us do what we want to do implies that we value our autonomy – the ability to make decisions for ourselves and then put them into effect.

Books have been written about each of these understandings of the good life – and others besides. Our interest is on the contribution that our sexual activities play in what we get from life. Specifically in this chapter we shall look at the role of sex in pleasure, recreation, health and well-being.

But first we need to clarify what we mean by sex or more precisely 'sexual activity'. Producing definitions has its problems but sexual activity can be described – albeit somewhat circularly – as actions involving two (or more) people which at least one of them considers sexual. The advantage of the latter part of this definition is that it would include, for example, an adult inappropriately (i.e. for sexual gratification) caressing a child, even if the child didn't realise that, from the adult's perspective, a sexual motive was involved (or experience being had).

Our definition requires a subjective construction for what is meant by sexual, and this too, we would argue, is an advantage. After all, depending on context and the participants, a kiss on the cheek can be sexual, a mark of friendship, a token between relatives or a social custom. Objective attempts to define what is meant by sexual activity also encounter the difficulty that there is a lack of culturally unambiguous terminology for sexual activity other than sexual intercourse (which term itself seems, in the absence of sex aids, to assume at least one partner is male) (Spencer *et al.* 1988). (A well-known illustration of this was the case a few years back of the US President who was able (just) to maintain that he had told the truth when he had claimed that he hadn't 'had sex' with someone other than his wife even when it subsequently transpired that the two of them had engaged in oral sex.)

Finally, our definition is not so much meant to exclude masturbation as to avoid giving it the same prominence as other sexual activities. One suspects – though we don't know any reliable research on the topic – that nearly all 'solitary' masturbation is fuelled by sexual fantasy about someone else or by erotic representations of another.

Sex and pleasure

The notion that the chief aim of life, including sexual activity, should be to accumulate pleasures is the most common form of utilitarianism. Utilitarianism itself exists in various forms, but it begins with the assumption that most actions lead to pleasure and/or displeasure. In a situation in which there are alternative courses of action, the desirable (i.e. right) action is the one which leads to the greatest net increase in pleasure.

There are two great strengths of utilitarianism. First, it provides a single ethical framework in which, in principle, any moral question may be answered. It doesn't matter whether we are talking about the legalisation of cannabis, the disposal of nuclear waste or the age of sexual consent; a utilitarian perspective exists. Second, utilitarianism takes pleasure seriously. People sometimes suspect that ethics is all about telling people what not to do; utilitarians assert that people should do what maximises the total amount of pleasure in the world.

However, there are difficulties with acknowledging utilitarianism as the sole arbiter in ethical decision-making. For one thing, an extreme form of utilitarianism in which every possible course of action would have consciously to be analysed in terms of its countless consequences would quickly bring all human moral thinking to a stop. Then there is the question as to how precisely pleasure can be measured. Is it to be equated with happiness or the satisfaction of preferences, for example? And what are its units? How can we weigh different types of pleasure, for example sexual and intellectual? Then, is it always the case that two units of pleasure should outweigh one unit of displeasure? Suppose two people each need a single kidney. Should one person (with two kidneys) be killed so that two may live (each with one kidney)?

Utilitarians claim to provide answers to all such objections (e.g. Singer 1993). For example, rule-based utilitarianism accepts that the best course of action is often served by following certain rules – such as 'Tell the truth' and 'Remain sexually faithful', for example. Then, a deeper analysis of the kidney example suggests that if society really did allow one person thus to be killed so that two others could live, many of us might spend so much of our time going around fearful that the sum total of human happiness would be less than if we outlawed such practices.

So, at the risk of appearing banal, what sorts of pleasures we may ask are connected with sexual activity? For a start, the immediate physical ones, through such intimacies as looking, touching, kissing, caressing, intercourse and orgasm – though even to produce such a list, while hardly deeply controversial, risks locking one's thoughts into a somewhat narrow and genital-aimed view of sexual activity.

Pleasure, of course, is an intensely subjective experience. You may derive great pleasure from rock climbing, clubbing, vegan cooking and attending hunt saboteur meetings. I may dislike all of these, preferring bird watching, Gregorian chants, black pudding and grouse shooting. Nevertheless, if you and I live together we might (just) manage to organise our lives so that each of us could enjoy these activities without the other. However, if the two of us are in a sexual relationship, my pleasure – unless I have no consideration for you at all – depends on your pleasure and vice versa. This truth isn't restricted to sexual relationships – after all, the pleasure enjoyed in any friendship depends on the sharing of experiences and some degree of mutuality – but it is especially apposite for sexual relationships. After all, to take a rather extreme example, if the only way I can find sex really satisfying is for others to acquiesce in my every demand of sexual position while you prefer sexual relationships to be based on a more equitable footing, the two of us are unlikely to enjoy a mutually satisfying sexual relationship unless one of us changes.

The merging of one's self with the other in a relationship is emphasised by Robert Solomon in one of the few philosophical treatments of erotic love when he says: 'one might well quote Cathy's climactic revelation in *Wuthering Heights*: "I *am* Heathcliff – he's always, always in my mind – not as a pleasure, anymore than I am a pleasure to myself – but as my own being."' (Solomon [1988] 1995: 252). The notion that in a sexual relationship one joins oneself to another so that the two become one is central to a Christian understanding of marriage (see Chapter 6). Here we can simply note one view of erotic love which sees the extent of physical intimacy to be such that those involved cannot, without a psychological cost, maintain an emotional divide between themselves.

Maintaining that sex is about the maximisation of pleasure is all very well but the sad truth is how little pleasure some people get from their sexual relationships. There is little doubt that some people would be happier if their sex lives were better (e.g. Hite 1994). Perhaps the best known authors who attempt to demystify sex and make it more likely that heterosexual couples will enjoy sexual intercourse are William Masters and Virginia Johnson (Masters and Johnson 1966; Masters *et al.* 1994).

In their most recent book, described on the cover as 'The up-to-date, comprehensive book of male-female love, pleasure, health, and well-being by the world's foremost team of sexual researchers-therapists', Masters *et al.* (1994) go on to describe carefully what couples, single women and single men can do to tackle such difficulties as not enjoying sex much, finding sex painful, ejaculating too soon, not reaching orgasm and preferring masturbating on one's own to sexual intercourse with one's partner. For example, in the chapter titled 'Female sexual dysfunctions' after reviewing the research evidence on the proportion of women who have orgasms, they discuss 'some specific suggestions for women to help identify and deal with common obstacles to sexual arousal' (Masters *et al.* 1994: 185):

1   Don't shut off your erotic potential by locking yourself into negative prophecies.
2   If there's something about your lovemaking style that doesn't suit you, take an active role in making a change.
3   Many problems with sexual arousal are a result of the tendency to think too much and touch too little.
4   Use fantasies to jump-start your sexual arousal or boost your turn-on once it's underway.
5   Emphasize the playfulness of sex instead of turning it into a chore or a mission.
6   Don't be afraid to experiment with different types of sensual stimulation.

(Masters *et al.* 1994: 185–7)

Sex and recreation

The category 'sex and recreation' overlaps with 'sex and pleasure' – a lot of recreation is pleasurable – but the two can usefully be distinguished. In everyday language, a married couple might find sex extremely pleasurable but would be unlikely to characterise it as recreational whereas someone on holiday might find novel sexual activity somewhat less pleasurable than they had hoped but describe the holiday and all its activities (including the sexual ones) as recreational, not in the etymological sense (i.e. making something anew) but with the associations of 'fun' and 'non-permanent' (to many people golf is a recreation, but not to Tiger Woods).

Historically there has long been an association between going away from home and sexual activity. Once most people went away from home only to make pilgrimages, for long-distance trade or to fight wars. All of these afforded opportunities for sexual indulgence (see Chaucer's *Canterbury Tales*). Nowadays it is holidays for many people and business trips for some.

There is a literature on tourism and sex. A useful distinction can be made between 'sex tourism' and 'sex in tourism'. Sex tourism involves journeys to a distant place primarily with the intention to have sex, typically sex with those who are much younger and poorer than oneself (bring to mind, despite the dangers of stereotyping, a middle-aged western male having sex and little else with a variety of teenage sex workers in Thailand). Sex in tourism, on the other hand, involves more of a typical holiday and the sexual partners are on a more level footing (think of loads of '2wenties' going on a package holiday from the UK to Ibiza, for example – there will be clubbing, sand and sea as well as sex with others on holiday themselves).

Feminists and others have pointed out that a flourishing sex tourist industry requires a labour market where women (as well as girls and some boys and men) can earn significantly more from prostitution than from more socially sanctioned employment, 'male travellers from affluent countries who are able to draw on a racialized ideology in which foreign women are imagined to be more available and submissive than women in their own countries' (Carter and Clift 2000: 10) and tacit support from local governments and western travel agents.

Of course, recreation need not involve sex. Furzana Khan and her colleagues, armed with clip-boards, questionnaires and tape-recorders (but also sun cream, swimsuits and holiday money – participant research can be arduous), accompanied 203 ravers on a package holiday to the Mediterranean (Khan *et al.* 2000). Alcohol and drug use was higher on the holiday but, contrary to the stereotype, the ravers were less likely to have sex when on holiday and had fewer sexual partners than at home.

However, even in this piece of research, there were many for whom one of the main aims of the holiday was sexual activity:

Liz: They're only here for one thing, eh? Pure on the hots, and everything.
Ann: The lads and that, they're all on the go looking for women.
Liz: Same with the girls, they're the same.

Ann: They're worse.
Interviewer: How?
Rob: 'Cos they are!
Ann: 'Cos they're looking for men, the crowd of lassies that are
                  sitting at the back there on the pool, you see them? I don't
                  know them, the lassie there [Ann points to another woman]
                  that's what she says to me. I says, 'Enjoying the holiday?',
                  she says, 'No! I've no' had a man yet!' So she's saying that's
                  what she wants, a man. Here it was even, 'Aye you can do it
                  on holiday, nobody will find out' and that.

                                                      (Khan *et al.* 2000: 229)

Prostitution can be seen, from the client's point of view, as a form of
recreation whether the client is a tourist (Aggleton 1999; Clift and Carter
2000) or closer to home (McKeganey and Barnard 1996; Aggleton 1999;
Bailey 2002; for a moral geography of prostitution see Hubbard 1999).
In McKeganey and Barnard's ethnographic work on street prostitution in
Glasgow, clients gave five reasons for the appeal of sex with a prostitute,
most of which can be interpreted within a framework of sex as pleasure
and/or recreation.

• The capacity to specify particular forms of sexual activity:

> Anal, I've only done that once with a prostitute, but it's perhaps
> more difficult to ask a girlfriend to do. Also I quite enjoy dressing
> up in ladies' underwear which again I would not ask a partner to do.
>
>   (McKeganey and Barnard 1996: 51)

• Being able to have sex with a range of different women:

> I used to have different partners before I met my wife and it's just
> something I missed.
>
>   (McKeganey and Barnard 1996: 52)

• The ability to seek out women with specific physical attributes or
  presenting certain images:

> she's got to have long legs or she looks a bit of a bitch. If she stand
> there and looks really nice that would be a complete turn-off, she's
> got to look a bit bitchy, a bit of a tart.
>
>   (McKeganey and Barnard 1996: 52)

• The limited and unemotional nature of the contact:

> It was just the fact that here were women who would do anything, you know that was required, no bones about it plus the fact that there was no commitment at all. You know, it was for a specific purpose that you became involved, then it was all over and you could go back to work.
>
> (McKeganey and Barnard 1996: 52)

- The clandestine nature of the contact:

> It's the thrill of it being illicit, unknown and the fact that you can be a bit more adventurous.
>
> (McKeganey and Barnard 1996: 53)

Recreational sex need not entail intercourse. Professional strippers have precise rules of conduct that may avoid any physical contact with clients unless the club permits lap dancing or the strippers decide to make extra money by permitting punters to touch them (Pasko 2002). The great majority of strippers are female and the great majority of clients are male. The limited amount of research that has been undertaken on women at male strip shows (e.g. the Chippendales) certainly indicates that the event is recreational and entertaining but suggests that it is perhaps rather different in character and meaning from many female strip shows:

> [it is] quite difficult to define the Chippendales act: on one level it sets itself up as a striptease – clothes come off and the body is revealed. Yet it never seems to really work in that way – if to work in that way is to encourage members of the audience to stare or gaze upon a sexual object. The music is too loud, fracturing the concentration that seems so necessary in, for example film theory's objectifying gaze; the audience is too loud, again a distracting element; the stage is too 'busy' with as many as 12 performers on stage at one time (where and who to look at?); the strip is never consummated, in that although glimpses of the genitals are just a breath away, the lights dim, the towel is snatched back just in time, or the sleight of hand is accomplished just at the crucial moment.
>
> (Smith 2002: 79)

Among 16–24 year olds, Ford (1991) identified two distinct sexual philosophies: 'relational-romantic' and 'casual-recreational'. The latter philosophy is more likely to be found in males than in females. Indeed, in their work with 9 and 10 year olds, Halstead and Waite (2001b) found elements of this as the boys talked about playing with condoms, experimenting with sex lines, watching other boys expose themselves, looking at 'girlie' magazines and watching adult and pornographic videos (see Chapter 3).

Sex and health

The connections between sexual activity and health are generally viewed within a framework of certain kinds of sexual activities being threats to health.

Pregnancy and health

Pregnancy among young (teenage and younger) and older women (late thirties and above) is riskier for the physical health of both mother and baby. Teenage mothers are more likely to experience anaemia, toxaemia, eclampsia, hypertension and prolonged and difficult labour (Social Exclusion Unit 1999). Further, in the UK teenage mothers, compared to older mothers:

- usually go to their doctors much later in pregnancy (as three-quarters of them aren't intending to become pregnant)
- often miss out on pre-conception health measures such as taking folic acid supplements
- are much more likely to smoke during pregnancy
- are 25 per cent more likely to have a baby weighing less than 2500 grams
- have a 60 per cent higher infant mortality rate for the 12 months after birth
- are three times as likely to suffer post-natal depression
- are only half as likely to breastfeed
- have children who are twice as likely to be admitted to hospital as the result of accidents or gastro-enteritis.

(Social Exclusion Unit 1999)

More careful analysis shows that many of the above correlations are due largely to poverty (see Hardwick and Patychuk 1999) rather than age but that teenage pregnancy has an additional, independent effect.

Sexually transmitted infections

Human have always had sexually transmitted infections (STIs) but the movement of people assists in the spread of STIs. In Europe, for example, syphilis may have been absent before the late fifteenth century. A doctor of the time in Barcelona, Dr Diza de Isla, wrote that syphilis was unknown until after Columbus returned from his first voyage to the Americas in 1493 (Reiss 1993a). In 1494 Charles VIII of France crossed the Alps into Italy and undertook the Siege of Naples. It seems that some infected Spaniards joined his army as mercenaries and in 1495 a dreadful plague, thought to be syphilis from contemporary descriptions of the symptoms, broke out among Charles VIII's men. The siege of Naples was abandoned and a disorganised retreat followed.

As with AIDS (Acquired Immune Deficiency Syndrome) today, the blame for syphilis was put on foreigners and 'others'. The English called it *morbus gallicus* (the French disease), the French called it the Italian disease, the Italians called it both the French disease and the Spanish disease, while the Spanish blamed people from Haiti.

Today, of course, it is HIV (Human Immunodeficiency Virus) that receives the most attention. Unknown to medical science until 1981, by the end of 2001 AIDS had already killed 25 million people with another 40 million alive but infected with HIV (Lamptey 2002). With a vaccine still not available, lowering the price of HIV drugs (Berwick 2002) and education are likely to be the two main means of tackling AIDS for the foreseeable future.

While most media attention about STIs has been on HIV/AIDS, a number of other countries, including the UK, have seen increases in recent years in the rates of other STIs. In England and Wales, the number of diagnoses of gonorrhoea at STI clinics more than doubled between 1995 and 2002 – with the greatest rises among 16–19 year olds (Nicoll and Hamers 2002). Syphilis had reached an all-time low in England and Wales in the mid-1990s. By 2000, cases had more than doubled (Doherty *et al.* 2002; Nicoll and Hamers 2002). Gonorrhoea and syphilis can both be treated successfully with antibiotics, if detected early enough. A number of other STIs are more difficult to detect and/or treat, yet these too have seen comparable increases. The number of instances of chlamydia more than doubled between 1995 and 2000, though some of this increase may have been due to increased testing. There have also been rises in genital herpes and genital warts. As the British Medical Association has concluded:

> The sustained rise in diagnoses of acute STIs over the last six years is probably attributable to the increasing practice of unsafe sexual behaviour, particularly in young heterosexuals and homo/bisexual men. In view of the severe longer-term complications associated with untreated STIs, as well as their potential role in facilitating HIV transmission, these latest data emphasise the need to improve current STI prevention strategies.
>
> (British Medical Association Board of Science and Education 2002: 10)

Violence and sex

Sex may be one of the most pleasurable activities open to us but as with anything that has the capacity to result in great good, it also has the capacity to result in great harm. One such harm is the violence or threat of violence that all too often accompanies sex. In Chapter 3 we saw that sex and violence are often linked in the thinking of boys as young as 9 and 10.

We have already mentioned the pleasure many men obtain from prostitutes. From many prostitutes' perspectives, though, violence is never far away. In McKeganey and Barnard's three-year study they contacted over 300 women prostitutes in Glasgow and 'violence was reported by nearly all of the women interviewed' (McKeganey and Barnard 1996: 70):

> We met up with Candy whom we had seen earlier that evening shouting the odds at a guy who was walking away from her. She said that she had been in the alley doing business with him when without any warning at all he had punched her hard in the side of her face and made a grab for her bag. She was still holding on to her bag as she recounted this, her lip and cheek bruised and swollen.
>
> (McKeganey and Barnard 1996: 71)

> [We] were approached by a woman who we have chatted to on many nights. She had a black eye and heavily swollen cheekbone. She explained that she had been set upon by a punter earlier that week. He had stopped and asked her for business. Although she had been a bit wary he had used her name. Once in the car she had given him her usual directions to the place she normally used but he had turned off near the fruit market, pulled the car up by some darkened factories, ordered her to strip and then tied her hands with bin liners. He then punched her in the face and pushed her out of the car. She thought for sure he had intended running her over but she had managed to scramble over a fence and into a nearby field.
>
> (McKeganey and Barnard 1996: 72)

Nor need we restrict our account of violence to prostitution to encounter sexual violence. Homophobic violence against men and boys is widespread (Warwick and Douglas n.d.), date rape is now a recognised phenomenon (Hollway and Jefferson 1998) and the world-wide statistics and stories of sexual violence among girls, boys, women and some men are extensive and horrific (e.g. Michael et al. 1994; Reavey and Gough 2000; Human Rights Watch 2001; Phasha 2002; Shumba 2002). We could fill this book with quotes. Here is just one, from a 15-year-old high school student in the northern suburbs of Johannesburg:

> I was walking with [a] friend and [the teacher] asked me to come to his room . . . I thought, he's a teacher, it'll be fine. He gave me a key so that I could get to the boys' hostel [where he lived]. I went to his dorm and walked to the lounge. He gave me a hooch [an alcoholic

drink]. I was lame. I knew what was happening to me, but I couldn't move. He picked me up and took me to his room and started taking my clothes off. He took his clothes off. He's twice my size and like five times my weight, and has so many muscles. Then he penetrated me. When I came to, I got up and went to my dorm. My friend said I looked high. I went to bed. Then I just left it. I was scared to tell anyone because I was afraid no one would believe me.

(Human Rights Watch 2001: 37)

Sex and well-being

The previous section on 'Sex and health' concentrates on *physical* health and the threats to it posed by sexual activity. But, of course, health can be understood more broadly and sex can have positive rather than only negative consequences for health, particularly when health is construed holistically in terms of the contribution it makes to a person's well-being. Simply having, not having or losing a boyfriend or girlfriend, whatever one's age, can make one feel good or bad about oneself, giving rise, as almost all of us know, to emotions that may surprise us in their intensity.

In an article titled 'Coming, coming, gone: a feminist deconstruction of heterosexual orgasm', Annie Potts (2000) interviewed women and men in Aotearoa/New Zealand in same-sex groups about the meanings that they attached to sexual health. Some of her interviewees talked in what Potts described as 'quasi-spiritual or existentialist terms' (Potts 2000: 62):

> *Alice*: [Sexual fulfilment is] kind of like where both of them had achieved a kind of moment of ecstasy, I can only imagine what it is like for a man but I – yeah again it's when I feel that I've achieved a kind of bond I think, when you have kind of intercourse and . . . you're kind of reaching that other person's soul that you're not able to achieve at any other moment . . . when you look into their eyes you feel as if you're looking into their soul and it's a bond – I see my vagina as being my soul too . . . and when we connect it's kind of like a joining of the souls sort of thing, and so it's that kind of bonding and then the sensation – feelings that you have that creates that feeling of sexual fulfilment.
>
> (Potts 2000: 62)

The notion that a sexual relationship is about more than recreation, physical health or pleasure is pretty widespread. We talk about 'meaningful relationships', implying that a sexual relationship without meaning falls short not just of an ideal but of a common expectation. Some indication of the prevalence of this expectation is realised when one reads the occasional attempts of philosophers to defend promiscuity, notably by

Elliston ([1975] 1995). Objections to promiscuity are obvious – it risks physical health, it can be argued to be ultimately less pleasurable than spending a lifetime (or, at any rate, a number of years) with one partner (at a time), it falls short of any religious ideals for marriage and it often leads to deception and exploitation. Elliston ends up arguing for promiscuity partly on standard liberal grounds (see Chapter 4) and partly on the grounds that 'in many areas, such as clothing, vocation, and recreation, the need for experimentation and diversity is recognized and conceded' (Elliston [1975] 1995: 153).

Actually, Elliston would have done better not to mention 'vocation' since one of the characteristics of vocations is precisely that they are often life-long (Reiss [1990] 1991). That aside, the weakness of his argument in many people's eyes – despite its evident sensibleness – is best indicated by quoting one of his defences for it:

> Strict adherence to the Western norm places our sex lives in a straight-jacket that curtails body language to 'I love you', the *only* message to be delivered, to just *one* person, with *fixed* diction and intonation – until the disillusioned pair have become bored by the repetition.
>
> . . . Consider a society where the following etiquette is operative. Each man is allowed to dine with only one woman. Before their first meal begins, each receives a solemn injunction: 'Thou shalt dine with none other, so long as you both shall live.' . . .
>
> Loosening the restrictions of the Western norm . . . is tantamount to permitting, if not promulgating, promiscuity. The ensuing changes promise to make our sex lives not only physically more satisfying, but also more meaningful.
>
> (Elliston [1975] 1995: 153–4, original emphases)

Are changing sexual and dining partners equivalent? Even on empirical grounds, aside from any reasoning about existentials, the answer, for most people, however much they enjoy food and eating with others, is clearly 'no'. I may remember with relish the first time I ate avocado and a gourmand may deeply regret being advised no longer to eat pâté de foie gras on health grounds, but for most of us a new sexual partner is more significant than a shift in diet.

There may be a link between sexual activity and well-being but there are arguments about well-being in favour of the renunciation of sex, i.e. celibacy (Abbott 2001) too (though recognising that in some societies, Islamic ones for instance, life-long celibacy for adults is culturally unacceptable). In the Christian tradition, for example, celibacy has been honoured since New Testament times. It is true that arguments for celibacy have included ones few would accept nowadays – those to do with original sin, understood literally, for example – while celibacy among nuns may have sometimes been, at least in part, an instance of partiarchal control over the lives of women. Nevertheless, the continued existence of celibacy, whether life-long or more bounded and whether within a religious or a secular framework, can serve both as an authentic home for some – with elements of self-discovery and/or service to others – and as a critique against the oversexualisation of society.

Sexual ethics

Having surveyed the possible contribution of sexual activity to pleasure, recreation, health and well-being, we can ask whether there is such a thing as a distinctive sexual ethics – i.e. right set of ways to behave sexually – or not.

At first the answer may seem obvious. Surely sexual behaviour has its own ethics! People, at different times and in different cultures, argue about the acceptability of polygamy and homosexuality and the age of consent and whether rape can exist within marriage and so on.

However, it can be argued that sex has no particular (i.e. distinctive) moral significance. Igor Primoratz (1999), for example, holds that sex is morally neutral, so that moral guidance regarding sexual behaviour is provided by the same general moral rules and values that apply in other areas:

> Thus adultery is not wrong as extramarital *sex*, but only when it involves breach of promise, or seriously hurts the feelings of the non-adulterous spouse, etc. Prostitution is not wrong as commercial *sex*, but if and when the prostitute is forced into this line of work by the lack of any real alternative. Paedophilia is not wrong as adult–child *sex* but because even when the child is willingly participating, its willingness is extremely suspect in view of the radical asymmetries of maturity, knowledge, understanding, and power of children and adults. Sexual harassment is not wrong because it is *sexual*, but because it is *harassment*. Rape is not wrong as *sexual* battery, but as sexual *battery*.
>
> (Primoratz 1999: 173–4, original emphases)

The reasoning is convincing and (as we shall argue in Chapter 12), there is much to be said for young people discussing such issues. To a certain extent, though, it could be held that the argument about whether there is such a thing as a distinctive sexual ethics is semantic. Analogously, are there such things as a distinctive business ethics or environmental ethics or reproductive ethics (governing the new technologies of *in vitro* fertilisation, surrogacy, designer babies and so on)? Perhaps all ethics can be subsumed under a small number of broad principles – such as autonomy, beneficence, non-maleficence and justice (see Chapter 4). However, just because chemicals obey the laws of physics and no other laws, this doesn't mean that we can't have a science of chemistry; just because all living organisms obey the laws of physics and chemistry and eschew vitalism, this doesn't mean that we don't have the biological sciences. In the same way, we can talk about sexual ethics even if there are no special considerations that apply to sexuality and sexual behaviour and to nothing else. And anyway, as Chapter 6 shows, there are many who do hold that there is such a thing as a distinctive sexual ethics.

In any event, what is clear is that, whether distinctive or not, there is such a thing as sexual ethics. In particular, there are certain limits to acceptable sexual behaviour set by the harms caused to others. In some cases, such as rape and sexual abuse, these harms are clear-cut; in others, such as visiting commercial sex workers (prostitutes) or leaving one sexual partner and changing to another, there are arguments on both sides. We would want young people, at the appropriate age, to reflect on and discuss their sexual values. There is much, therefore, to be said for them considering such issues.

Summary

1   One view of life is that our chief aim in it should be to accumulate pleasures. Pleasures are best understood subjectively. One of the particular features of mutually pleasurable sexual relationships is the degree to which each person's pleasure both depends on and enhances that of the other. However, many people experience little sexual pleasure.

2   Sex can be viewed as recreation, even entertainment. By and large, males are more likely than females to see sex as recreational.

3   Sexual activity is often seen as being a threat to health. Teenage pregnancy is more risky for mother and baby alike than is pregnancy for women in their twenties or thirties, though this is partly because of poverty. HIV and other sexually transmitted infections are on the rise and many girls and women, and some boys and men, experience sexual violence and abuse.

4   Sex can have positive as well as negative consequences for health, particularly when health is construed more holistically in terms of the contribution it makes to a person's well-being. For a considerable number of people, sexual intimacy can be profoundly meaningful.

5   Whether there are particular ethical rules and values that apply exclusively to sexual activity is contentious. Some argue that sex is morally neutral, so that moral guidance regarding sexual behaviour is provided by the same general moral rules and values that apply in other areas.

Issues for discussion

1   Is the aim of life to maximise the amount of pleasure in the world? If not, what else might life consist of?
2   Why does the recreational understanding of sex seem to be more prevalent among males than among females?
3   Why does sexual activity often seem to be accompanied by violence?
4   Is celibacy a second-best option?
5   Draw up a list of ethical rules to govern (a) patterns of sexual activity within a relationship; (b) good conduct in a doubles partnership in tennis. Comment on similarities and any differences between the two lists.

Further reading

For clear introductions to moral philosophy where the concept of the good life is discussed see:

- Blackburn, S. (2001) *Being Good: A Short Introduction to Ethics*, Oxford: Oxford University Press.
- Singer, P. (1993) *Practical Ethics*, 2nd edn, Cambridge: Cambridge University Press.

For sociological accounts of the realities of sexual experiences for people see:

- Hite, S. (1994) *The Hite Report on the Family: Growing up under Patriarchy*, London: Bloomsbury.
- Humphries, S. (1988) *A Secret World of Sex*, London: Sidgwick and Jackson.
- Johnson, A. M., Wadsworth, J., Wellings, K. and Field, J. (1994) *Sexual Attitudes and Lifestyles*, Oxford: Blackwell Scientific.

- Michael, R. T., Gagnon, J. H., Laumann, E. O. and Kolata, G. (1994) *Sex in America: A Definitive Survey*, London: Little, Brown.

Valuable philosophical analyses of sex are provided by:

- Primoratz, I. (1999) *Ethics and Sex*, London: Routledge.
- Scruton, R. (1986) *Sexual Desire: A Philosophical Investigation*, London: Weidenfeld and Nicolson.
- Stewart, R. M. (ed.) (1995) *Philosophical Perspectives on Sex and Love*, New York: Oxford University Press.

Chapter 6

Religious values

The significance of religion

There are many factors that unite people, and there are many factors that divide them. Religious belief falls into both camps. For some people, their religious faith is absolutely the core of their being: they could no more feel comfortable acting or thinking in a way that conflicted with their religious values than they could feel comfortable not breathing. For others, religious faith is either an irrelevancy – an historical anachronism – or positively harmful with many of the ills that befall humankind being placed at its door.

Religious believers need no arguments to be voiced in favour of taking religious values seriously, both generally and with particular reference to sexual ethics and behaviour. Agnostics and atheists might be tempted to ignore religious values but this would be a mistake. For a start, it is still the case that even in countries, such as the UK, where the national significance of religion is in decline, the majority of people when asked affirm a belief in God, including about a half of young people (McGrellis *et al.* 2000). Although a stated belief in God may not translate into any overt religious activity, such as communal worship, it often connects with what people feel about important issues in life and occasionally manifests itself, for example in wishing to get married in church (e.g. Davie 1994).

Then there is the fact that most of the world's religions, while they may not have anything very direct or clear to say about certain of today's ethical questions – such as the legitimacy of human reproductive cloning or globalisation – do have a great deal to say about sexual values. Religious values still permeate, for historical reasons, much of society and need to be understood. Of course, those with a religious faith also need to understand something of secular reasoning about sexual ethics: it is still too often the case that those with a religious faith assume that only they really know what is good sexual behaviour, and only they can put such knowledge into effect.

What might be the relationship between religious faith and ethical behaviour? One possibility is that ethical behaviour depends on religious belief. Such a possibility may seem absurd – most of us know too many people without a religious faith but with strong moral principles that translate into right actions. However, there is a possible defence for the thesis 'all ethical reasoning and right action depends on religious belief'. For instance, it might be that good atheists are good because they inherit a set of views, for example that hurting other people is wrong, that derives from the historical pervasiveness of religious values. A consequence of this argument would be that should good atheists awaken and realise that their moral actions are merely the inherited legacy of religious values, they might discard them, free thereafter to lead a life of pure selfishness.

One problem with this chain of reasoning – aside from its, to most people, inherent improbability – is that it requires that actions and intentions are good not in themselves but because they are deemed good by God or some other source of religious teaching. This is to raise again the question posed by Plato in the *Euthyphro*: 'Do the gods love holiness because it is holy, or is it holy because they love it?' Doesn't it seem unacceptable to say that right is right and wrong is wrong only because God deems them so? Even if it somehow seems to limit God, there must be some sense in which, for example, justice, compassion and honesty are good not merely because God considers them so in arbitrary preference to injustice, selfishness and dishonesty (Berg 1993).

Given this argument, a different view of the relationship between religious and secular values can be advanced. Such a view divides behaviours and thoughts, including sexual ones, into three categories. First, there are those that are good irrespective of religious teachings: consideration for others is an example. Second, there are those that are right only for adherents of a religious faith: the keeping of certain food laws is an example. Third, and most contentiously, there are those actions that are held by many religious believers to be right for *all* people, whether or not they have a religious faith, even though such actions may not be acknowledged as right by all non-believers. The requirement, or at least the ideal, for marriage to be life-long is an example.

Here we shall proceed on the assumption that religious views about sexual values need to be considered for two main reasons. First, that a not inconsiderable number of people have them; second, that if we wish to live together in a pluralist society, it behoves all of us to understand at least something of what it is that motivates others. Such understanding is both intrinsically respectful and instrumentally useful. In addition, many people are still, consciously or otherwise, influenced by religious perspectives on sexual values, even if they have no overt religious commitment. Further, it is hard to understand some of the dilemmas represented in the literature about sexual ethics without some knowledge of religious teaching about sex.

Religious values in the context of school sex education

Until fairly recently, relatively little has been written in any detail about religious values and school sex education. Even such a valuable book as Ron Morris's (1994) *Values in Sexuality Education* has almost nothing on the issue beyond a telling anecdote that needs no interpretation:

> My first experience with a formal lesson on sexuality was as a senior high school student in the early seventies. Our school had a special sex education class in which the school nurse would visit all grade 10 and 11 classes. She would give a presentation on male and female anatomy, ovulation, conception and contraception. I remember being quite bored by the countless facts and clinical diagrams until she did something that was extremely unusual, especially in a Catholic school. She distributed a condom for each student to examine and manipulate. Most of us seemed rather uncomfortable. Some students appeared disgusted while others just giggled. Much to my surprise the nurse looked quite comfortable with the topic and with our response to the flabby instrument.
>
> The nurse then asked if we had any questions. I will never forget that moment. Dead silence. It was a silence which may have lasted 30 seconds but felt like more than 30 minutes! Finally one courageous student raised his hand. 'Miss,' he asked, 'now that you have shown us all this, does this mean that we can go out and do it?' 'All right,' I thought, 'right on, yes, what a great question!' I could sense a fever of anticipation and excitement rising throughout the class. Although others might have had a different question, I sensed that we were all eager to hear her answer. For the first time, however, she seemed somewhat uncomfortable. This was her answer: 'That's a really good question. But unfortunately I can't answer that. That's something you're going to have to decide for yourself. I suggest that you ask your parents when you get home.' What a disappointment!
>
> (Morris 1994: xv–xvi)

In recent years, though, there has been an increasing acknowledgement from all sex educators, whether or not they themselves are members of any particular religious faith, that religious points of view need to be taken into account, if only because, as pointed out, a significant number of children and their parents have moral values significantly informed by religious traditions. Further, it has been argued that religion is increasingly becoming a means through which identities are articulated on the public stage (Thomson 1997).

The first major attempt in the UK among believers from a number of religious traditions to agree a religious perspective on sex education resulted in an agreed statement by members of six major UK religions (Islamic Academy 1991). This statement provided a critique of contemporary sex education, listed principles which it was felt ought to govern sex education and provided a moral framework for sex education. This framework 'enjoins chastity and virginity before marriage and faithfulness and loyalty within marriage and prohibits extramarital sex and homosexual acts', 'upholds the responsibilities and values of parenthood', 'acknowledges that we owe a duty of respect and obedience to parents and have a responsibility to care for them in their old age and infirmity' and 'affirms that the married relationship involves respect and love' (Islamic Academy 1991: 8).

Another early UK project to look at the importance of religion and ethnicity for sex education was the Sex Education Forum's 'religion and ethnicity project'. A working group was set up which 'was concerned to challenge the view that religions offer only negative messages around sex, wanting to explore the broader philosophy and rationale behind specific religious prescriptions' (Thomson 1993: 2). Each participant was sent a total of 28 questions (e.g. 'Are there different natural roles for men and women, if so why?' and 'What is the religious attitude towards contraception and/or "protection" for example, safe sex re: STDs, HIV?') and the project chose to present a range of views, rather than attempting to reach a consensus. The outcome was a pack described on its title page as 'A resource for teachers and others working with young people'. One apparently minor, though noteworthy, feature of the pack – which has chapters on Anglican, Hindu, Islamic, Jewish, Methodist, Roman Catholic, secular and Sikh perspectives – is its postscript which reads:

> We would like to draw readers attention to the absence of a perspective in this pack that addresses Caribbean or African cultural attitudes to sex and sexuality. The primary concern of the pack is to explore religious perspectives on sex and sexuality, which inevitably also involve questions of ethnicity and culture. The absence of such a perspective that specifically addresses the cultural beliefs and practices of the large Caribbean and African communities in the United Kingdom should not be taken to obscure the existence or relevance of such traditions. It is hoped that schools and others working with young people will use this pack to initiate dialogue with parents and the community at a local level. We hope that schools will include Caribbean and

African communities in such consultation. We apologise if the title of
the pack is misleading.

(Thomson 1993: 125)

The postscript indicates a difficulty in writing in the field of religious
values. One steers forever between the Scylla of generalities, emphasising
the commonalities between the outlooks of the world's various religions,
and the Charybdis of specificities, stressing the particular viewpoints of
each religion and acknowledging the considerable diversity of opinion to
be found within each of them too.

At the same time as Rachel Thomson was compiling her pack, Gill
Lenderyou and Mary Porter of the Family Planning Association were putting together a booklet arising from the 'Values, faith and sex education'
project (Lenderyou and Porter 1994). At a four-day residential event in
this project, a bill of pupils' rights was drawn up by 22 people of different
religious faiths, and agreed statements on sex education were produced
under the headings of: Respect and difference, Faith and change in
society, Male and female equality, Relationships and marriages, Homosexuality, Cohabitation, Disability and sexuality, and Celibacy. The bill of
pupils' rights is more liberal and the agreed statements are more tentative
than the contents of the Islamic Academy's (1991) statement. For example,
included in the bill of pupils' rights are the assertions that pupils have
the right to sex education that 'provides full, accurate and objective information about growth and reproduction on topics including puberty,
parenthood, contraception, child care and responsible parenthood' and
that pupils have the right 'to be consulted about the manner in which
sex education is implemented in the classroom in connection with issues
such as whether it takes place in single sex or mixed groups or which
topics can be included in the programme' (Lenderyou and Porter 1994: 37).

More recently Michael Reiss and Shaikh Abdul Mabud edited an
academic book titled *Sex Education and Religion* which concentrated on
Christian and Muslim views about sex education (Reiss and Mabud 1998),
and publications have also resulted from two projects funded by the
Department of Health's Teenage Pregnancy Unit: *Faith, Values and Sex and
Relationships Education* (Blake and Katrak 2002) and *Diverse Communities*
(Katrak and Scott in press).

The approach we take for the remainder of this chapter is first to look at
what most religions have in common and then to concentrate on Christian
and Muslim perspectives on sex education. Focusing on just two religions
allows a more in-depth treatment in the space available than can be
obtained by looking at the full range of religions. We have chosen
Christianity and Islam partly because there is more literature on these
two religions (with respect to sex education) than on any others, partly
because between them Christians and Muslims account for a high propor-

tion of the faith communities of the UK (Katrak and Scott in press) and partly because of our own experience and expertise. We are both late-twentieth-century, early-twenty-first century white, male, middle-class academics. One of us is a priest in the Church of England; the other has a particular knowledge of Islamic values. Others will inhabit different vantage points; the best any of us can do is to acknowledge from where we come and try to maintain dialogue with those of other persuasions, always providing that we do not feel another's position to be so different from our own that we may be corrupted by exposure to it. Each of us should not feel embarrassed about inhabiting a particular set of cultural norms, but nor should we feel so defensive that we cannot learn from other traditions.

What do religions have in common?

No attempt is made here to define with any precision what is meant by a religion. There are those who maintain that Marxism, US nationalism, scientism and even atheism are all religions. We are content to use the word in its everyday sense. Most religious adherents have a sense of the transcendent, frequently of a God, or gods, who exists and has some connection with our everyday lives. A standard classification (Smart 1989; see also Hinnells [1984] 1991) argues that most religions have the following dimensions:

- the practical and ritual dimension (e.g. worship, prayer, meditation)
- the experiential and emotional dimension (e.g. visions of the divine, a feeling of the presence of God)
- the narrative or mythic dimension (e.g. the discourses between Lord Krishna and the warrior-prince Arjuna in the *Bhagavad Gita* of Hinduism)
- the doctrinal and philosophical dimension (e.g. the doctrine of the Trinity in Christianity)
- the ethical and legal dimension (e.g. the Ten Commandments and other regulations in the Jewish *Torah*)
- the social and institutional dimension (e.g. the *Sangha* – the order of monks and nuns founded by the Buddha to carry on the teaching of the *Dharma* – in Buddhism; the *umma* – the whole Muslim community – in Islam)
- the material dimension (e.g. synagogues, temples, churches, icons, the river Ganges, Mount Fuji and Ayer's Rock).

Most religions make distinctive claims to knowing what is right and what is wrong. For a start, most religions have sacred scriptures believed to contain teachings either of God or of pivotal early leaders of the faith. Then, religions have teachings and traditions assembled over many years (e.g. those contained in the Jewish *Talmud* and the teachings of the Roman Catholic *Magisterium*). Finally, most religions maintain that our consciences have some divine justification.

Christian views of sex and sex education

The phrase 'Christian views' suggests that there may be more than one Christian view about this subject. Now, the very suggestion that there can be a diversity of Christian views about sex and sex education, as opposed to a single, definitive view, will cause some Christians to be suspicious. After all, it might be felt, is not the acceptance of the notion that there may be more than one Christian view about so important an issue as human sexuality and sex education tantamount to the denial of a straightforward reading of the Christian scriptures as the word of God? Does it not amount to the adoption of a relativistic view of morality in which no unified, objective set of moral principles can be defended (Reiss 1998a)?

A full response to this point of view would require us to deal with the whole issue of conservatism and liberalism in the Christian Church and other religions too. In an important book James Barr (1984) argues that what is generally termed 'fundamentalism', and also known as the doctrine of scriptural inerrancy, is untenable precisely because taking literally the words of the (Christian) scriptures shows that the scriptures themselves do not take themselves literally (Barr 1984).

At the same time, it needs to be acknowledged that the liberal position can be held as dogmatically as the conservative one! Religious liberals are sometimes as dismissive of the conservative position, and those who hold it, as religious conservatives are of the liberal position, and those who hold it. For some, the advent of postmodernism offers a resolution to this impasse. Not the form of postmodernism that dismisses all knowledge as wholly subjective and relative but the postmodernism that rejects the notion of there only being a single way of discerning truth. This latter version not only is more tolerant of a diversity of coexisting viewpoints but also requires them, generally rejecting the single grand metanarrative.

Christian views about sex

Christian views about virtually everything derive from perhaps five main sources: first, the writings of the Bible, containing both the Jewish and New Testament scriptures; second, the teachings of the Church down the ages; third, the conscience of individuals informed, they believe, by the Holy Spirit; fourth, their God-given, though imperfect, powers of reason;

fifth, the particular cultural milieu they inhabit. This catalogue alone makes it likely that there will be a diversity of Christian views about almost any important subject.

To illustrate Christian views about sex, we concentrate on marriage and homosexuality. This is partly because both subjects are extremely important ones, but also because more of a consensus exists among Christians on one than on the other. Christian teachings about marriage are widespread in the New Testament and the doctrine of marriage has been very widely debated over the last two millennia with considerable agreement resulting. On the other hand, the New Testament teaching about homosexuality is sparser and it is only in recent decades that it has been analysed in any great depth. Indeed, there currently exists a very wide diversity of opinion on the subject in Christian circles, as we shall see.

Christian views about marriage

Traditional Christian understandings of marriage are outlined in the marriage services of the various Christian denominations. In the Church of England the following, since the early 1980s, has been the most widely used form of words proclaimed at a marriage by the officiating minister to the congregation as the bride and bridegroom stand near the beginning of the service:

> The Scriptures teach us that marriage is a gift of God in creation and a means of his grace, a holy mystery in which man and woman become one flesh. It is God's purpose that, as husband and wife give themselves to each other in love throughout their lives, they shall be united in that love as Christ is united with his Church.
>
> Marriage is given, that husband and wife may comfort and help each other, living faithfully together in need and in plenty, in sorrow and in joy. It is given, that with delight and tenderness they may know each other in love, and, through the joy of their bodily union, may strengthen the union of their hearts and lives. It is given, that they may have children and be blessed in caring for them and bringing them up in accordance with God's will, to his praise and glory.
>
> In marriage husband and wife belong to one another, and they begin a new life together in the community. It is a way of life that all should honour; and it must not be undertaken carelessly, lightly, or selfishly, but reverently, responsibly, and after serious thought.
>
> (Alternative Service Book 1980: 288)

Of course, each sentence in this quotation could be the subject for a chapter in itself. However, several points can be stressed. Marriage is something that two adults, a man and a woman, choose to enter. It is life-long, exclusive and the only proper place for sexual intercourse. Further, it has a mystical element to it, the relationship between a married couple reflecting the relationship Christ has with his Church. Indeed, in the Roman Catholic tradition marriage is one of the sacraments.

This is not, of course, to maintain that every Christian marriage lives up to this high calling. Enough is known of sexual behaviour within and without marriage both in history (Goody 1983; Porter and Hall 1995) and more recently (Humphries 1988; Moore and Rosenthal 1993; Johnson *et al.* 1994) to appreciate that this is far from the case. Further, issues such as polygamy, divorce, cohabitation and contraception have been signifi-cant sources of tension, both doctrinally and pastorally, for the Christian Church at different times and in different places (e.g. Commission on the Christian Doctrine of Marriage 1971; Spong 1988; Pope John Paul II 1993; Thatcher 1993). In recent decades, a feminist perspective has developed critiquing hitherto unquestioned assumptions about the relationships between the sexes (e.g. Evans 1983; Laffey 1988; Dowell 1990; Webster 1995; Isherwood 2000). And, of course, the institution of marriage has been viewed as under threat as fewer couples choose to get married, as the divorce rate climbs and as the various new reproductive technologies such as *in vitro* fertilisation and surrogacy pose new ethical dilemmas (Dickenson 2002).

Nevertheless, it is still the case that a considerable consensus about marriage exists both among theologians and among the public at large, whether or not people describe themselves as practising Christians. Indeed, the majority of adults still choose, at some point, to get married (most people still hoping that their marriage will be permanent), only a minority (albeit a large minority) divorce and most children are still con-ceived in the time-honoured manner – but see Duin (1988) and Dyson (1993).

One significant shift in Christian views about marriage, though, is in the attitude taken towards people who live together (cohabit) before marriage. Although many Christians still see this as a second-best option, cohabita-tion is increasingly being accepted. A 1995 report on the family from a Working Party of the Church of England Board of Social Responsibility resulted in furious debate, exemplified by the front-page headline in the *Church Times* of 9 June 1995 'Living together no longer a sin'. The chief offending passage was as follows:

> the widespread practice of cohabitation needs to be attended to with sympathy and discernment, especially in the light of the enormous changes in western society that have taken place recently and the effect these have had on the understanding and practice of personal relationships. Anxiety among churchgoers about cohabitation is best allayed, not by judgemental attitudes about 'fornication' and 'living in

sin', but by the confident celebration of marriage and the affirmation and support of what in cohabiting relationships corresponds most with the Christian ideal. Being disapproving and hostile towards people who cohabit only leads to alienation and a breakdown in communication. Instead, congregations should welcome cohabitees, listen to them, learn from them and co-operate with them so that all may discover God's presence in their lives and in our own, at the same time as bearing witness to that sharing in God's love which is also available within marriage.

(Working Party of the Board for Social Responsibility 1995: 118)

Critics of the report argued that it had lost any substantive theological underpinning, reducing itself, instead, to a sociological commentary on contemporary mores. Advocates of the report argued that not only had its conclusions on cohabitation pastoral and historical support (there is no formal marriage ceremony in the Jewish or Christian scriptures; Jewish law, technically, regards cohabitation as a legitimate form of marriage; until the Hardwicke Marriage Act 1753, marriage 'without benefit of clergy' was the practice for most couples in the UK), there is a theological justification too. The theological justification is that the defining element in a sexual relationship is arguably not so much the marriage ceremony but the first act of sexual intercourse. As St Paul wrote 'You surely know that anyone who joins himself to a prostitute becomes physically one with her, for scripture says, "The two shall become one flesh"' (1 Corinthians 6.16). In other words, some would argue that the distinction between cohabitation and marriage is smaller than generally supposed. Of course, one logical consequence of this view is that the ending of a relationship characterised by cohabitation (assuming that both parties are still alive) is closely analogous from a theological perspective to the ending of a marriage by a divorce. A different contemporary Christian perspective is offered by Adrian Thatcher (2002) who argues that marriage is to be understood not as a sudden event that starts with a wedding or cohabitation, but rather as a gradual process, so that a wedding is seen as the authentication of what has gone before.

Christian views about homosexuality

The relative degree of consensus that exists among Christians about marriage does not exist among them about homosexuality. The traditional view is that homosexuality is, at best, a sin that can be cured by repentance, prayer and Christian counselling; at worst, an abomination, an instance of humankind at its most depraved. While homosexuality receives relatively little attention in the scriptures, the references to it are, at least on initial inspection, unambiguously condemnatory – notably the story of Sodom in *Genesis* 19:4–11, the prohibition against it in *Leviticus* 18:22 and 20:13, and Paul's recitation of God's judgement in *Romans* 1:27.

Since the late 1970s, however, a tremendous amount of scholarship has questioned this traditional view (General Synod Board of Social Responsibility 1979; Boswell 1980; Scroggs 1983; Countryman 1988; Nelson 1988; Coleman 1989; Reiss 1990; General Synod of the Church of England 1991; Vasey 1995; E. F. Rogers 1999). This re-evaluation has tackled the question from a range of viewpoints: hermeneutical, scientific, sociological, ethical and pastoral.

The hermeneutical approach has concentrated on a detailed reassessment of the scriptural position on homosexuality. It has been argued that some of the classic 'proof' texts have been overinterpreted. For example, while the story of Sodom in *Genesis* 19 does include reference to homosexuality, the chief sin of the men of that city was their inhospitality and their various religious and social sins (*Jeremiah* 23:14; *Ezekiel* 16:49). This is not to conclude that homosexuality is celebrated or even condoned in this passage; rather that this *locus classicus* of the scriptural condemnation of homosexuality has been seriously overemphasised. After all, few commentators conclude from the near parallel account in *Judges* 19 (in which a woman is raped to death) that heterosexuality is denounced.

Then there is the argument that much of the repugnance expressed by writers both in the Jewish scriptures and in the New Testament stems from the importance attached to Jews and Christians standing aside from certain customs and practices of Canaanite and Graeco-Roman culture. Further, it can be maintained that the writers of scripture were probably mostly unable to envisage a state of homosexuality in which two adults of the same gender freely enter into a monogamous relationship. The authors of the Jewish scriptures implicitly associated homosexuality with cult-prostitution; those of the New Testament mainly with paederasty.

The scientific reassessment of homosexuality has failed, as yet, to produce any very definite conclusions as to the cause of a person's sexual orientation, whether homosexual or heterosexual. It is frequently maintained that a person's sexual orientation is a result of their upbringing. For example, the classical Freudian position is that the relationship a child has with its parents in the first few years of life determine its future sexual orientation. The same conclusion is reached both by social learning theory and by Kohlberg's cognitive development theory. Others hold that genetic and/or hormonal influences are crucial in the determination of a person's sexual orientation – see Ruse (1988) for a philosophically informed discussion of the various theories.

On the other hand, many people argue that there is a spectrum of sexual orientation, with 'pure' homosexuality at one pole and 'pure' heterosexuality at the other. Some of us unambiguously find ourselves at one or other pole; others of us, though, sit between the two extremes. A different point of view is that rather than finding ourselves somewhere along this spectrum, we position ourselves on it. In other words, our sexuality is not entirely a 'given'; it is, at least to some extent, something we determine for ourselves. Queer theory – with its perspective that none of us fits securely into a set of objectively defined sexual boundaries – can be seen as an extension of this analysis (e.g. Garber 1994). A related point of view, deriving from Foucault, and discussed further below, is that what we now see as 'homosexuality' and 'heterosexuality' are social constructions, terms whose meanings are contingent on their historicity (Foucault 1990).

Finally, contemporary Christian views about homosexuality have been influenced by the personal testimonies of many gay and lesbian Christians. Both scripture and tradition place a high value on what an individual's conscience tells that person, while the Bible and Church history contain a number of accounts of people who fail to act in accordance with tradition or the injunctions of scripture, yet are subsequently blessed by God (e.g. Peter at Joppa in *Acts* 10). Listening to people's stories about themselves can be an effective way of discerning what God is saying in a situation.

For all these reasons a consensus among Christians about homosexuality currently does not exist. Some Christians are moving towards an official position in which mutually faithful homosexual relationships – though typically only among the laity rather than among the clergy – are considered acceptable. Time alone will tell whether this is merely a further sign, as some would maintain, of the spiritual decline of institutionalised Christianity, or the beginnings of a full acceptance of all people, whatever their sexual identity.

Christian views about sex education

Until recently, surprisingly little had been written about sex education from an explicitly Christian perspective. However, the 1990s have seen a reaction to this state of affairs and a number of authors have written about sex education within a Christian framework – e.g. Vickerman (1992), Brown (1993), chapters by David Cleland, David Lankshear and Margaret Vincent in Thomson (1993), Catholic Education Service (n.d.), Clark (1998) and Reiss (1998a).

Two extreme, opposite positions with respect to Christian views about sex education can be rejected. One is that a Christian perspective on sex education is wholly distinct from a secular one; the other is that a Christian perspective differs only marginally, if at all, from a secular one. As is so often the case in life, the truth lies between the extremes.

Of course, precisely what a Christian holds as the Christian position on sex education differs according to the particular form of their faith. One person, of a conservative theological persuasion, may hold that the teachings of scripture can straightforwardly be applied to today's moral situations. Such a person is not likely then to be persuaded by a liberal Christian position which argues that the particular cultural situation in which anyone lives is so significant that laws, however divinely inspired, of two or more thousand years ago cannot simply be translated directly into today's settings.

This polarisation between the conservative and liberal positions is not restricted, in Christian circles, to issues to do with sex and sex education. Related debates have taken place at different times in Church history over questions as diverse as usury, slavery, the ordination of women and human attitudes to the environment.

Islamic views of sex and sex education

There is probably more of a consensus among those who write about sex and sex education from an Islamic perspective than among those who write about sex and sex education from a Christian perspective. Feminism and liberalism, in particular, have had only a limited influence among Islamic theology and educational theory. It is customary for Islamic scholars to argue that a clear distinction can be drawn between Islamic practices and cultural customs, for example 'Islamic practices are quite distinct from cultural customs in that those of Islam are constant, steadfast, unchangeable whilst ethnic practices vary from country to country' (Noibi 1993: 41). This makes valid sociological generalisations about Muslim sexual attitudes and practices difficult (Halstead 1997) though the *Qur'an* and the authenticated *Hadith* reports of the sayings, action and practices of the Prophet Muhammad (p.b.u.h. [peace be upon him]) – form the basis for the religious practices and daily lives of Muslims world-wide.

Muslim views about sex

In order to maintain the ongoing process of creation, God created sexual duality – i.e. male and female – in creation. Even things which come out of the earth are said in the *Qur'an* to have this duality (Ashraf 1998). Man and woman are said to be of the same nature and to have a desire for complementary love. In both men and women there is therefore a natural desire for companionship with the other sex. Accordingly, celibacy is not praised. Rather, sexual union gives a foretaste of the joys of paradise – with the pleasures of paradise sometimes being portrayed in strikingly erotic terms (Bouhdiba 1985) – and sexual relations are recognised as one of the great signs of the blessings Allah has bestowed on humankind:

And among His signs is this: He creates for you mates out of your own kind, so that you might incline towards them, and he engenders mutual love and compassion between you.

(Qur'an 30: 21)

Muslim views about marriage

An Islamic marriage is:

- an act of *taqwa* – piety
- a form of *ibadah* – worship of Allah and obedience to His Messenger
- the only legitimate means of emotional and sexual fulfilment
- a means of legitimate procreation
- an approach to inter family alliance and group solidarity

(Noibi 1993: 44)

Early marriage is encouraged and marriages may be arranged in Islam, as in many cultures, but should not be forced, though such marriages do still occur in the UK as elsewhere (Home Office Communications Directorate 2000; Shah-Kazci 2001). Some Islamic jurists hold that a father may arrange a marriage on behalf of his daughter, to be consummated when she attains maturity.

It is a religious obligation of married couples to try to fulfil each other's sexual needs. The wife is to make herself as attractive as possible to her husband just as he too should make himself attractive to her (Noibi 1998). Within a marriage, as within Islamic societies more generally, gender divisions of roles are standard. Husbands are assigned the responsibility of providing sustenance and general welfare for their wives, children and other dependants. At the same time, husbands and wives have the same religious duties and men and women are both encouraged to acquire knowledge from the cradle to the grave. Married women retain their legal identity, keep their family name and may enter into contracts in their own name (Noibi 1998). They keep their own property and can acquire new ones; they are guaranteed a fixed share of inheritance when their husbands or relatives die. As HRH Prince Charles noted in a speech on 'Islam and the West' given in Oxford on 27 October 1995, the rights which Islam accorded women from its inception far surpassed those enjoyed by women in the west.

Islam takes very seriously both fornication and adultery – with the same word, *zina'*, referring to both (Noibi 1998). Women are to avoid displaying their beauty and using strong-smelling perfume, for instance, or conducting themselves in a seductive manner when in the presence of men other than their husbands (or close relatives). At the same time, men are not to look lustfully at women. More generally:

Unguarded intermingling between the sexes, engaging in or listening to amorous talk, lustful touch, watching pornography and any other things of this sort are forbidden as they arouse the sexual appetite and could lead to *zina*'.

(Noibi 1998: 86)

Muslim views about homosexuality

While there is a gay and lesbian Muslim movement called Al-fatiha and a lesbian and gay support organisation for South Asian communities, including Muslims, called SHAKTI, there is overwhelming support in Islam for the teaching that homosexuality is unnatural and abhorrent. As the *Qur'an*, referring to the people of the Prophet Lot (p.b.u.h.), says:

Do ye commit lewdness such as no people in creation committed before you? For ye practise your lust on men in preference to women: ye are indeed a people transgressing beyond bounds.

(*Qur'an* 7: 80–1)

It can be strongly argued that the Arabic language and Muslim worldview do not make the distinction customarily made in the west (as discussed earlier) between homosexuals and heterosexuals. From an Islamic perspective there is no such thing as a homosexual orientation, just homosexual acts (Halstead and Lewicka 1998). Foucault (1990) tells us that the contemporary, western understanding of homosexuality came into being in two stages. First, the sexologists of the late nineteenth century sought to redefine homosexuality from a secular perspective. Previously throughout Christendom it had been considered sinful behaviour and a violation of natural law. However, once it was medicalised, case histories were gathered and theories were developed that homosexuals belong to a common sexual species which could only be understood through scientific investigation. In the second stage, the minority group which had been created by the sexologists began to turn the identity it had been given to its own advantage by transforming it into a source of strength and solidarity. Homosexuals, now self-defined, discovered advantages in this new classification, and began claiming rights alongside other minority groups in a democratic society.

The Muslim view of homosexuality is therefore close to the earlier Christian perspective based on natural law: that God created an order in the world which was designed to bring everything to fulfilment and that to understand the natural purpose and function of something is to understand God's will for it (Halstead and Lewicka 1998). Accordingly, most Muslims strongly condemn any public avowal of homosexuality as constituting a public transgression of Islamic morality. It seems though that something of a blind eye is turned on homosexual activity if it takes place in private. Indeed, it has been claimed that in some Muslim countries homosexual behaviour among males is widespread – between men and boys, older and younger boys, masters and apprentices, teachers and pupils, in religious brotherhoods, within the extended family, in public baths and in bars and other meeting places (Schmitt and Sofer 1992). From a religious perspective it might not be a matter of turning a blind eye so much as leaving it to God to judge the behaviour and give it its due reward in the world to come (Halstead and Lewicka 1998).

Muslim views about sex education

In the UK the first significant publication about sex education from a Muslim perspective was provided by Sarwar (1989). Sarwar pointed out that:

> To all intents and purposes, British society is largely secular and materialistic and non-mundane matters such as *'the spiritual and moral'* aspects of life remain almost ignored in the actual curriculum of our schools, notwithstanding the objective set out in sec 2 of the ERA [Education Reform Act], 1988.
>
> (Sarwar 1989: 5, original emphases)

Sarwar went on to assert that the need for sex education is not in doubt but that 'It is probably fair to say that the majority of Muslim parents would be happy if there was no sex education at all in schools' (Sarwar 1989: 7). In particular he noted that 'Sex education in schools invariably includes a study of contraception methods' and concluded 'Islam, as earlier stated, does not allow any extra-marital sex and also prohibits the free-mixing of grown-up boys and girls. It closes all doors to the growth of extra-marital sex. So contraception becomes almost unnecessary' (Sarwar 1989: 11).

Fatima D'Oyen's (1996) *The Miracle of Life* is described on its back cover as 'a practical guide on sex education and traditional family values for young Muslims growing up in today's world'. A note to parents at its beginning explains the context in which it was written and includes the following:

> With few exceptions, sex education in public secondary schools has become a series of lessons in how to use condoms, get abortions, and avoid diseases; the prevailing attitude seems to be 'young people are going to have sex anyway, so we should just help them do it in a

"safe way".' A moral or ethical perspective is rarely given, and if it is, there are no references to pleasing Allah. Mixed-sex classes remove a young person's natural sense of shyness. Even in the single-sex classes with a biological focus which are often held in the upper grades of primary school, both boys and girls are encouraged to experiment and given tips of a variety of sexual activities such as kissing techniques or masturbation as part of a 'natural exploration of sexuality'. Muslim children who have not had any previous exposure to such topics will be at a loss as to how to respond, and may be too embarrassed to ask their parents about it.

(D'Oyen 1996: 3)

Sarwar's and D'Oyen's concerns about school sex education are echoed by other Muslim writers. Mabud (1998) provides a detailed account of what sex education would be like if it embodied Islamic values. Mabud begins from the premise that education regarding sexual matters occupies a central position in Islam and points out that, traditionally, sex education has never featured as a separate subject in the school curriculum in Muslim countries but has been integrated into religious education:

It has always been taught through lessons on cleanliness, family values, human dignity, modesty and praiseworthy and prohibited activities using a modest and indirect language. Young Muslims learn about sexual manners, etiquette, virtues, vices and taboos not through a formal curriculum but from society. Strict social pressure and segregation of sexes have never necessitated the inculcation of the Western type of sexual education whether at the primary or secondary level. That primary children do not know how babies are formed or that secondary children are not aware of different methods of contraception is not seen as a deficiency but as perfectly normal.

(Mabud 1998: 99)

Accordingly, Muslims feel uncomfortable about sex education conducted within a secular framework. There are three main aspects of contemporary practice in school sex education which are legitimate targets for Muslim opposition:

- some sex education materials offend against the Islamic principle of decency and modesty
- sex education tends to present certain behaviours as acceptable which Muslims consider sinful
- sex education is perceived as undermining the Islamic concept of family life.

(Halstead 1997)

Decency and modesty are considered in Islam to be natural instincts created by Allah to regulate all aspects of relations between the sexes. Modesty affects not only dress but also one's attitude to all sexual matters. The use of pornography is clearly incompatible with the principle of modesty as is staring 'at people of the opposite sex whom we find attractive' or 'watching people kissing on TV or in the street' (D'Oyen 1996: 78). Teaching about sex does not in itself offend against modesty, nor does the use of diagrams as appropriate. Indeed, parents are urged not to feel shy or guilty about providing necessary information about sex to their children (Noibi 1993). However, some materials used in school sex education, most obviously videos showing fully naked bodies, do offend against the principle of modesty and are unacceptable from a Muslim point of view. In the debate on sex education at the UK Muslim Parliament in November 1994, one member described his shocked reaction on viewing a BBC video on human anatomy designed for school use which showed a mother getting up from bed, naked, to take her young child to the bathroom, and the naked father following after. He asked if this was the normal scene in the average British household (Bodi 1994).

Islamic law provides clear guidance about what is acceptable and unacceptable for Muslims in the area of sexual behaviour. Because of this it is unacceptable from a Muslim point of view that Muslim children should be taught that pre-marital, extramarital or same-sex sexual relationships are valid alternative lifestyles, or that how one should behave sexually is entirely a matter of personal choice or mutual agreement by a couple. Of course, in a multicultural society such as the UK, Muslim children will be perfectly aware that non-Muslims may hold sexual values or adopt sexual practices different from their own; it is appropriate for education in a pluralist society to encourage Muslim children to adopt an attitude of toleration towards certain behaviours which, though un-Islamic, are acceptable in the broader society. However, there is a difference between the *toleration* of difference and the kind of *celebration* of difference which, for example, Lenderyou (1995) recommends. Toleration implies a conscious decision not to interfere with behaviours of which one disapproves, whereas it is not possible to celebrate something one finds unacceptable (Halstead 1996c).

Fundamentally what underlies Muslim objections to much contemporary practice in sex education is that this is based on a humanistic interpretation of the wills of individuals rather than on religious foundations. Muslims see Islam as a whole way of life, in which the will of Allah unites the social, moral, intellectual, cultural, sexual and religious dimensions of human existence into a harmonious whole. Human beings have a natural tendency to go astray, but Allah has revealed his will in the *Qur'an* and in the sayings and traditions of the Prophet Muhammad (p.b.u.h.). Alliances may be forged between religious traditions in the face of secularism. As Abdul Mabud puts it: 'It is necessary to think, assess the situation and try to learn from the common heritage shared by all three Abrahamic faiths, Islam, Christianity and Judaism' (Mabud 1998: 120). In the mean time, Mabud suggests six measures that Muslim parents can take 'in order to protect their children' (Mabud 1998: 121):

- as an extreme measure, withdraw them from sex education lessons
- limit the extent to which they mix with those who might have an anti-Islamic influence on them – though too strict a parental control can be counterproductive
- prohibit them from going out with friends of the opposite sex
- encourage them to take part in activities that enable them to feel a sense of unity with other Muslims
- send them to mosques
- teach them Islamic values at home.

Summary

1   Religious views about sexual values need to be considered for two main reasons. First, because a not inconsiderable number of people have them; second, because if we wish to live together in a pluralist society, we should understand at least something of what it is that motivates others. Such understanding is both intrinsically respectful and instrumentally useful.

2   Religions have much in common in their attitudes towards human sexuality and their views about what should be included within school sex education. At the same time, there are significant differences between religions in these matters, and most religions contain within themselves a considerable variety of views.

3   Christian perspectives on school sex education have a considerable amount in common with secular perspectives but place more weight on the teachings of the Church and on Christian tradition. In particular, marriage may be understood sacramentally while abortion and homosexuality are highly contentious.

4   Muslims generally feel uncomfortable about school sex education in the UK. Some sex education materials offend against the Islamic principles of decency and modesty while sex education classes tend to present certain behaviours as acceptable which are considered sinful and as undermining the Islamic concept of family life.

Issues for discussion

1 What is the relationship between religious faith and ethical behaviour?
2 Should marriage be life-long, exclusive and the only proper place for a sexual relationship?
3 Propose arguments for and against the view that parents with a religious faith should be able to affect the content and teaching of the sex education in a school even if they are in a minority.
4 How might you try to explain to a teenager without a religious faith some consequences of having one? How might you try to explain to a teenager with a religious faith some consequences of not having one? Would it be a good thing to put either or both of these suggestions into practice?
5 Defend the notion (a) that religion subjugates women sexually; (b) that religion enables women to lead sexually flourishing lives.

Further reading

Two standard introductions to the world's major religions are:

- Hinnells, J. R. (ed.) ([1984] 1991) *A Handbook of Living Religions*, London: Penguin.
- Smart, N. (1989) *The World's Religions: Old Traditions and Modern Transformations*, Cambridge: Cambridge University Press.

For books and packs that examine positively the contributions of religions to sex education see:

- Blake, S. and Katrak, Z. (2002) *Faith, Values and Sex and Relationships Education*, London: National Children's Bureau.
- Lenderyou, G. and Porter, M. (eds) (1994) *Sex Education, Values and Morality*, London: Health Education Authority.
- Reiss, M. J. and Mabud, S. A. (eds) (1998) *Sex Education and Religion*, Cambridge: Islamic Academy.
- Thomson, R. (ed.) (1993) *Religion, Ethnicity and Sex Education: Exploring the Issues – A Resource for Teachers and Others Working with Young People*, London: National Children's Bureau.

The following books explore Christian perspectives on sexuality and feminism:

- Countryman, L. W. (1988) *Dirt, Greed and Sex: Sexual Ethics in the New Testament and their Implications for Today*, Philadelphia, PA: Fortress Press.
- Isherwood, L. (ed.) (2000) *The Good News of the Body: Sexual Theology and Feminism*, Sheffield: Sheffield Academic Press.
- Rogers, E. F. Jr (1999) *Sexuality and the Christian Body: Their Way into the Triune God*, Oxford: Blackwell.
- Thatcher, A. (1993) *Liberating Sex: A Christian Sexual Theology*, London: SPCK (Society for Promoting Christian Knowledge).

For an examination of sexuality in Islam see:

- Bouhdiba, A. (1985) *Sexuality in Islam*, London: Routledge and Kegan Paul.

Chapter 7

Family values

The problem of teaching family values

The relationship between sex education and the family is an important and intimate one. On the one hand, the family is the first provider of sex education for young children and (as we have seen in Chapter 3) a major influence (alongside peers and the media) on the developing sexual values and sexual understanding of children and young people. On the other, the family is itself inevitably part of the content of sex education. Topics such as family relationships, parenthood and family planning are all well established elements in any sex education programme. Indeed, one of the main intentions of sex education is to prepare children for family life as adults.

All of this is obvious and uncontroversial. What *is* controversial, however, is the teaching of 'family values'. The term 'family values' is itself an ambiguous one. In a national survey in the USA, respondents linked it to a broadly conservative set of values such as 'respecting one's parents', 'being married to the same person for life' and 'respecting authority' (Mellman *et al.* 1990). In the UK the term is associated with recent pressure from central government to add a more explicitly moral dimension to teaching about the family within sex education, based on a fairly narrow, traditional view of the family. Guidance issued by the Department for Education in 1994 speaks of the need for pupils to 'be encouraged to appreciate the value of stable family life, marriage and the responsibilities of parenthood' (DfE 1994: 6), and more recent guidance also lays stress on 'learning the value of family life, marriage and stable and loving relationships for the nurture of children' (DfEE 2000a: 5).

This guidance is part of a broader political initiative to support the traditional family (Home Office 1998), an initiative also seen in recent legislation such as the Family Law Act 1996. The latter sets out in an introductory section the general moral principles on which it is based, including, for example, the principle 'that the institution of marriage is to be supported' (Oldham 1997: 402). The phrase 'family values' thus appears to be a politicised concept referring to the value of the traditional family and the values implicit in the lifestyle of such a family. It carries a strong symbolic value, conjuring up cosy images of decency and respectability and a belief in the family as the cornerstone upon which society rests.

The inclusion of a moral dimension in both legislation and educational guidelines relating to the family is justified primarily in social and economic terms, though it does happen also to coincide with a conservative religious agenda. The family is perceived as making an important contribution to public welfare by taking responsibility for the care of dependents, both young and old (Cherlin 1996: ch. 1). It is clear that families who live together make far fewer financial demands on the state than would each individual member of the family living separately. The attacks in recent years on unmarried and teenage mothers who are seen as a financial burden on the state (Brown 1990; Murray 1990; Phoenix 1991), and on absent fathers who do not support their children financially must be understood in this light (Dennis and Erdos 1992).

However, recent research suggests that many teachers are unhappy about being expected to promote marriage and family values in schools in this way (Passy 2003). In particular, they are concerned that such teaching, however justifiable it appears in terms of public policy, may fail to meet the needs of individual children with diverse private family circumstances. Teachers sometimes also claim that:

- such teaching implies the moral superiority of certain kinds of family relationship, and this conflicts with the teachers' view that they should be non-judgemental about things that belong to the pupils' private lives
- such teaching stigmatises children from single-parent families, renders them more vulnerable and may potentially damage their self-esteem
- such teaching is based on an idealised, static and backward-looking notion of family life and pays inadequate attention to contemporary attitudes and lifestyles or to the complexity and instability of some children's family lives
- families are in any case not always based on love, care, support and commitment, but may equally embody violence, deceit, neglect, abuse, manipulation, rejection, overprotection, dominance and mistrust
- one of the aims of school-based education, particularly at the secondary level, is to encourage children to move towards a greater degree of personal autonomy, and this may include becoming more independent of their families.

The importance of these points cannot be overstressed. However, we believe that it would be a mistake if teachers were to draw the conclusion that it is wiser to avoid the topic of the family altogether in schools.

In research into family values in English schools, Passy (2003) quotes one teacher who found it very difficult to talk to pupils about the family:

> There's such a diverse range of what is at home really; there are a lot of them [pupils] who have your nuclear family, and then there are those that . . . I don't actually know if there's a dad at home . . . So I find it very difficult . . . because . . . there are some here that have got really difficult situations at home and I don't want to make them feel that they're missing out on something . . . cos I think it's hard to talk about it without making it sound as though this is how it should be . . . So that's the main reason I avoid it. And also it's difficult, there's so much else that we've got to do – I mean it's easier not to do it.

One of the effects of avoiding any direct teaching about the family in this way is simply to drive the topic into the hidden curriculum, where (as indicated in Chapter 3) the influences on children are haphazard and generally unexamined and where children pick up values and moral messages that may be unintended. For example, modern language or mathematics textbooks may present stereotypical views of family life, whereas literature and drama activities may overemphasise family violence (which makes good drama but not necessarily a valid introduction to family life). It is clear that schools can achieve a policy on family values that is coherent, consistent and justifiable only if teachers have thought through their own values, if they know what values their pupils are learn-ing both in and out of school and if teachers and pupils are able to engage in a systematic discussion of these values at a developmentally appro-priate level.

In this chapter we argue that children need to be given opportunities in schools to discuss and reflect on the nature and value of family life, since the family (whatever form it takes) plays a hugely important part in the lives of most children. We also argue that such discussion should reflect the diversity of family structures that exist in contemporary society rather than focusing exclusively on the traditional nuclear family. We argue further that the value of the family as an institution and the values asso-ciated with being a member of a family are not tied exclusively to any particular family structure or definition of the family but are linked to the benefits that derive from living on intimate terms with others, and that these values have a clear place in education. Finally, we argue that sex education is an obvious place for many issues to do with family and family values to be raised.

The rest of this chapter therefore falls into three sections. The first examines the concept of the family and compares the popular image of the (traditional) nuclear family with more inclusive definitions which acknowledge the diversity of families existing in contemporary society.

The second considers the values implicit in the notion of family life and the reasons why the family continues to be valued as a social institution. The third explores how family values can be approached in sex education and concludes with some comments on how children learn values and how teachers can influence children's personal development.

What is a family?

Most writing on the family assumes that this question can be answered in one of two main ways. The first defines the family as *a heterosexual, legally married couple plus their dependent children*. This normative definition is usually called the 'traditional nuclear' family. The concept may be expanded to include other generations (for example, grandparents) and a wide range of other relatives by blood or marriage, in which case it may be called the 'traditional extended' family. The second defines the family more loosely as *a group of two or more people who live together on intimate terms in the same household and who normally have a socially approved sexual, filial, parental or other kinship relationship*. This descriptive definition clearly covers a much wider variety of attachments and relationships than the first. For example, the term 'socially approved sexual relationship' allows for the fact that an unmarried couple, whether heterosexual or homosexual, may be considered a family in societies which recognise such relationships. We may call this definition the 'inclusive' or 'socio-logical' family.

The appeal of the first definition depends partly, as we have seen, on its powerful symbolic value, conjuring up images of moral decency and respectability. There is no doubt that marriage is still valued by many people as 'the fundamental building block of the family' (Newman 1999: 9), and Muncie and Sapsford (1995) claim that the idea of the traditional nuclear family 'clearly retains a potency such that all other forms tend to be defined with reference to it' (1995: 10). A major study of values in Britain, albeit one conducted in the early 1980s, confirmed continuing widespread support for the traditional family and for the belief that children need a home with both a father and a mother to grow up happily (Brown *et al.* 1985). This view of the family is often justified as in the best interests of society and in the best interests of the individual child. Its claim to be in the best interests of society depends, as we have seen, mainly on economic and social reasons, and to be in the best interests of the child mainly on evidence from social research which seems to suggest that children from traditional two-parent families are more likely to do well at school and less likely to be involved in disruptive, antisocial or criminal behaviour than children from single-parent families. The educational implications of this view are that if the traditional family is an institution of vital importance to the well-being of society, the school has a responsibility to play its part in seeking to reverse the decline of the traditional family.

The second definition is more concerned to recognise the reality of the diversity of family forms which exists in contemporary societies (Gelles 1995; Silva and Smart 1999), and to ensure that children from single-parent families, step-families, foster families, adoptive families and the many other kinds of non-traditional families that are on the increase in many western countries (Lamb 1999) are not stigmatised because of family circumstances over which they have no control. The definition is thus related to a number of fundamental liberal values, including toler-ance, pluralism, freedom, equality, justice and inclusion. Proponents of this view point to the fact that only a small proportion of families in the UK or the USA strictly match the definition of the traditional nuclear family (Bernardes 1997: 9–10). One of the problems with the traditional model, it is claimed, is that it tends to maintain inequality and the exploi-tation of women (Gittins 1985; Delphy and Leonard 1992; Balswick and Balswick 1995). On this view, the traditional image of the family lacks sufficient validity in present-day society to have educational value or policy implications (Wringe 1994) and a more inclusive definition is required.

The debate between these two distinct, value-laden definitions is potentially interminable because people are prioritising different values and arguing from the basis of incompatible cultural beliefs and assump-tions. In these circumstances we conclude that it is not the role of the common school to take sides in a politicised debate about the definition of the family. This is not to deny the right of the religious school to teach its own distinctive beliefs about the family. But the best the common school may be able to do is to help children to be aware of the different beliefs people hold about the family (as about other areas of life) and to encourage them to reflect carefully on the debate, considering arguments from all sides and, over time, reaching their own conclusions in a way which remains open to challenge and change. On the other hand, it is clear that the common school does have a duty to develop the self-esteem of all the children in its care, and part of this involves helping them both to celebrate the positive values in their own diverse family circumstances and to demonstrate understanding, tolerance and respect towards those whose family circumstances differ from their own. In fact, to understand the phrase 'family values' only in connection with the teaching of the value of the traditional nuclear family is to trivialise it. There are very many ways in which the family is of value to the child which are not related at all to the debate about the traditional family. The value of family life is not entirely tied to any particular family structure or definition of the family but is linked to the benefits that derive from living on appropriate intimate terms with others. The exploration of these values is part of the contribution that schools can make towards children's spiritual and moral development.

An alternative approach to the issue of defining the family which avoids the sterility of the debate about the traditional nuclear family from an educational point of view involves a distinction between the denotation and the connotation of the word 'family'. The denotation of the term – what it precisely refers to and the boundaries of the definition – is important in legal, social and economic contexts, such as inheritance law, adoption, housing, health care, family allowances or family income support, but is not of central educational significance. The connotations of the term 'family', on the other hand, include strong positive emotions. When head-teachers, for example, describe the school community as a 'family' (as they often do, particularly in primary schools), this carries connotations of warmth, loyalty, commitment, caring for each other, and a sense of belonging. Similar connotations are seen in phrases like 'blood is thicker than water' and 'like one of the family'. As we saw in Chapter 3, family members feature almost universally when children are asked to list 'the people most important to me'. From the point of view of sex education, the value of the family is more apparent in the rich connotations of the term than in debates about the precise denotation.

Values in family life

We have already seen that the family is justifiably viewed as a valued institution in our society. Part of that value lies in the fact that the family provides a context in which basic human needs such as love, care and a sense of belonging are most likely to be met. Much has been written about the values which hold families together, including loyalty, trust, fidelity, cooperation, commitment, mutual support, respect and understanding. Families are where children first learn (whether through guidance and instruction offered by older family members or through observation of and participation in the activities of older members) values such as caring, sharing, respect for individuality, and a sense of common purpose and a common bond, which are all central to the notion of family life.

Before looking more closely at the relevance of these values to sexual development and sex education, however, we need to examine two possible objections to this rosy view of families. The first is that the values mentioned in the last paragraph are not universally shared, and indeed there is a darker side to family life including violence, neglect, abuse, hostility, rejection, overprotection and dominance which should not be ignored. The second is that families actually hold a wide diversity of values. As Leichter (1974) points out:

The family is an arena in which virtually the entire range of human experience can take place. Warfare, love, violence, tenderness, honesty, deceit, private property, communal sharing, power manipulation, informed consent, formal status hierarchies, egalitarian decision-making – all can be found within the setting of the family.

(Leichter 1974: 1)

This diversity of experiences and values is sometimes linked to a particular worldview, religion, class, ethnicity, culture or gender, sometimes to the idiosyncratic personalities, attitudes, beliefs and commitments that are found in an individual family (see Halstead 1999a). In response to the first objection, we would point out that the fact that not all families share these values or exemplify them in practice does not invalidate them as educational goals. Few if any values are universally shared, and the fact that there are dishonest people is no reason for schools to give up teaching the value of honesty. It is largely through education which presents positive alternatives to children that the darker side of family life ceases to be self-perpetuating. In response to the second objection, we would argue that in addition to the wide diversity of values found in individual families and particular cultural groups, there is a core of values implicit in the notion of family life itself which does not vary so much from family to family or from culture to culture. These values mainly relate closely to the practicalities of living on intimate terms with others. For example, research among Chinese immigrants to the USA (Chen 1988) found that their family strengths and values – including respect, trust, love, mutual understanding and support, loyalty, commitment, communication and encouragement – did not differ significantly from those identified in studies of families from many other cultures (see Olson and DeFrain 1994: ch. 2). There are four clusters of such values which appear particularly relevant to sexual development and sex education, and we shall now examine these more closely.

The first cluster relates to the family as a primary source of children's identity and self-concept. Children usually develop a sense of their own personal identity from their relationships and interactions with their parents and other family members. Hand in hand with this goes the development of feelings of self-importance and self-worth as an individual; the extent to which children feel confident, successful, useful and wanted usually depends on the amount of time and attention families give them. Unless children develop a sufficiently strong sense of themselves as worthy of love and respect in childhood, it is likely that they will find it more difficult to form successful sexual relationships in adulthood.

The second includes the values associated with living with others – values such as loyalty, trust, sharing, reliability, commitment, legal and moral obligations and mutual support and care. Children often learn these values through participation in shared activities – mealtimes, family discussions, jokes, leisure activities, play, care during illness, family holidays, and a wide range of other cooperative activities. They learn much about the nature of close relationships (and the permanence of such relationships) through both experience and observation of family life; they learn how a husband and wife interact, a parent and child, a brother and sister, and so on. Family life is also likely to teach much about the need to communicate, to compromise, to cooperate, to give praise and show appreciation, to be open to change, to deal with stress, to respect others.

The third cluster of values is linked to the emotional dimension of close relationships. The family provides a secure framework within which children's early emotional development takes place and within which their need to share their feelings and their desire for intimate response can best be satisfied. Children are able to experience and observe an extensive range of feelings and learn the difference between appropriate and inappropriate expressions of feeling in different contexts. They can learn ways of expressing love and affection as well as ways of coping with negative emotions such as anger, jealousy and depression.

Fourth, the family introduces children to important transitions and rites of passage including birth, marriage and death and helps them to understand sexual attraction and sexual activity as part of the cycle of life. It provides models of parenthood and child-rearing and makes children aware of the inevitability of growing older. It also introduces children to issues of gender as they learn gender roles based on their own sexual identity and as they observe the degree of gender equality or subordination and the structures of power, authority and control in their own family. In this way children are provided with opportunities to think through their own priorities and values, especially as they come into contact with other families whose values and experiences differ from their own.

Teaching family values in sex education

It is sometimes maintained that there are certain values associated with being a member of a family which are so important both to individuals and to the broader society that they merit universal transmission to the next generation. Although the two of us place great store on family values, we are unhappy with this approach because it shows inadequate respect for the developing autonomy of children and assumes that they should be passive recipients of adult values. An alternative approach to the teaching of family values within sex education puts more emphasis on children's personal construction of values (see Moore *et al.* 1996: 3). From a constructivist perspective, knowledge and values do not consist of fixed objectivised 'truths' that are external to the child, nor does learning consist of harvesting these 'truths' and making them one's own. On the contrary, knowledge and values are constructed by children through the interaction between their existing knowledge and values and the new situations, experiences and ideas they encounter at home, in the media, at school or among peers. New learning is the outcome of this interaction. This may not be how all learning occurs, but it seems to be a particularly good way of understanding the way that learning goes on within sex education, where the knowledge which is learned is intimately connected with the personal development of the learner. Of course, constructivism does not imply that children will always develop different values from their parents or that they will always become critical of the values of their parents and other adults, but it allows for that possibility.

If the purposes of sex education include meeting the present and future needs of individual children, preparing them for family life, and respecting their individuality and developing autonomy, family values clearly cannot be taught by deciding what values underpin the ideal family life and then looking for the most effective ways of instilling these values into children. Rather, children have a right to have their horizons extended during education at school in a way that empowers them to grow as individuals and develop their own family values. This entails being given opportunities in school to learn about:

- marriage and different kinds of intimate relationships
- other kinds of families than their own
- different kinds of relationships, ways of forming, maintaining and ending relationships, and the value of relationships
- parenthood, and the differing values that individuals place on parenthood
- the economic values underpinning family resource management
- family communication and problem-solving
- domestic violence
- divorce and remarriage
- the relationship between the family and other social institutions
- the values that underpin national policies on the family
- inter-generational issues in the family and the family life of older people (see Arcus et al 1993)

They also have a right to expect some guidance and support as they try to make sense of the differing beliefs and values they are faced with and work at the task of constructing their own values.

This approach to family values in sex education makes many demands of teachers. Teachers need experience themselves of the process of reflection, so that they can in turn guide children through the process. They need to recognise opportunities that occur in the existing curriculum, so that they are not missed and so that children are not left to make sense of things unaided. Where opportunities do not arise naturally, they need to know how to introduce certain topics and how to capture children's interest and desire to explore family issues more fully. They need to know when to be neutral and when not, so that, for example, children understand and respect different kinds of family structures, but at the same time are left in no doubt that an abusive family is not as good as a caring family. They need to ensure balance; it is possible that an overemphasis on one or two objectives may distort the overall learning that goes on through sex education. For example, where teachers have seen the reduction of sexually transmitted infections as their primary goal, there is the possibility that the concept of 'responsibility' might be reduced to a willingness to wear a condom. Similarly, the goal of reducing teenage pregnancy has led in some schools to the practice of giving young teenage girls a doll to take home that wakes up every two hours in the night. This is designed to put girls off having a baby too young (and there is some evidence that it is often very successful in so doing), but there is clearly a danger that it might put them off having a baby altogether. Certainly it does nothing to help pupils to understand the joy that many people feel at the birth of a child, or the deep bond that mothers commonly feel with their newborn child. Teachers need above all to reflect on the hidden messages that pupils are picking up from the things they choose to teach and not to teach, from their teaching styles and relationships within the school and from the example they set. Good sex education, whether formal or informal, *can* strengthen and enrich the individual and family well-being of pupils. But there are many pitfalls along the way.

Summary

1   There is pressure from many governments and conservative groups for schools to teach traditional family values. Many teachers have resisted this pressure, believing that such teaching would not be in the interests of individual children. But it would be a mistake to allow such misgivings to result in the total abandonment of teaching about the family.
2   The polarised debate between the traditional nuclear family and the more diverse, inclusive family can be unproductive from an educational point of view. The value of the family for children is not necessarily tied to any particular family structure, but is linked to the benefits that derive from living on appropriate intimate terms with others.

3 Many of the values associated with being a member of a family
   are directly relevant to sex education. These include the values
   associated with having a positive self-concept, the values linked
   to living with others, the values linked to the emotional dimension of close relationships and the values linked to an understanding of sexual roles, parenthood and gender issues.
4 On topics like the family, children construct their own values on
   the basis of all their experiences in and out of the school. It is
   the role of the teacher to facilitate this process by encouraging
   balanced discussion and reflection on family life and family
   values while at the same time respecting the developing autonomy of the child.

Issues for discussion

1 Cherlin (1996) distinguishes between the public family (which is
   defined in terms of the family's contribution to public welfare by
   caring for dependents) and the private family (defined in terms
   of the intimate relationship of two or more people who live
   together). Does this distinction help to clarify different senses of
   family values?
2 Consider one or more of the following questions

   (a) What is the value of marriage in your opinion? Consider
       arguments for and against (i) marriage, (ii) the single life,
       and (iii) cohabitation.
   (b) Are homosexual partnerships a valid form of family?
   (c) What do you think are the most important ethical values that
       guide family life?
   (d) What difference would it make to family life if we lived in a
       matriarchal rather than a patriarchal society?

   Think about the process you went through in answering these
   questions. Was your thinking fair, open-minded and critical? If
   so, think about ways pupils could be helped to adopt the same
   approach in their own reflections on family values.
3 Some schools talk of teaching family values to their pupils, others
   of teaching *about* family values. What precisely is the difference
   between these, and which is preferable?

4   How can sex educators respect the diverse family values of different cultural groups, and are there limits to such respect and tolerance?
5   What values are presupposed in the claim that good sex education can strengthen and enrich individual and family well-being?

Further reading

There are many excellent sociological textbooks on the family. Among the best are

- Bernardes, J. (1997) *Family Studies: An Introduction,* London: Routledge.
- Cherlin, A. J. (1996) *Public and Private Families: An Introduction,* New York: McGraw-Hill.
- Newman, D. M. (1999) *Sociology of Families,* Thousand Oaks, CA: Pine Forge Press.
- Olson, D. H. and DeFrain, J. (1994) *Marriage and the Family: Diversity and Strengths,* Mountain View, CA: Mayfield.

There are not so many texts on family values. Some worth reading are:

- Donnellan, C. (ed.) (1994) *Family Values,* Cambridge: Independence.

and from a more feminist perspective:

- Hite, S. (1994) *The Hite Report on the Family: Growing up under Patriarchy,* London: Bloomsbury.

Halstead discusses the diversity of values in contemporary families:

- Halstead, J. M. (1999a) 'Moral education in family life: the effects of diversity', *Journal of Moral Education* 28: 265–81.

The following adopts a broadly traditional approach to the family:

- Davies, J. (ed.) (1993) *The Family: Is It Just Another Lifestyle Choice?* London: IEA (Institute of Economic Affairs) Health and Welfare Unit.

Wringe strongly rejects the traditional concept:

- Wringe, C. (1994) 'Family values and the value of the family', *Journal of Philosophy of Education* 28: 77–88.

Finally, children's views on the family are discussed in:

- Moore, M., Sixsmith, J. and Knowles, K. (1996) *Children's Reflections on Family Life*, London: Falmer Press.

Chapter 8

Love

Love: the missing dimension of sex education

Nowhere is sex education so out of tune with the thinking of young people as it is on the topic of love. Love is a powerful emotion in the lives of many adolescents. Love is the overarching reason why people in the west – and in many other societies – get married (Gelles 1995: 166–7). As we saw in Chapter 3, love features extensively in the discussions of children about relationships, and appears fundamental to their worldview. Yet love gets little attention in government guidelines either on sex and relationship education (DfEE 2000a) or on personal, social and health education (QCA 2000), and little attempt is made to incorporate love as an underlying value into mainstream programmes of sex education. For example, in using a phrase like 'once they [children] are old enough to want to have a sexual relationship', Lenderyou (1993: 87) appears to take inadequate account of love as a motivating factor in young people's first sexual experiences. This general neglect of love and the emotions contributes to the frustration felt by many teenagers at the sex education they are offered at school, as noted by several researchers (e.g. Measor *et al.* 2000: 123–6).

It is true that this reluctance to talk about love is not exclusive to sex education, or to contemporary society. Love is equally neglected in many theories of emotion, as Shaver *et al.* (1996) have shown; one researcher has pointed out that even in the Middle Ages only 2 out of the 25 theological writings he studied on marital sexual activity had anything at all to say on the subject of love (Flandrin 1985). But it is worth reflecting briefly on the possible reasons for this neglect of love in sex education. One reason that may be put forward is that love is not relevant to the key aims of sex education as defined in government planning and legislation, such as reducing teenage pregnancy and STIs. However, it will be abundantly clear from what has been written so far in this book that we do not believe that such aims can be achieved in isolation from a more holistic sex education based on explicit values. Several more deep-seated reasons for the neglect may also be suggested.

First, love is hard to define. For some writers (such as Peck 1985) love is not a feeling but an act of the will, a choice to give of oneself even when one does not 'feel' like it. On this view, 'falling in love' is an illusion, nature's trick to make us get on with the task of having children, and true love is what is left when the initial excitement passes, involving commitment, caring and the exercise of wisdom. For others, love is a pure dynamic force, or a moment of crazy wisdom and insight, opening up new perceptions of reality and touching people to the very depths of their being. For others again it is a matter of uncontrollable magnetic attraction, or a risky form of self-surrender, or a 'dance on the razor's edge' (see Welwood 1985). Teachers may feel vulnerable or embarrassed to talk to their pupils about love in these terms, and may fear 'baring their soul' in front of pupils.

Second, linked to this is the belief that love is a private matter, one of the few remaining areas where teachers have no right to intrude in pupils' personal lives. Weeks (1995) has rightly pointed out that in certain respects (such as control of the spread of AIDS) public intrusion into the private domain can be justifiable, but many teachers may still believe that they should exercise great caution when entering what Weeks calls 'the sphere of the intimate'.

Third, attitudes to love may also vary with age and gender. Brehm (1992) concludes from various research evidence that love and romance may have a curvilinear association with age, decreasing towards middle age, then increasing again. Some middle-aged teachers may therefore have developed a cynical attitude towards young love which makes it difficult to relate to young people's experiences and attitudes. Frequent gender differences (such as men's more carefree attitude and women's greater caution in love) add further complications (see Dion and Dion 1985; Brehm 1992: ch. 4).

Fourth, in addition to the wide diversity of personal experiences of love, there is much cultural variation. For example, Dion and Dion (1996) have shown that romantic love plays a more important part in intimate relationships in western individualist societies than in non-western collectivist societies, though some western feminists have in turn developed significant critiques of romantic love. In a society marked out by increasing cultural diversity in attitudes to love, teachers may find it hard to do justice to the diversity, but may at the same time feel it is inappropriate to adopt a monocultural perspective.

Finally, to many people love is a mystery, not open to rational discussion. As Peck points out, it is too large, too deep ever to be truly understood or measured or limited within the framework of words. To try to teach children about love may thus be to attempt 'to examine the unexaminable and to know the unknowable' (Peck 1985: 81).

Whatever the causes, there are many problems that result from the neglect of love in sex education. In the absence of adult guidance, children's learning about love may be inappropriate, unreflective and unsystematic. Their learning often derives from pop music, TV, teenage magazines, films, books, peers, observation, jokes, and perhaps from parents and family. As we saw in Chapter 7 on family values, it is not good education to leave children to try to make sense by themselves of such a haphazard array of influences. Indeed, there are few topics that generate as much confusion as love. Schools need to provide children with carefully planned opportunities to discuss and reflect on the nature and value of love at a developmentally appropriate level.

This chapter is written in the belief that love *can* be talked about safely and that we *need* to talk about it. Indeed, as Wilson (1995) points out, it is dangerous to avoid talking and thinking about love, because this leaves untouched our prejudices, fears, fantasies and self-deceptions, and may leave us prey to a wide range of myths and untruths (see Fromm 1956; Peck 1985). The key question is not *whether* love should feature among the values which are discussed within sex education, but *how* to encourage appropriate reflection and discussion. Teachers have to find ways of talking about love which avoid feelings of vulnerability and embarrassment and respect individual and cultural differences. In the next section we shall suggest that certain approaches, such as the examination of historical attitudes, the use of stories, and investigations grounded in the social sciences or conceptual analysis, enable discussions to begin without either intruding unduly on pupils' private lives or destroying the mystery and excitement of love.

Thinking and talking about love

As with the other groups of values examined in this book, we wish to argue that teachers cannot help children to discuss and reflect on the value of love unless they have engaged in serious discussion and reflection on the topic themselves. Such discussion requires an understanding of alternative perspectives on love. This section therefore examines a number of different ways of starting to think about love and related concepts which avoid the difficulties outlined in the last section. Each of the approaches brings distinctive insights and ways of understanding love and is designed to challenge readers to think through their own values from a different perspective. Clearly, different approaches will appeal to different people, and some approaches will be found more suitable than others when working with children.

Approaches through history

Even the briefest and most superficial survey of the history of love in the west is enough to draw attention to the diversity of experiences which go under that name. In Ancient Greek literature, for example, instances of loving marriages are sometimes found, but love was more commonly thought of as a kind of torment and frenzied passion. An alternative concept – platonic love – emphasised a spiritual form of communion and passion in which physical contact played no part. The purest kind of love was sometimes seen as that which occurred between two men or a man and a boy. In both Greece and Rome marriage was often thought likely to destroy love, though the Romans also developed the view of love as a game, something that demanded great concentration while it lasted, but that was ultimately not to be taken too seriously. In the Middle Ages, courtly love became an elegant ritual in which knights rendered devoted service to their noble mistress in the hope of gaining her favour. The Church disapproved of passionate love even in marriage and encouraged the view that passion was doomed to end in unhappiness. A period of greater sexual openness in England in the seventeenth century was gradually replaced by an emphasis on married love and finding companionship and fulfilment in family life. The revival of puritanism in the Victorian era redefined marital love as a spiritual relationship in which the wife's role was in part to limit the sexual passions of her husband. The start of the twentieth century saw a renewed emphasis on the connection between romantic love and marriage, and as the century progressed (as shown in Chapter 2) a loving marriage was increasingly defined in terms of husbands and wives meeting each other's needs. Love became more associated with sexuality than spirituality, and a good sex life was taken to be an important indicator of a successful marriage.

The perspective offered by historical approaches to the understanding of love, and the wide variations that are revealed, help to make clear that contemporary attitudes to love are unlikely to remain unchanged in the future and that children need to be helped to become autonomous, flexible and open-minded if they are to cope with these changes. But they also raise crucial questions: do the different historical manifestations of love sketched out above all refer to what is basically the same phenomenon? Or are there actually different kinds of love? As we shall see shortly, contemporary psychologists have come up with different answers to these questions.

Approaches through story

Stories fall into two categories: those that have an origin that is external to us (i.e. stories that we hear or read or observe), and those that come from within (i.e. stories that we write or tell). Those that are outside ourselves expand our horizons by making us aware of the diversity of human experience, emotions and ways of relating to others. Since so many stories – whether in films, magazines, novels, drama, poetry or other media – are about love, they become a major way of increasing one's understanding of love, especially if they become the subject of reflection and discussion. In school, the study of fiction, drama, poetry and film (and to some extent all of the arts and the humanities) thus has an important contribution to make to learning about love. Similarly, the stories that we write or tell draw on our own experiences, and the act of telling involves reflection which is itself educative. When children and young people reflect on their own personal experiences and observations of love, this provides not only a way to self-knowledge but also an entry to the wider context of social customs, history and traditions in which their own beliefs about love are developing. It is the potential of personal narrative to promote self-discovery and to create holistic knowledge that has increased its popularity as a method of inquiry particularly in North America in the 1980s and 1990s.

In a sense, the central concern of all ethnographic research is to get people to tell their stories. The research reported in Chapter 3 (see Halstead and Waite 2001b: 191) shows how children respond to a love relationship in a soap opera, expressing strong views on the 'rights' and 'wrongs' of the characters' actions and taking for granted the power of love as a motivating force. Other researchers have listened to children's reflections on family life, showing how they see families in terms of caring, affection and commitment. Kajan and Lewis (1996), for example, quote a boy who says, 'Family is where I feel safe. Loved, I suppose', and Rout *et al.* (1996) quote a girl talking about what it is like to live in a family: 'To know people care, people want you around, lots of love and bonding.'

Some writers (see McAdams 1993) go further and claim that we live by stories. Sternberg (1996) suggests that love is a story that people create in their lives out of their particular context of beliefs, values, ideals, life-styles and experiences, and that different stories emerge from different contexts. He tentatively identifies a taxonomy of 24 such love stories. These include the Art model, in which it is important for one's partner always to look good; the Business model, in which relationships are seen as a partnership in a business proposition; the Gardening model, in which the relationship needs to be constantly nurtured and tended to; the Travel model, in which the relationship is a journey of discovery; and the Fantasy model, in which one partner may be viewed, for example, as a knight in shining armour. According to this theory, we 'construct' the characters in these stories – both ourselves and others – and 'construct' the kind of relationship the characters have. We are thus creating our own love story, though we may think of it as external reality, as something that just happens to us. Sternberg (1996) acknowledges that this is just one of a number of metaphors or models through which one can understand love, but argues that it is a helpful way to think about love and to strive to make sense of the diversity of its manifestations.

Psychological approaches

At a popular level, psychologists have produced any number of checklists and self-administered questionnaires, mainly for teenagers' and women's magazines, designed to help readers to know whether or not the feelings they have for a person are truly love. Often such questionnaires are amusing or trivial, but Wilson offers a more serious variant, based on a careful analysis of the concept and meaning of love (1995: 192–5). More academic psychological research has sought to identify the components of love, to investigate the different styles of love and to explore the links between individuals' personalities and love experiences.

Psychologists commonly identify three different elements that make up love, though they may define these differently. Here we examine them under the headings of need fulfilment, emotional attachment and passion. First, love is commonly described as the child of want or need: the lover needs the other to feel complete or whole. Human beings naturally have needs which can be satisfied only through loving relationships: the need for intimacy, the need for someone we can care for, the need for reassurance of our own worth, the need for someone to support us, the need to experience the commitment of someone else to us, and perhaps the need for interdependence (see Brehm 1992: 4–5). Love may not satisfy all of these needs, but perhaps it is the awareness of such needs that drives people to look for love in the first place and makes them willing to meet their partners' needs in turn. In this sense, need fulfilment may be viewed as the most rational of the three components of love. Second, emotional attachment involves feelings of closeness and affection. Some characteristics may be shared with friendship, such as mutual trust, respect, acceptance, sharing and understanding and the enjoyment of each other's company (see Davis and Todd 1985). But the emotional attachment which is characteristic of love goes beyond mere friendship: it involves emotional dependence, the sharing of intimate feelings, a high level of self-disclosure, and a willingness to base one's identity at least in part on one's attachment to one's lover. The third component of love is passion – the excitement at the thought of the lover, the sexual attraction, the feeling of being 'turned on', the desire to touch, to kiss, to abandon oneself to the lover in an ecstasy of physical intimacy. A slight variation on these three components can be seen in Sternberg's triangular theory of love (Sternberg and Barnes 1988), which suggests that the three basic components of love (commitment, intimacy and passion) can be combined in different ways to produce different types of love relationships. Thus romantic love combines intimacy and passion but lacks commitment, while companionate love combines commitment and intimacy but lacks passion, and consummate love combines all three.

Lee (1988) has produced a typology of love using colour as a metaphor for ways of loving. He proposes that there are three primary love styles (eros, ludus and storge) which form the basis for a wide range of combinations. Prominent secondary love styles include pragma, mania and agape. These six ways of loving differ in terms of degree of commitment, intensity of passion, patterns of behaviour and expectations of the lover and the relationship. Eros is intense, passionate, sensual, erotic love. Ludus is the game of love, where following the rules may be important (and the main rule is to be carefree and have fun) but there is little commitment or depth of feeling. Storge is the steady growth of affection leading to lasting commitment. Pragma is a more calculating love in which the lover adopts a clear-headed, business-like approach to the search for a partner and the assessment of a relationship's chances of success. Mania tends to be a possessive relationship in which the lover is likely to be highly demanding and 'living on the edge'. Agape is altruistic, self-giving love, the willing of someone else's personal well-being without demanding anything in return. Other researchers have found that differences in love styles are associated with personality differences. Thus people with high self-esteem were more likely to be eros-oriented while those with lower self-esteem tended towards mania.

One of the aspects of love that is most widely discussed by psychologists is the relationship between personality and love. The Freudian view that loving someone is a kind of substitute for having a high self-concept (in that one projects onto the lover one's own ego ideal) has been widely challenged, and the weight of evidence now supports the view that high levels of self-esteem, personal security and independence contribute significantly to the confidence to pursue love relations, while lower levels might make one feel more in need of love (Dion and Dion 1988; Brehm 1992: 118–22).

Another aspect of love which is the focus of much psychological research is intimacy, which in its narrow sense of sharing in another's psychological and physical self is seen as the goal of most love relationships. Psychologists have been concerned to explore how intimate relationships get started, the stages in the development of intimacy, the relationship between romantic love, courtship and intimacy, the stages of sexual arousal, barriers to intimacy, fear of intimacy, destructive and constructive intimacy games, the darker side of intimacy, including jealousy, physical abuse and sexual violence, and the ways of maintaining an intimate relationship (see Brehm 1992: ch. 3; Olson and DeFrain 1994: ch. 5; Strong *et al.* 1996: ch. 7; Newman 1999: ch. 2).

Sociological and sociobiological approaches

Is love biologically determined or socially constructed? Sociobiologists might argue that love has evolved as a highly elaborate form of essentially sexual ritual, and that it has come into being as a result of the distinctive biological make-up of human beings. The fact that women have a much higher investment (in terms of time and other things) than men in the process of reproduction, combined with the fact that offspring require an extended period of parental care before they are capable of independent survival, requires some mechanism to encourage the permanent or at least semi-permanent pairing up of the males and females, in order to maximise the number of offspring that are reared to independence. The notion of love serves this purpose very well. It encourages loyalty to the sexual partner, not as a moral imperative but as a desire. In their experiences of love, therefore, human beings are on a sociobiological view merely fulfilling their genetic destiny (see van den Berghe 1979).

Sociologists, on the other hand, are much more likely to claim that love is largely socially constructed. The assumptions that individuals carry round with them about the nature of love derive from the beliefs and expectations of the broader society or cultural group, and their individual experiences of love are understood and interpreted in the light of those beliefs and expectations. For example, belief in romantic love (encapsulated in phrases like 'being head over heels in love' or 'being swept off your feet' or love being 'bigger than both of us') is likely to lead to different outcomes or love experiences from belief in companionate love (where the main emphasis may be on providing a stable, loving home). Cancian (1987) traces two ideas that are dominant in the history of the social construction of love in the west, and in particular in the USA: the socialisation of gender roles and the feminisation of love. The socialisation of gender roles refers to the expectation that women should be dependent, emotionally sensitive and preoccupied with relationships, while men should be strong, competent, independent, assertive and preoccupied with work or sport. The feminisation of love is based on the idea that men and women have different ideals and expectations, but that love has come to be seen as the domain of women and is therefore defined in terms of verbal self-disclosure, vulnerability, warmth, affection and the expression of tender feelings (see Noller 1996). The rhetoric of western love also tends to emphasise individual freedom to choose a partner, though social research has revealed the major parts played by social class, religion, ethnicity and economic factors in 'mate selection'. Of course, much bigger cultural differences can be seen when western beliefs about love are compared to those in other parts of the world. When students from ten countries were asked the question 'Would you marry someone with all the right qualities if you did not love them?', the overwhelming majority of North American and Brazilian students said no, but three-quarters of the Indian and Pakistani students did not see this as a problem (Levine 1993). Romantic love is less significant in those countries where the choice of a marriage partner depends mainly on family and economic considerations (see Dion and Dion 1996).

Philosophical approaches

The role of philosophy is to bring precision and clarity to our thinking about a subject, but in fact comparatively few philosophers in recent times (notable exceptions are Scruton 1986; Wilson 1995; White 2001) have turned their attention to love. Typical philosophical approaches include analysing a concept and breaking it down into its component parts, exploring the way that language is used and making distinctions or drawing comparisons with related concepts. Many concepts related to love have already come up in this chapter (passion, romance, intimacy, affection, attachment, desire, caring, attraction, arousal, commitment, friendship, possessiveness) and others could be added (sex appeal, sexual appetite, sexual urges, animal magnetism, fancying, going out with, coquetry, seduction, infatuation, tenderness, unrequited love, addiction). Wilson (1995: 9) makes the point that these are not concepts or ideas which can be easily isolated. Love comes into intimacy, and vice versa, and friendship comes into both. So it is difficult to determine just what ground each concept covers in relation to other concepts. For instance, if A and B appear to love each other, but are given to outbursts of uncontrollable jealousy, should we say that they cannot really love each other? Or is it that this is just one of a range of different kinds of love? A philosophical exploration of the concept of jealousy may help to clarify whether jealousy is an inevitable consequence of love, or whether it is not related to love at all, and may also help to clarify the relationship between jealousy, sexual desire and love (see Scruton 1986: 162–7).

Wilson (1995: ch. 1) argues that ultimately there is only one kind of love, and that the constant feature of this love is a deep and strong desire for the person loved. This enables him to answer a series of questions which further clarify the concept. 'What is the difference between loving X and wanting X?' Wilson's response is that love involves a degree of permanence of desire, and also desire 'for its own sake' rather than for any extrinsic reason. 'What is the difference between "loving" and "fancying", "infatuation" or "being in love"?' For Wilson, the key is again the permanence or durability of love: in contrast, 'fancying' implies only a passing erotic attraction, 'infatuation' an excessive and perhaps illusory attraction, and 'being in love' a great surge of desire which may burn itself out much faster than love itself (see Peck 1985: 84–93). 'What is the difference between loving X and caring about X?' Here the difference lies in the strength of feeling; 'caring' implies compassion, tenderness and the wish to protect, but 'love' combines this with desire, attachment and delight. 'What is the difference between loving X and desiring to do various things with X?' Wanting to do various things with X, Wilson suggests, may be a sign of love, or may be a sign simply of wanting the other person for some external purpose (such as the relief of boredom or sexual frustration). What makes the difference is whether the fundamental signs of love are present: wanting to be close to each other, taking pleasure in each other's company, touching, kissing, smiling, looking on the other with affection and passion, opening their minds and hearts to each other in talk and other kinds of sharing and communication, being concerned about the other's health, happiness and general welfare, and missing the other when apart. Such questions as these, though presented here as part of a philosophical process of conceptual clarification, are of great interest to many young people, and providing the opportunity to think through such issues is a central part of a worthwhile sex education.

Each of these approaches – the historical, the narrative, the psychological, the sociological and the philosophical – illuminates the topic of love from a different angle and draws attention to the richness of the concept, and together they illustrate the diversity of ways of understanding love. It is also intended that the different approaches will inspire a range of different teaching activities, such as discussing a love affair in a soap opera, devising a questionnaire about love for a teenage magazine, comparing attitudes to love in different literary texts, historical periods or cultural groups, discussing love styles and ways of expressing love and analysing the cultural influences which determine young people's taken-for-granted assumptions about love. In the concluding section we move from an exploration of the complexity of love to a brief consideration of why love is an important value in sex education.

The value of love

Love as sexual enrichment

Though love is a wider-ranging concept than sexuality – for love can create the closest of ties for families and friends as well as for partners – it is clear that love and sexuality are very closely intertwined. Love is a powerful force in the intimate relationships of both heterosexuals and homosexuals. Love is a profound feeling – perhaps the most profound of human emotions – and many people describe the experience of love as the most important and memorable experience in their lives. Though men and women may experience love differently, very many people of both sexes see love as an important element in their sexual relationships, because it adds a distinctively human dimension to sexual relations and makes sex a more holistic experience by adding a moral and spiritual dimension to what might otherwise be a purely physical activity.

The question is often raised whether love is necessary for sex. Woody Allen probably hits the nail on the head when he says that sex without love is a meaningless experience, but as meaningless experiences go it's a pretty good one. In other words, there can be sexual relationships (particularly brief ones) where erotic pleasure rather than love is the central feature. But the lesson of history, many people's experience and formal research all suggest overwhelmingly that the combination of sex and love is both enriching and elevating. For many women and some men sexual activity without love is undesirable, perhaps even inconceivable, and even men who separate sex and love report that their most erotic experiences take place in the context of love (Levine and Barbach 1983; see also Strong *et al.* 1996: 186–9).

Love as moral guidance

Wilson (1995: 14) rightly warns us about the dangers of moralising the idea of love at the expense of desire (by claiming, for example, that agape is the only reputable form of love). Nevertheless, there are various ways in which love does introduce a moral dimension into sexual relations. First, love is a major motivator of various kinds of virtuous behaviour: caring for the other, trusting the other, and tolerating characteristics in the other that one does not like or approve of. Second, since love is not an abstract feeling but is directed towards another person, we have to do justice to the reality of that person as a person while still retaining our desire for the person and the pleasure we get from them. Wilson argues that this involves treating the beloved as an equal (1995: especially ch. 7), and Scruton (1986) goes further, claiming that sexual desire gets its focus, its principal pleasures and its long-term rewards from the inherent constraints of a personal morality, and that sexual fulfilment depends upon our capacity for sexual restraint. Third, love is taken by many people today as the moral justification for any sexual activity, whether within or outside marriage. When people are no longer subject to tight sexual regulation by religion, society or culture, the choice whether or not to have sexual relations is an individual rather than an institutional one. And since love is the standard by which many individuals judge the rights and wrongs of sexual activity, this makes love an even more important part of being human.

Love as spiritual fulfilment

Part of the feminisation of love mentioned above is the reinterpretation of sexuality as spirituality (though of course the link between these two dimensions of human experience has a long history: see Halstead 2001b). This does not mean that spirituality replaces sexuality as the preferred way of expressing love (as may have happened in some circles in Victorian times) but that sexuality is itself seen as a spiritual activity. 'Making love' is thus more than a synonym (or euphemism) for sexual intercourse: it draws attention to the fact that humans express their deepest love sexually, and that sexuality is the physical manifestation of love. This is perhaps easiest to understand in a religious context. In Islamic teaching, the soul's desire for union with God is usually expressed symbolically in terms of human love and sexual desire. In Christian teaching, God is love, and love is the cure for alienation and loneliness: both sexual intimacy and holy communion are a celebration of love. For many Christians, sexual passion, desire and intimacy are the basis of the spiritual life of a married couple, not merely something to tolerate as weakness (Gallagher *et al.* 1983: 49–50), and sexual intimacy in a human relationship is an image of spiritual intimacy with God. Even many people without religious belief see in the union of bodies a symbol and reflection of the union of souls. Perhaps it is here that the mystery of love resides.

Summary

1   For many people, both children and adults, sex is intimately connected with love, but there is little teaching about love in most sex education programmes. This may be because teachers feel vulnerable or embarrassed talking about sexual love, or because they believe it is hard to do justice to a topic on which there are so many different views. In any case, they may feel that love is a private matter, or too much of a mystery to be really open to rational discussion.

2   However, children need guidance and support if they are to make sense of the wide range of influences outside school where they learn about love. Schools can introduce their teaching about love from various perspectives: the historical, the narrative, the psychological, the sociological, the conceptual. Each approach offers distinctive insights into love and helps to develop an understanding of the rich diversity of ways of thinking about love.

3   The justification for including love as a fundamental value in sex education lies in its capacity to enrich our sexual experiences. Love also brings a moral dimension to sexual relations, and provides for many people the basis on which to choose whether or not to have sexual relations. Love can also make sexual relations a more holistic experience, aimed at the union of souls as well as bodies.

Issues for discussion

1   It has been said that love is impossible to define (though many people have tried). Consider the arguments for and against defining love as a feeling; an attitude; a way of behaving; a social construct; a matter of choice; an act of the will; an illusion; a kind of madness.
2   Do men and women have radically different expectations as far as love is concerned?
3   Is sex without love ever desirable? Is sex a necessary part of love between the sexes?
4   Take one or two episodes of love relationships in soap operas and examine their key features. Do you think that soap operas accurately reflect our society's views about love relationships?
5   Design your own checklist for love, to help readers find out whether or not they really love someone.

Further reading

There are comparatively few books on love and related topics. Three helpful philosophical books are:

- Scruton, R. (1986) *Sexual Desire: A Philosophical Investigation*, London: Weidenfeld and Nicolson.
- White, R. (2001) *Love's Philosophy*, Lanham, MD: Rowman and Littlefield.
- Wilson, J. (1995) *Love between Equals*, London: Macmillan.

Textbooks on human sexuality often include a useful chapter on love:

- Brehm, S. S. (1992) *Intimate Relationships*, 2nd edn, New York: McGraw-Hill.
- Strong, B., DeVault, C. and Sayad, B. W. (1996) *Core Concepts in Human Sexuality*, Mountain View, CA: Mayfield.

A number of popular psychological and religious texts take love as their theme, including:

- Gallagher, C. A., Maloney, G. A., Rousseau, M. F. and Wilczak, P. F. (1983) *Embodied in Love: Sacramental Spirituality and Sexual Intimacy*, New York: Crossroad.
- Peck, M. S. (1985) *The Road Less Travelled*, London: Rider.
- Welwood, J. (ed.) (1985) *Challenge of the Heart: Love, Sex and Intimacy in Changing Times*, Boston, MA: Shambhala, pp. 253–6.

Finally, two special issues of journals contain useful articles:

- Understanding Love, special issue of *Personal Relationships* 3 (1) (March 1996) edited by K. K. Dion and K. L. Dion.
- Sexuality and Spirituality, special issue of *International Journal of Children's Spirituality* 6 (2) (August 2001) edited by J. M. Halstead.

Part 3

Chapter 9

Aims for school sex education

A diversity of aims

While there is a growing academic literature on the aims of sex education (Went 1985; Reiss 1993b; Epstein 2000; Clark 2001), it is still the case that in most guides to sex education, the aims are not analysed. Examination of policy guidelines and the resources used for teaching school sex education suggest that the following main ones are found:

- helping young people to know about such biological topics as growth, puberty and conception
- preventing children from experiencing abuse
- decreasing guilt, embarrassment and anxiety about sexual matters
- encouraging good relationships
- preventing under-age teenagers from engaging in sexual intercourse (abstinence education)
- preventing under-age teenage girls from getting pregnant
- decreasing the incidence of sexually transmitted infections
- helping young people question the role of women and men in society.

These aims are not entirely distinct but there is worth in examining them one-by-one. This chapter will look at the educational and philosophical arguments for these aims and at the extent to which they are compatible.

Helping young people to know about such biological topics as growth, puberty and conception

In many countries there has long been a tradition at both primary schools (typically for 5–11 year olds) and secondary schools (typically for 11–16 year olds) of teaching about such biological topics as growth, puberty and conception. This aim is occasionally denigrated as 'teaching about the plumbing', which we take to mean that sex education should be

about more than this rather than that it should not include such fundamental biology.

Precisely what is covered under this heading depends on the age of the
pupils concerned. For example, for older juniors in primary school Sanders
and Swinden (1990) suggest that a teacher photocopies a line drawing
(provided by Sanders and Swinden 1990: 124–5) of a naked female and
one of a naked male, cuts them up into parts and distributes the frag-
mented parts to pairs of children. The children are then asked to piece
the bodies together and to name at least 15 parts. As is so often the case
with sex education, one can imagine teachers and classes where an
exercise like this would work wonderfully, and one can imagine teachers
and classes where it might be a disaster. So much depends on what
parents consider appropriate, on the pre-existing relationship that the
teacher has with the class and on how an exercise such as this is introduced and managed.

Assuming, though, that such an exercise 'goes well' in the sense that
the children learn more about their bodies without anyone getting upset
or more than a normal amount of misbehaving, what might be the worth
of such knowledge? One possibility, to be looked at later (see pp. 140–2)
is that guilt, embarrassment and anxiety about sexual matters is decreased
– or, put more positively, that one feels good about oneself and one's
sexuality. Here, though, we can concentrate simply on anatomical knowledge. Well, one argument would be about 'knowing oneself'. Just as one
should learn something about the history and geography of one's country,
one should learn something about the history and geography of one's
body. Equally, girls should learn about boys' bodies and vice versa. At the
very least, such knowledge will often be of instrumental value. One of
us recalls a middle-aged man (with four children) admitting that he
knew nothing about women's periods. It is also the case that every year a
surprisingly large number of couples, even in this day and age, end up
going for infertility treatment only for sensitive questioning to reveal that
they haven't actually attempted penial–vaginal sexual intercourse, not
realising that this is what heterosexual couples do when the woman
wants to conceive.

One of the great values of school sex education, at least in theory, is that
it can allow a place for teaching to take place that may be thought difficult
in other everyday circumstances – e.g. between a parent and a child –
precisely because teaching about developmental and sexual matters is
personal. Given the understandable propensity for people, including young
people, to maintain that they 'know it all already' (see Chapter 3), careful
teaching that makes no such automatic assumptions, but takes into
account what really is known, can achieve a great deal of good.

Preventing children from experiencing abuse

In Isobel Allen's (1987) study 82 per cent of teenagers and 61 per cent of their parents reported 'Not going with strangers' as having been covered more than any other topic when they (or their children) were in primary school. The need for such education has not diminished. However, we are all more aware now that much (very probably most) abuse, including sexual abuse, takes place not at the hands of strangers but by family and friends (Braun 1988; Russell 1995).

How realistic is it to expect schools to prevent children from being abused? Some teachers will have stories of where following the various guidelines about detecting and responding to child abuse – whether the guidelines are statutory (e.g., in England and Wales, DfEE 1995) or not (e.g. Wonnacott 1995) – led to positive outcomes. Sadly, other teachers will have stories where the opposite proved to be the case and despite the best efforts of social services or the police, one ends up feeling that more harm than good resulted (see Webb and Vulliamy 2001).

No one would deny that, if feasible, schools should help prevent children from experiencing abuse. Mostly this entails teachers and other school staff detecting and responding to signs of abuse, including attempts by pupils to tell adults in school about the abuse. Here sex education is not education provided by teachers to pupils; rather it is teachers and other adults in school being educated to notice and react appropriately to evidence of abuse, including sexual abuse. In addition, it is possible that good quality school sex education might lead to it being less likely that those who have received such education will go on to abuse others – though we are unaware of any empirical evidence for this. Indeed, what data there are suggest that work with both young people and with adults who sexually abuse others can lead to such abuse becoming less frequent but that the work is intensive and highly skilled, often requiring specialist psychotherapy (Lamb 1996; Erooga and Masson 1999).

While much of what is classified as sexual abuse is about as clearly and non-controversially wrong as anything can be, it would be possible with certain groups of older students (say, 14–18 year olds) to discuss such questions as:

- Should there be a cut-off age below which sexual intercourse is always wrong? (A useful distinction is between paedophilia, which refers to sexual activity between adults and pre-pubescent children, and sexual activity between adults and those defined by the law as being under the age of sexual consent but who are physiologically well beyond puberty, e.g. many 14-year-old girls nowadays.)
- Should the law treat more leniently (as it does) a 17-year-old who has sexual intercourse with a 15-year-old than a 25-year-old and, if so, why?

- Does showing pornographic videos to 14 year olds count as sexual abuse? (And what is meant by 'pornographic' – how, for instance, is it to be distinguished from 'erotic'?)
- If female circumcision (often labelled 'female genital mutilation') is unacceptable, should male circumcision be banned? (For ethical analyses of female genital mutilation see Sheldon and Wilkinson (1998) and Miller (2000); for ethical analyses of male circumcision see Harrison (2002) and Miller (in press).)

Decreasing guilt, embarrassment and anxiety about sexual matters

Many sex education programmes aim to reduce guilt, embarrassment and anxiety about sexual matters (e.g. Mayle 1978; Went 1985; Greenberg 1989; Welbourne-Moglia and Moglia 1989; Cole 1993; Harris 1997). Few would deny that this is a worthwhile aim.

Nowhere is this truer than for teaching about puberty (Prendergast 1992; Alvarado and Power 1993). With improvements in nutrition and health – and possibly also as a result of the greater distribution of endocrine disruptors (Motluk 2002) and certain oestrogen-containing shampoos (Westphal 2002) – girls are reaching puberty earlier (e.g. Ng and Haeberle 1997) and there are many countries where 10 per cent or more of girls start their periods before the age of 11 (e.g. Whinchup *et al.* 2001). Partly for this reason, many girls start their periods without their mothers or any other family members telling them what to expect. This is often embarrassing, and occasionally is frightening, as it was for Farida:

> *Interviewer:* Can you tell me about when you first heard about periods as a girl? Whom you heard that from and what you learnt from it?
>
> *Farida:* I think my first experience was really frightening. I knew nothing about it before I started. I had only picked up that I would have periods but I was not prepared for that either from other institutions or from home. In fact I got most of my information from my friends who were older than me. I noticed there was staining on my underpants, it was not blood but like it. I thought, what has been happening to me for the past three days?
>
> (Alvarado and Power 1993: 53)

However, a number of points need to be made about the aim of decreasing guilt, embarrassment and anxiety. The first is that there are times when guilt is an appropriate response: one should feel guilty when one has done something wrong. A second point is that while one could spend a great deal of time dissecting the relationships between these three terms, the distinction between embarrassment and modesty is rarely made in any school sex education literature. For example, in an HIV and AIDS training pack for use with 16–19 year olds, Bain *et al.* (1989: 19) list as one of their aims 'To promote open and explicit communication about sexual issues'. In an exercise called 'Words we use', the following is suggested:

> Split into small groups. Give each group a large piece of paper on which is written one word (see suggestions below). Ask participants to write down as many other words that they think mean the same as the word on the piece of paper. Once each group has completed, share information in a large group and discuss.
>
> Penis
> Urinate
> Menstruation
> Intercourse
> Vagina

- How did this exercise feel?
- Were there any words you didn't like?
- Did they make you feel passive, aggressive, etc.?
- Were there any words you hadn't heard before?
- Is there a common language with different people? When would it vary and why?

(Bain *et al.* 1989: 21)

Exercises such as this can be of value with certain groups of young people – though they will not be acceptable to some parents and young people. However, they can run the risk of implicitly carrying the message that we should feel as uninhibited talking about words to do with sex and sexuality as about any other words (see Figure 9.1). In contradistinction, matters of sexuality are for most people deeply and appropriately personal. It is not the case that what is private and personal ought necessarily to be easy to talk about. Wendy Shalit (1999) titles her book *A Return to Modesty: Discovering the Lost Virtue* and argues that we have lost much of the notion of modesty. Naomi Wolf's (1997) *Promiscuities: A Secret History of Female Desire* doesn't discuss the word but, perhaps surprisingly, provides an implicit argument for it.

A third point is that a teaching approach and philosophy that aims to decrease guilt, embarrassment and anxiety about something may have the effect of condoning it. This general point is a familiar one to counsellors and those who teach about controversial issues. That which is intended to be non-evaluative and spoken from a position of neutrality

Figure 9.1 'Condom on the Patio' by Ros Asquith

Source: © Ros Asquith, published by Cath Tate Cards, PO Box 647, London SW2 4JX (reference CTF66)

may be heard more positively (try to be non-evaluative to someone who tells you that they enjoy hurting pets).

Encouraging good relationships

In England and Wales, the changes to the National Curriculum that were introduced into schools from September 2000 included a shift in language from 'sex education' to 'sex and relationship' education. At Key Stage 3 (11–14 year olds) the framework for personal, social and health education (PSHE) stipulates:

Developing good relationships and respecting the differences between people

3 Pupils should be taught

a about the effects of all types of stereotyping, prejudice, bullying, racism and discrimination and how to challenge them assertively

b how to empathise with people different from themselves

c about the nature of friendship and how to make and keep friends

d to recognise some of the cultural norms in society, including the range of lifestyles and relationships

e the changing nature of, and pressure on, relationships with friends and family, and when and how to seek help

f about the role and importance of marriage in family relationships

g about the role and feelings of parents and carers and the value of family life

h to recognise that goodwill is essential to positive and constructive relationships

i to negotiate within relationships, recognising that actions have consequences, and when and how to make compromises

j to resist pressure to do wrong, to recognise when others need help and how to support them

k to communicate confidently with their peers and adults

(Qualifications and Curriculum Authority 1999: 190)

The move from sex education to sex and relationship education came about, according to the Department for Education and Employment, partly because of criticisms by young people of 'the lack of any meaningful discussion about feelings, relationships and values' (DfEE 2000a: 11). We welcome this broadening of sex education. Of course (as we discussed in Chapter 1) one of the 'attractions' to many of attempting *not* to include values in sex education is that this apparently simplifies what one is trying to teach. Certainly, the paragraph in the draft consultation from the Department for Education and Employment on relationships came in for a huge amount of comment and feedback:

Relationships

1.21. Young people, when asked about their experiences of sex education at school, often complain about the focus on the physical aspects of reproduction and the lack of any meaningful discussion about feelings, relationships and values. Sex and relationship education set within the framework for PSHE across the four key stages will significantly redress that balance. It will help young people to respect themselves and others, and understand difference. Within the context of talking about relationships children should be taught about the nature of marriage and its importance for family life and for the bringing up children. The Government recognises that there are strong and mutually supportive relationships outside marriage. Therefore, children should learn the significance of marriage and stable relationships as key building blocks of community and society. Teaching in this area needs to be sensitive so as not to stigmatise children on the basis of their home circumstances.

(DfEE 2000b: 8)

Conservative commentators felt strongly that this down-graded marriage; liberal commentators felt equally strongly that to put any greater stress on marriage would be unacceptable. In the event, the only changes that were made in the published version were to improve punctuation and grammar (see DfEE 2000a: 11). As we saw in Chapter 6, even within one religion (Christianity) there is today a very considerable divergence of opinion about the need for sexual relationships to be confined within marriage. Although there are certain contemporary societies where marriage is almost universally regarded as the norm (e.g. Islamic societies, and to a certain extent secular Japan), in most societies this is no longer the case. Research among young people in the UK shows a very wide range of views about marriage (McGrellis *et al.* 2000; Sharpe 2001).

Preventing under-age teenagers from engaging in sexual intercourse (abstinence education)

In 1996, as part of welfare reform legislation, the United States Congress established an abstinence education programme. Section 510(b) of Title V of the Social Security Act, P. L. 104–193 provides an eight point definition of abstinence education:

For the purposes of this section, the term 'abstinence education' means an educational or motivational program which:
1. has as its exclusive purpose teaching the social, psychological, and health gains to be realized by abstaining from sexual activity;
2. teaches abstinence from sexual activity outside marriage as the expected standard for all school-age children;
3. teaches that abstinence from sexual activity is the only certain way to avoid out-of-wedlock pregnancy, sexually transmitted diseases, and other associated health problems;
4. teaches that a mutually faithful monogamous relationship in the context of marriage is the expected standard of sexual activity;
5. teaches that sexual activity outside of the context of marriage is likely to have harmful psychological and physical effects;

6. teaches that bearing children out of wedlock is likely to have harmful consequences for the child, the child's parents, and society;
7. teaches young people how to reject sexual advances and how alcohol and drug use increase vulnerability to sexual advances; and
8. teaches the importance of attaining self-sufficiency before engaging in sexual activity.

No waffle here about the difficulties of identifying a common set of values for sex education (see Chapter 2)! Further, by 2002 Congress had allocated over $300 million to fund abstinence programmes (Mabray and Labauve 2002). Obtaining these funds therefore means that, for example, teaching about contraception is excluded.

One could not have a clearer illustration of the centrality of values to sex education. Advocates of abstinence education see it not only as effective but also as the right way to be educating young people about sex. Opponents of abstinence education see it as fear-based, failing to take into account student diversity and divisive (Blake and Frances 2001). One point sometimes not appreciated by Europeans is how central religious values still are in the USA both for young people and for adults: 83 per cent of US teenagers say that religion (nearly always Christianity) is an important part of their lives and by a wide margin they say that morals, values and/or religious beliefs affect their decisions about whether or not to engage in sexual intercourse more than concerns about sexually transmitted diseases (STDs) or pregnancy, sex education or attachment to their partners (Whitehead *et al.* 2001).

Teenagers in the USA who avow a religious faith are more likely to delay having sex (Whitehead *et al.* 2001). However, the research evidence about the efficacy of abstinence education is surprisingly thin (Kirby 2001). In the most careful review of the field, only three evaluations met methodological criteria and it was concluded that 'None of the three evaluated programs showed an overall positive effect on sexual behaviour' (Kirby 2001: 5).

Preventing under-age teenage girls from getting pregnant

Abstinence education is one way of preventing under-age teenage girls from getting pregnant. We deliberately refer to girls, partly because the emphasis has all too often been on females rather than on both females and males (but see Salisbury and Jackson 1996; Blake and Laxton 1998; Hilton 2001) and partly because the word is used, we suspect, to suggest immaturity. One of the longest-running aims of school sex education has been to decrease the incidence of teenage pregnancy; in Britain, sex

Table 9.1 Birth rates for 15–17 year olds in OECD countries per 1000 women in that age range in 1998

Country	Birth rate
USA	30.4
UK	16.6
New Zealand	15.4
Hungary	14.1
Portugal	11.8
Slovak Republic	11.4
Iceland	11.2
Canada	10.8
Australia	9.5
Ireland	8.2
Poland	5.8
Greece	5.3
Germany	5.3
Austria	5.1
Czech Republic	5.0
Spain	4.2
Norway	4.0
France	3.4
Belgium	3.4
Luxembourg	3.0
Italy	2.9
Finland	2.6
Denmark	2.5
Netherlands	2.2
Sweden	2.2
Switzerland	1.5
Japan	1.4

Source: based on UNICEF (2001: 4)
Note: Mexico and Turkey were excluded because of their high overall fertility rates

education in the early 1930s strove to prevent illegitimacy (Barry 1979). Although the aim of sex education is rarely described thus today, the majority of educators would envisage a reduction of teenage or below-age (typically under the age of 16 years) pregnancy as a result of good school sex education.

There are various ways of calculating the 'teenage birth league' – should one include 18 and 19 year olds, for example? But however the data are presented, the USA comes out as having by far the highest teenage birth rate in the developed (rich) world, and the UK comes out having the highest teenage birth rate in Europe. In 1998 – the most recent year for which valid international comparative data are available – 52 out of every 1000 15–19 year olds in the USA gave birth (that's 5.2 per cent). Another way of putting this is that almost a quarter of women in the USA have a child while they are in their teens.

The data for 15–17 year olds are perhaps most relevant (after all, there are plenty of 19 year olds who are in a stable relationship or married, want to have a baby and have the support of their partners or husbands and society in this). Data for births for this age range for countries in the OECD (Organisation for Economic Co-operation and Development – the group of countries that produces two-thirds of the world's saleable goods and services) are given in Table 9.1.

Although one might not realise it from the regular tirades in some sections of the media about teenage births, in most countries births to teenage mothers more than halved between 1970 and 2000 (UNICEF 2001). In the USA, for example, teen birth rates declined for the tenth straight year in 2001 and are now at record low levels (Anon 2002). In the UK, however, the 1990s showed little change in the figures (Social Exclusion Unit 1999). This was despite the fact that the 1992 Strategy for Health in England, *The Health of the Nation*, presented to Parliament by the then Secretary of State for Health, set as one of its 15 targets 'To reduce by at least 50 per cent the rate of conceptions amongst the under 16s by the year 2000 (*Baseline 1989*)' (Secretary of State for Health 1992: 19).

Why should countries aim to reduce the incidence of teenage births? As reviewed in Chapter 5, there are physical health arguments in favour of this aim. However, the major arguments are not to do with health. For a start, young mothers are more likely in almost all rich countries to end up with fewer educational qualifications, to be unemployed or low-waged, to live in poor housing conditions and to suffer from depression. Their children are more likely to live in poverty, to grow up without a father, 'to do less well at school, to become involved in crime, to abuse drugs and alcohol, and eventually to become a teenage parent and begin the cycle all over again' (UNICEF 2001: 3).

Then there is the argument that a 16- or 17-year-old young woman can't know what she is letting herself in for by becoming pregnant; it would be better to wait a few years. Technically (not intended derogatorily) this is a patronising argument about informed consent – that I know better than the person concerned that in the future she will look back and realise that she didn't understand at the time what the consequences of her actions were, whereas had she waited a few years she would have understood more fully.

So the arguments against teenage births include valuing the physical and mental health of mothers and their children, believing that reducing teenage pregnancies would be beneficial for the wider society both financially and in terms of crime reduction, and that teenagers cannot give informed consent to become pregnant. There are several ways in which teenage birth rates might logically be lowered:

- reducing the incidence of heterosexual intercourse (discussed under abstinence education on pp. 144–5)
- increasing the use of effective contraception
- increasing the abortion rate.

Of course, each of these has profoundly different consequences and raises significantly different issues to do with values. The one possibility that needs contradicting here is that countries with low teenage birth rates achieve this by high rates of abortion. The opposite is the case (UNICEF 2001: 20 – data are for 1996). The USA and Hungary have the highest teenage abortion rates (30.2 per 1000 women aged 15 to 19 years), followed by Australia (23.9), New Zealand (22.5), Canada (22.1) and the UK (21.3). At the other end of the scale are Greece (1.3), the Netherlands (3.9) and Spain (4.9).

Decreasing the incidence of sexually transmitted infections

Sex education programmes frequently aim to reduce the incidence of sexually transmitted infections (STIs). With the success of antibiotics in the treatment of syphilis and many strains of gonorrhoea, the aim was often a fairly minor one in the 1950s, 1960s and 1970s. However, the arrival of AIDS in the 1980s meant that this aim of sex education under-went something of a renaissance. There was a flood of HIV/AIDS education packs for use in schools or by youth and community workers (e.g. Sketchley 1986; British Medical Association 1987; Harvey and Reiss 1987; Gordon and Klouda 1988; Massey 1988). Most of these made little effort to connect with broader aims and principles of sex education.

As reviewed in Chapter 5, STI rates are currently rising in the UK, as they are in a number of countries. To a certain extent this is not surprising. Ages at puberty are still falling, we live in more sexualised societies than used to be the case (Chapter 2); religious and other societal restrictions on sexual activity are less than they used to be and in most countries (other than those in sub-Saharan Africa) HIV/AIDS is still in its early stages. Age at first sexual intercourse has fallen considerably in many countries (UNICEF 2001; Wellings *et al.* 2001; Nash 2002) and people are almost certainly having, on average, more sexual partners over their lifetime.

Precisely how school sex education programmes might seek to reduce the incidence of STIs is open to debate. As discussed above, abstinence education adopts one approach. Another approach, taken by many programmes, particularly in the light of HIV/AIDS, is to attempt to increase the use of condoms (Ray 2001). For example, in the Scottish SHARE (Sexual Health And RElationships) study, condom demonstrations are undertaken with 15 year olds at the end of a two-year programme of sex and relationship education. In one study, interviews undertaken with 16–19 year olds revealed two contrasting strategies that were used to ensure condom use at first intercourse with a new sexual partner: verbal and non-verbal (Coleman and Ingham 1999). Men were more likely than women to adopt the non-verbal strategy. This might indicate the power relationships that exist in many relationships – with women feeling less able to adopt such a strategy – or might simply be because men are less likely to talk about things before doing them!

Many sex education programmes take what is often termed a 'non-judgemental approach' to sexually transmitted infections, stressing, for example, that what matters in terms of one's likelihood of becoming infected is one's behaviour rather than what group of people one belongs to. In the most extreme cases there are illogical arguments about viruses not having morals. The advantages of stressing behaviours rather than the group one belongs to are several: such an approach should be less likely to lead to stereotyping ('only gays and drug injectors gets AIDS') or a false sense of security ('I don't inject therefore I needn't worry) and encourage agency and autonomy. However, it is worth emphasising the common-sense point that human nature is very judgemental. In a study of the psychosocial impact for women as being diagnosed as having chlamydia, perceptions of stigma were still strongly associated with infection. As one woman put it when talking about disclosing the diagnosis to others:

> You don't phone up everyone and say I've got a sexually transmitted disease you know, I'm not feeling too good come round and see me, cheer me up . . . From that point of view you feel very isolated because you can't really talk about it, I suppose you could but you know other people's reactions would put you off talking about it.
>
> (quoted in Duncan *et al.* 2001: 196)

Helping young people question the role of women and men in society

Some current sex education programmes encourage students to examine the roles played by women and men in society. The aim is generally for students to realise the existence and extent of sexual inequality and become committed to such fundamental values as justice, fairness and respect for others – seen through a gendered lens (e.g. Singh 1989; Herbert 1992; Blake and Laxton 1998).

Feminist critiques of sex education have pointed out how easy it is for sex education simply to reinforce some of the gender inequalities in society (Wolpe 1987; Szirom 1988; Baker and Davies 1989; Holly 1989; Francis and Skelton 2001). Many sex education programmes examine gender roles. Yet such examinations may fail to challenge injustice. Baker and Davies (1989) analysed a lesson on sex roles which took place in an Australian coeducational secondary school. They concluded that the teacher's intention to teach a lesson for equality was undermined by his own theorising and his teaching methodology. As a result, the pupils heard a lesson that confirmed the fact that women and men are not equal. Francis and Skelton (2001) argue that men teachers can use mis-ogynist and homophobic discourses of gender and sexuality to construct their sexuality and that this can manifest in the harassment or seduction of pupils. Girls 'may sometimes be gratified by male objectification while simultaneously experiencing such behaviour as harassing' (Francis and Skelton 2001: 18).

In the mid-1980s, Wolpe (1987) pointed out that for a hundred years female sexuality and its fulfilment, as defined in terms of middle-class values, had been located within marriage and the bearing of children. Male sexuality, on the other hand, she argued, had been represented quite differently, as a primordial urge which need not be gratified within marriage. Wolpe concluded that sex education at the time placed female sexuality firmly in the context of marriage and the family.

By now, there are more sex education programmes that avoid assump-tions of heterosexuality for all – we discuss these in Chapter 10. At the same time, there are an increasing number of sex education programmes that attempt actively to challenge the stereotypes identified by Wolpe (1987). There has also been a growing emphasis on the need for young men to be challenged or helped to examine common assumptions about what it is to be male. Davidson (1990) pointed out that for a long time the burden of society's sexual problems was carried by women, with young men traditionally being seen as too far beyond the pale to be worth bothering much about.

> 'Boys will be boys' reflects a common belief that men are incapable of change in relation to sex. This results in a similar 'damage limitation' approach to our current problems. If men cannot change, so the argu-ment goes, then we must protect women and children from them by better 'policing' and more severe punishment. Inevitably this leaves many women feeling fearful, angry and frustrated and many men feel-ing confused, defensive or guilty.
>
> (Davidson 1990: 7–8)

Non-sexist sex education with boys and young men aims to encourage them to examine themselves and their hopes and desires and break out of the cycle of oppressive behaviour. It is a sex education which encourages the sharing of thoughts, feelings and behaviours which might otherwise not be discussed. It aims to liberate young men – and so, ultimately, young women – from the restrictive effects of sexism and hetero-normativity by, *inter alia*, providing a safe environment to explore feelings of inadequacy and to challenge standard ideas of what is involved in becoming and being a man (e.g. Whyld 1986; Davidson 1990; Segal 1990; Whyld *et al.* 1990; Blake and Laxton 1998; the journals *Achilles Heel* and *Working with Men*).

From aims to frameworks

The range of aims for sex education has widened over the years and the relationships between these aims are rarely considered. In the next chapter we identify four overarching frameworks for sex education, beneath which the various aims are located.

Summary

1   There are a number of aims for school sex education. A common one is to help young people to know about such biological topics as growth, puberty and conception. Occasionally denigrated as 'teaching about the plumbing' we take this criticism to mean that sex education should be about more than this rather than that it should not include such fundamental biology.

2   Sex education may also attempt to prevent children from experiencing abuse. Here sex education entails teachers and other adults in school being educated to detect and react appropriately to evidence of abuse, including sexual abuse. In addition, it is possible that good quality school sex education might lead to it being less likely that those who have received such education will go on to abuse others.

3   Sex education can also intend to decrease guilt, embarrassment and anxiety about sexual matters, though a useful distinction can be drawn between embarrassment and modesty.

4   Sex education may try to encourage the development of good relationships. In England and Wales the move from sex education to sex and relationship education came about partly because of criticisms by young people of the lack of meaningful discussion about feelings, relationships and values in much sex education.
5   Sex education programmes generally try to reduce teenage pregnancy rates and decrease the incidence of sexually transmitted infections. There are a wide variety of ways in which this may be attempted, reflecting very different value judgements.
6   Some recent sex education programmes attempt to help young people question the role of women and men in society.

Issues for discussion

1   Is it realistic to expect schools to reduce the incidence of sexual abuse?
2   When, if ever, are feelings of guilt desirable?
3   What is meant by a good sexual relationship?
4   Should schools be required to practise abstinence education, be forbidden from practising it or given a choice? Why?
5   Draw up a list of reasons (a) for and (b) against encouraging young people to use condoms.
6   Should we expect men and women to behave in the same ways?

Further reading

For a detailed consideration of the aims of menstruation education (which range from provision of biological knowledge, through empowering young people to challenge sexual harassment, to putting pressure on manufacturers of sanitary products to make healthy and environmentally friendly products) see:

• Alvarado, S. and Power, P. (1993) *The Inside Story: Menstruation Education for Young Men and Women*, Wisbech: LDA (Learning Development Aids).

For suggestions about how schools can deal with sexual abuse see:

- Gillham, B. and Thomson, J. A. (eds) (1996) *Child Protection: Problem and Prevention from Preschool to Adolescence – A Handbook for Professionals*, London: Routledge.
- Smith, G. (1995) *The Protectors' Handbook: Reducing the Risk of Child Sexual Abuse and Helping Children Recover*, London: Women's Press.
- Whitney, B. (1996) *Child Protection for Teachers and Schools: A Guide to Good Practice*, London: Kogan Page.

For thorough reviews on attempts to reduce teenage pregnancy rates see:

- Kirby, D. (2001) *Emerging Answers: Research Finding on Programs to Reduce Teen Pregnancy*, Washington, DC: National Campaign to Prevent Teen Pregnancy.
- Social Exclusion Unit (1999) *Teenage Pregnancy*, London: The Stationery Office.
- UNICEF (2001) 'A league table of teenage births in rich nations', *Innocenti Report Card* 3, Florence: Innocenti Research Centre. Available at www.unicef-icdc.org

Chapter 10

Frameworks for school sex education

Identifying frameworks

A number of competing frameworks for school sex education can be identified. Oversimplifying somewhat, these are that school sex education should

- not occur
- promote physical health
- promote autonomy
- promote responsible sexual behaviour.

This chapter will examine each of these frameworks and consider how they relate to one another.

School sex education should not occur

In many ways, the most straightforward position to take in respect of school sex education is that it should not occur. For example, an article in *Family Matters*, the newsletter of the Conservative Family Campaign, states that:

> Under the banner of education, teachers have become seducers – corrupters of innocence who usher young people into forbidden sexual experiences that lead to teenage pregnancy, abortion, sexual diseases, and mental and emotional problems.
>
> (Masters 1992)

The main point made by those who believe that school sex education should not take place is that sex education is the responsibility of parents. Schools, it may be argued, do not have the right to deal with such matters. Nor do they have the abilities. All too often, it is maintained, schools adopt an amoral, or even an immoral, approach. It is sometimes argued or implied, as in the above quote, that childhood is a time of innocence and that that time should not be shortened through a premature exposure to the world of adults. Further, teachers may lack the skills and abilities needed to teach sex education and may hold very different beliefs and values from those held by parents.

A strength of this framework is that it places the onus for sex education firmly on parents. It therefore prevents parents shrugging their shoulders and leaving schools to 'deal with it'. Further, interviews with pupils and ex-pupils (Allen 1987; Langille *et al.* 2001; Buston and Wight 2002) and official inspections (Office for Standards in Education (Ofsted) 2002) suggest that schools all too often provide at best only mediocre sex education.

There are, however, a number of difficulties with this approach. To expand on a point we made at the beginning of Chapter 1, an immediate difficulty is that, in a sense, a school cannot avoid sex education occurring. It is impossible, for instance, to teach about almost any piece of literature without transgressing onto the field of sex education. Consider, for example, within the corpus of English literature, Shakespeare's *Romeo and Juliet* and Hardy's *Tess of the D'Urbervilles*. Each of these has sexual relationships at its heart. Similarly, it is difficult to conceive (an appropriate word) of biology without human reproduction, of geography without population studies, of history without the suffragette movement, or of religious education without a consideration of the gender-specific roles of men and women. Each of these subjects would be emasculated (if that is not too sexist a term) by the exclusion of such matters. Further, avoiding school sex education would not simply entail removing certain topics on the timetabled curriculum. Gender and sexuality issues are built into the very structure and ethos of a school. As anyone who has ever sat on an equal opportunities working party knows, every aspect of school life gives messages to pupils about what it is to be male or female.

Nevertheless, it can be pointed out that this objection to the suggestion that schools should not teach sex education is rather an overstated one. No one is suggesting that we should stop teaching the classics of literature or the fundamentals of biology, geography or history. All that is being claimed is that schools would be best to avoid any sex education other than the most basic biology.

A different argument in favour of having school sex education is that surveys generally show that this is what young people and their parents want. In her 1985 survey of 14–16 year olds and their parents in three cities in England, Isobel Allen found that 96 per cent of parents and 95 per cent of the teenagers felt that schools should provide sex education (Allen 1987) and much the same had been reported earlier by Christine Farrell (1978). More recently, the Health Education Authority (1995), Stone and Ingham (1998) and the Health Promotion Agency for Northern Ireland (1996) all found extremely strong support among UK parents for the provision of sex education by schools. In Stone and Ingham's study, there was least support for the suggestion that schools should teach about homosexuality but even here only 8 per cent of parents felt that this should not be taught or discussed at all in school. Strong support for the provision of sex education in schools is also found in a number of other countries, such as Canada (Langille *et al.* 2001), Greece (Kakavoulis 2001), Russia (Shapiro 2001) and the USA (Saul 1999).

However, there are societies where there is far more ambivalence about whether schools should provide sex education, for example rural Bangladesh (Cash *et al.* 2001). Even within societies where parental support for school sex education is generally very strong, there are parents who very firmly believe that their children should not receive it. While the Health Education Authority (1995) study found that 94 per cent of parents said schools should provide sex education, this figure fell to 49 per cent among Muslim parents with 27 per cent unsure and 24 per cent against it.

In some countries, including England, Wales and New Zealand, parents have a right to withdraw their children from most or all school sex education and a small minority of parents do exercise this right (e.g. Stone and Ingham 1998), whether for religious (see Chapter 6) or other reasons. Although this policy has difficulties – consider parents who are sexually abusing their children and for that reason do not wish them to receive school sex education – nevertheless we feel, on balance, that it is the best overall. Most schools take measures (which we discuss in Chapter 11) to ensure that parents at the very least get to review what pupils cover in their sex education lessons.

A final difficulty with the suggestion that schools should not provide any sex education is associated with the notion of 'lost childhood innocence'. Whether there ever was such an age is open to question (see Fletcher and Hussey 1999). It can be argued that:

> Historians date the modern, western, concept of an ideally innocent childhood to somewhere around the seventeenth century. Until then, children had been understood as faulty small adults, in need of correction and discipline, especially Christian children who were thought to be born in sin.
>
> (Higonnet 1998: 8)

Even, though, if we grant the possibility of a golden age of innocence, it is surely increasingly true that it lay in the past (see Halstead 1998). For a whole variety of reasons, even quite young children in many countries often have more experience of adult matters than most of us would wish them to have, as every sensitive piece of ethnographic research on the subject concludes. For example, in the study conducted with 9 and 10 year olds in two primary schools in the south-west of England (reported in Chapter 3), Halstead and Waite (2001a) found that girls in particular discussed the impact of alcohol and drugs on relationships. Drugs were seen as something that could take over your life. They did not want to marry drug-takers because they felt they could be dragged down by it. The girls were also very aware of male violence perpetrated against neighbours and acquaintances. One girl cited her babysitter who had family problems and had taken an overdose after being raped. Both girls and boys in the research appeared fascinated that condoms came in different flavours, and sometimes the boys bought them from machines to blow up or suck:

Boy: [J] brings in condoms. He blows them up – lucky dip, curry flavour.
Boy: Whenever we go out we always like find packets of condoms.
Boy: Me and L. found a pack, loads of different flavours.
Boy: Some stupid people buy them and shove them on their head, chocolate coloured ones, and some people suck them.
Boy: My friend, he always takes money, he just gets licorice ones, coconut ones, sucks 'em.

(Halstead and Waite 2001b: 196)

School sex education should promote physical health

If school sex education is to take place, perhaps it should simply promote physical health (i.e. health in a narrow sense, not including mental health, social health or spiritual health). This would mean schools teaching factually about such matters as conception, contraception, pregnancy and sexually transmitted infections. Indeed, the Royal College of Obstetricians and Gynaecologists, in its 1991 report on unplanned pregnancy, put sex education in schools at the top of its list of recommendations in the belief that school sex education is the most important factor in helping to reduce unplanned and unwanted pregnancies (Royal College of Obstetricians and Gynaecologists 1991). The British Medical Association has similarly strongly supported the provision of school sex education for all pupils (British Medical Association Board of Science and Education 1997).

It might be thought that the promotion by a school of the physical health of its pupils would be a relatively uncontroversial matter. However, it is frequently argued that sex education in general, and teaching about contraception in particular, leads to an increase in under-age sexual activity (White 1994; White 1998; Castro-Vázquez and Kishi 2002) and that this fact argues against the provision of school sex education.

In fact, major reviews of the evidence, whether sponsored by the World Health Organization (Grunseit and Kippax 1993) or the US-based National

Campaign to Prevent Teen Pregnancy (Kirby 2001), strongly conclude that sex education that includes teaching about contraception either has no effect or postpones initiation of sexual intercourse:

> In summary, the overwhelming majority of articles reviewed here, despite the variety of methodologies, countries under investigation and year of publication, find no support for the contention that sex education encourages sexual experimentation or increased activity. If any effect is observed, almost without exception, it is in the direction of postponed initiation of sexual intercourse and/or effective use of contraceptives.
>
> (Grunseit and Kippax 1993: 10)

> evaluations of many sex and HIV education programs strongly support the conclusion that these curricula do not increase sexual intercourse, either by hastening the onset of intercourse, increasing the frequency of intercourse, or increasing the number of sexual partners, and that some, but not all, programs can delay and reduce sexual activity.
>
> (Kirby 2001: 89)

The same conclusion holds in the UK (Wellings *et al.* 1995).

The belief that sex education should promote physical health may have certain surprising – to some – implications. Not only, if the above reviews are correct, should it include teaching about contraception, but also it should probably include some positive teaching about homosexuality. There is evidence that gay and lesbian pupils are more likely to commit suicide than their heterosexual counterparts (Khayatt 1994; Bagley and Tremblay 1997). It is certainly the case that many lesbians, bisexuals and gay men experience violence on account of their sexuality (Epstein 1994; Heron 1994; Rivers 1995; Mason and Palmer 1996) with teenagers being especially at risk. It is possible that a positive treatment of homosexuality in the classroom could reduce this (Stafford 1988; Unks 1995). We discuss teaching about homosexuality in the following section.

School sex education should promote autonomy

As we argued in Chapters 1 and 2, one of the roles of schools in sex education is to help pupils make sense of the diversity of sexual values which they acquire from a variety of sources and gradually, through a process of critical reflection, begin to shape, construct and develop their own values. In maintaining this we are in effect saying that an important function of school sex education is what it is for school education more generally, namely to enable the development of rational autonomy. In this we follow Harris (1971) and Jones (1989), among others, who write from a philosophical perspective and argue that sex education should promote rational sexual autonomy.

This position is argued for in many school sex education policies and guidelines. For example, Hampshire's guidelines for sex education state that one of the aims of sex education is that it should 'promote the ability to make informed decisions' (Hampshire Education n.d.: 4). Similarly, Surrey's curriculum guidance for sex education includes as one of its aims: 'To help young people to deal with their own circumstances and where appropriate to change both themselves and their environment' (Surrey Inspectorate 1987: 3). More recent policies and guidelines also advocate rational autonomy – sometimes described as skills of 'assertiveness and decision-making' (Lawrence et al. 2000: 24), 'learning to make choices' (DfEE 2000a: 5) or 'the ability of pupils to make informed choices' (Ofsted 2002: 14).

The concept of rational autonomy has a long history, being informed by Plato and other Ancient Greek philosophers and developed further by philosophers with such different presumptions as Kant and Mill. It is generally held that rational autonomy is displayed by individuals who act intentionally, with understanding and without external controlling influences that determine their actions (for a fuller discussion see Chapter 4 and Haworth 1986). However, each of these three criteria is problematic, especially when young people are considered. Is it realistic to expect actions, particularly sexual actions, to be undertaken intentionally, with understanding and without external controlling influences?

Three responses need to be made. First, these criteria, especially the latter two, can be met to various degrees. A successful sex education can therefore be envisaged as one that significantly enhances them. Second, and more substantively, the notion of 'with understanding' is not a trivial one. People are deeply divided about the 'facts' of such relevant issues as masturbation, homosexuality and lifetime monogamy. Third, it is obviously naive to equate 'without external controlling influences that determine their actions' with 'without being affected in any way by what others think, say or do'. No man is an island, entire of itself, and that is especially true of our sexual mores.

Teaching about homosexuality to promote autonomy

In recent years, whether and how schools should teach about homosexuality has become something of a *cause célèbre*. We have already said something about the varying Christian and Muslim understandings of and attitudes towards homosexuality in Chapter 6 and have mentioned the possibility that a school sex education framework for the promotion of physical health might require positive teaching about homosexuality. Here, within a framework of promoting autonomy, we will argue for a position that is unlikely to please either pole of the debate: namely that schools should teach about homosexuality but should treat it as a controversial issue.

Let us begin by assuming that it makes sense to talk about homosexuals (i.e. gays and lesbians) and heterosexuals – noting that, as we have already mentioned (see pp. 100–1), there are alternative viewpoints which concentrate on homosexual and heterosexual behaviours rather than dividing people into separate categories. Given this assumption, one powerful argument in favour of schools teaching about homosexuality is that the absence of such teaching is often deeply hurtful to homosexuals. Adult gays and lesbians, when asked, frequently tell of the pain that they felt by their apparent non-existence at school, in the structured silence that surrounded their sexual identity. Often, even explicit teacher-controlled discussions on sexuality omit any reference to gay and lesbian orientation and behaviour (e.g. Trenchard and Warren 1984; Khayatt 1994).

It is difficult to be certain, but a conservative estimate would suggest that in the UK and the USA around 4 per cent of adult males and 2 per cent of adult females are exclusively or predominantly homosexual (Johnson *et al.* 1994; Laumann *et al.* 1994; Johnson *et al.* 2001). In other words, while homosexuals are undeniably a minority, they are a sizeable one – comparable, in the UK, to the number of Muslims or Roman Catholics. As such they deserve the attention and curriculum space when teaching sex education that should be accorded to religious minorities when teaching religious education (Reiss 1997b). Further, even if the percentage of people who are exclusively or predominantly homosexual is not large, several times this number have at least some homosexual tendencies and this may be especially true of teenagers. White argues that a school should 'present homosexuality as a morally acceptable way of life which some of its student members may one day lead' (White 1991: 406).

On the other hand, there are arguments against teaching about homosexuality. One is the belief that such teaching cannot be balanced. Just as peace studies and environmental education promote peace and the responsible use of the environment, so, it might be held, teaching about homosexuality is likely to lead to its advocacy. Perhaps teaching about homosexuality, unless simply to condemn it, results in its implicit legitimisation. We do not teach at school in an even-handed way about slavery, murder or child abuse. Indeed to teach about such issues in a 'balanced' way is wrong, precisely because we hold such behaviours to lie outside the moral pale (see Archard 1998). Similarly, it can be argued, we should not even help students to consider the arguments in favour of homosexuality.

Further objections are that many teachers feel uncomfortable teaching about homosexuality and that a significant number of parents do not want their children to be taught about it, even though other aspects of sex education are widely supported (Allen 1987; Elam *et al.* 1996). In a 1996 US survey, when asked whether they favoured or opposed teaching about the gay and lesbian lifestyle as part of the public school curriculum, 34 per cent of respondents approved such teaching and 63 per cent opposed it. Probing further, the pole asked how the gay/lesbian lifestyle should be presented if it *were* included in the curriculum. Only 9 per cent thought it should be presented as an acceptable alternative lifestyle, while 27 per cent thought it should be presented as an unacceptable alternative lifestyle and the majority, 57 per cent, thought it should be presented simply as an alternative lifestyle with no moral judgement made (Elam *et al.* 1996: 54–5).

A different objection is that teaching in this area might even increase homophobia and prejudice. Halstead (1992) argues that three types of controversial issue can be distinguished: (a) where there is agreement over the existence of a particular moral imperative, but disagreement over how to interpret it; (b) where there are conflicting moral imperatives and uncertainty over which should take priority; (c) where disagreement arises because groups do not share the same fundamental moral principles. It isn't always easy to place any particular instance of controversiality into one of these three categories, but it seems likely that the issue of homosexuality may, at least for some people, fall into type (c). The significance of this is that discussions about type (c) controversies are especially likely to inflame the situation rather than inform the participants. Such discussions may be counterproductive.

Overall, and taking into account citizenship arguments (considered in the next section) as well as arguments about physical health and autonomy, our conclusion is that most secondary schools should teach about homosexuality. Such teaching should, first, be balanced (we discuss later what this might mean in practice), second, be undertaken only by suitably trained teachers who wish to teach about it, and third, be part, where possible, of the explicit curriculum so that parents do not suddenly find that such teaching has been foisted on their children without their being aware of it. Fourth, parents and guardians should have the right to withdraw their children from formal school sex education. Finally, teaching in this area should be evaluated, particularly in terms of its acceptability to those receiving it. If a sex education programme of any sort proves highly divisive or unacceptable to a significant number of recipients, it needs amending.

We have argued previously (Reiss 1997b; Halstead and Lewicka 1998; Halstead 1999b; Reiss 1999) that teaching about homosexuality should be considered as an instance of teaching about a controversial issue – a position that has the additional benefit that a substantial literature exists on the teaching of controversial issues (Dearden 1984; Stradling *et al.*

1984; Bridges 1986; Halstead and Taylor 1996). While there are various ways of teaching validly about controversial issues, these have in common that the teaching is balanced in the sense that the teacher neither favours nor disfavours that which is controversial. That homosexuality should be taught as a controversial issue is supported by Beck (1999, 2001) in contradistinction to John Petrovic (1999), who argues that teachers must not express any beliefs they have against it and must 'present and use materials that portray GLB [gays, lesbians and bisexuals] in a positive light' (Petrovic 1999: 205; see also Petrovic 2002).

It is clear why teaching about sexual orientation is so difficult. Our ideal, fantasised, teacher of sexual orientation might be someone knowledgeable about pedagogy, developmental psychology, sociology and moral philosophy, not to mention epistemology, theology, genetics and endocrinology (for pupils who want to ask questions about the 'causes' of sexual orientation). She would also be able to ensure that a classroom ethos prevailed in which differences of opinion, within certain limits, could safely be voiced while her character would be such that she would be respected by students, parents and community leaders. Her pupils would be personally affirmed and feel valued, and understand what it would be like to have a very different set of sexual values. Such teachers are not ubiquitous, nor are they always backed up by administrators and elected officials – whether at local or national level – anxious to pursue truth, well-being and justice.

Helping students enjoy their sex lives

It cannot be said that a central aim of school sex education in the UK or elsewhere has been to help students enjoy their sex lives in any very direct sense. As one of us noted, in an analysis of how school science textbooks for 14–16 year olds portrayed human reproduction:

> To be honest, some of the accounts also managed to make the whole undertaking sound boring, or at any rate devoid of all passion or excitement.
>
> (Reiss 1998b: 145)

Jackson (1982) argued that British educators saw sex education as preparing adolescents for the future rather than helping them to come to terms with sexuality here and now. 'Its chief aim, indeed, is apparently to dissuade them from expressing their sexuality at all' (Jackson 1982: 137–8).

The difficulties in teaching in school about sexual enjoyment are obvious. For one thing, the subject matter is intensely personal; for another, it does and should lie in the future for most pupils. Perhaps the latest edition of Alex Comfort's *The Joy of Sex* is a better tutor than one's school teacher in these matters. More fundamentally it can be argued from a psychoanalytical angle:

> Later, post-oedipally, armed with language, the child will try to make sense of what is now called 'sex', only to discover the impossibility of doing so. Well-meaning education and enlightenment may follow, but the erotic remains outside any educational process.
>
> (Weatherill 2000: 265)

In addition, one of us has argued that:

> The fullest way to learn about a marriage is in marriage; the fullest way to learn about the Eucharist is in receiving communion; the fullest way to learn about sexual intercourse is with one other person in private. Other learning can be preparatory – schools can help pupils to develop commitment, be true to themselves and to others, to manifest forgiveness and so on – but the fullest learning in these areas is ultimately that which is authentic and truly participatory. And the language of such learning is rarely the language of words but, whether we are talking about sex education or education about spirituality, the language of imagination, of experience, of touch and of the other senses.
>
> (Reiss 2001: 244–5)

On the other hand, Jones (1989), in addition to maintaining that sex education should promote rational sexual autonomy and the fostering of inquiry into, and critical reflection on, sexual issues, held that one of its desired outcomes was in

> working towards minimizing the unhappiness felt on account of sexual matters and helping people to achieve as much sexual satisfaction and pleasure as possible.
>
> (Jones 1989: 57)

More recently, Louisa Allen, working with New Zealanders aged 17 to 19 years, concludes that the type of sexual knowledge they were most interested in, and which they had found lacking in their school education, centred on a 'discourse of erotics' (Allen 2001: 109), for example:

> *Peter:* The stuff you want to know is, like, how is the best way to go about, maybe obtaining condoms or how to approach a girl and say, 'hey do you want to have sex', or even how to do it, like just the basics, like positioning or whatever or something like that I mean . . .

Amy: What makes it, you know with regards to positioning what makes it easier for both, you know, sexes . . . If you've got absolutely no idea, you're going to stuff around for ages and you know most times it's painful, if you don't know what you are on about.

(Allen 2001: 117)

Helping young people to develop skills of assertiveness

In order to make and implement an informed decision about an issue, a person needs at least three things: adequate relevant information, an appropriate ethical framework and the skills needed to translate the decision into action. It was the realisation that specific skills may be needed for people to put sexual decisions into practice that resulted in a tendency for many programmes of sex education to include or run alongside sessions on assertiveness.

Assertiveness involves telling someone what you would like in a way that appears neither threatening nor punishing. It is about standing up for your rights but not at the cost of violating the rights of others (Hopson and Scally 1980; Townend 1985).

Sex education programmes sometimes include assertiveness training exercises with the aim of enabling young people to say 'no' when confronted with unwanted sexual advances. This is to be welcomed. However, pretty much the same skills that may enable a 14-year-old person to resist the sexual advances of an 18-year-old person will help some 18 year olds to make such approaches to 14 year olds. Assertiveness training is of value provided it takes place in a framework that promotes responsible sexual behaviour.

School sex education should promote responsible sexual behaviour

Understood narrowly, promoting autonomy is all about enabling individuals to put their rational decisions into effect. Promoting responsible behaviour – for all that we may have responsibilities to ourselves – is principally taking the interests of others into account. Sex education policies and guidelines nearly always talk about promoting or enabling responsible behaviour, or respecting others. As the Canadian Guidelines for Sexual Health Education put it:

Sexual health education is concerned with the well-being of the individual while recognizing that individuals have responsibilities to, and are affected by, each other and by the social environment in which they live.

(Ministry of National Health and Welfare 1995: 6)

Similarly, the UK Sex Education Forum believes that sex and relationships education should:

> encourage personal and social development, fostering self-esteem, self-awareness, a sense of moral responsibility, and the confidence and ability to resist abuse and unwanted sexual experience.
>
> (Ray 2002: 2)

while the Department for Education and Employment in England and Wales states that:

> Pupils need also to be given accurate information and helped to develop skills to enable them to understand difference and respect themselves and others and for the purpose also of preventing and removing prejudice.
>
> (DfEE 2000a: 4)

Of course (as we have already noted) there is a very wide diversity of perspectives as to what is meant by responsible behaviour in general and sexually responsible behaviour in particular. Nevertheless, there are certain areas of agreement between most parties and (as we shall spell out more fully in Chapter 12) there is considerable value in pupils discussing what they understand by such terms as 'responsible sexual behaviour'.

Teaching for the promotion of responsible sexual behaviour requires a teacher to help students to see sexual situations and possibilities from the points of view of others. As the Department for Education and Employment official guidance puts it, sex and relationship education entails 'developing self-respect and empathy for others' (DfEE 2000a: 5). One problem with this is indicated by the case of a 26-year-old man in Florida who was arrested in 1996 *in flagrante delicto* with a plastic female porpoise in a sex shop into which he had broken. He had intended simply to rob the till but told the police that once in the shop he had become mesmerised by the various sexual appliances. 'I'm not a pervert', he said 'but I wanted to see what it felt like to be one'. (He was sent to prison where he chose to study for a degree in marine conservation.)

In other words, we would not normally envisage schoolteachers helping their charges to understand what it is like to be, for example, a prostitute, a child molester or a sado-masochist. We would, though, envisage pupils, at the appropriate ages (see Chapters 11 and 12), imagining what it is like to, on the one hand, believe that one's religious faith provides a complete framework for deciding what is acceptable and what is unacceptable sexual behaviour and, on the other hand, to believe that there are no God-given moral absolutes and that it is up to us in communities to determine what is acceptable and what unacceptable (see Mackie 1977; White 1990; Weeks 1995).

Behaving responsibly in society

Much sexual behaviour takes place between pairs of people so that my responsible sexual behaviour largely entails my considering one other person. However, we also have wider responsibilities as citizens. For example, one argument in favour of schools in many western countries teaching about homosexuality is a citizenship argument in that all of us, whether or not we are homosexual, need to know about homosexuality in order, as citizens, to understand and be able to make an informed contribution to such issues as 'Should homosexuals be permitted in the Armed Forces?', 'Should the age of consent be the same for homosexuals and heterosexuals?' and 'Should marriage be an option for homosexuals?' This argument would hold (with suitable linguistic amendment) even for those who deny that there are homosexual people, holding instead that there are, rather, some people who manifest homosexual behaviours.

The citizenship argument might entail teachers going on to explore with students whether there is a valid distinction between the public (civic) and the private sphere of morality (see Haydon 1995; McLaughlin 1995). For example, does it make sense for an individual to disapprove of homosexuality yet campaign against discrimination by the Armed Forces against lesbians and gays?

Summary

1   The argument that school sex education should not occur is difficult to accept in its full form in that schools can't help some sex education occurring. In addition, surveys generally show that both parents and pupils want sex education to take place in schools. Nevertheless, some parents do not want school sex education to occur and many have concerns about certain topics. Schools should heed these concerns and parents should be allowed to withdraw their children from formal sex education.

2   Through teaching about conception, contraception, pregnancy and sexually transmitted infections, schools can do much to promote physical health. Such teaching does not seem to lead to an earlier onset of sexual intercourse – if anything, the opposite is the case.

3   Schools should enable pupils to develop sexual autonomy. They should teach about homosexuality, treating it as a controversial issue.

4   School sex education should promote responsible sexual behaviour and encourage pupils to consider what is meant by 'responsible sexual behaviour'. Teaching for the promotion of responsible sexual behaviour requires teachers to help students to see sexual situations from the points of view of others.

Issues for discussion

1   Which should be more important in determining the content of a school's sex education curriculum: the wishes of pupils or of their parents? What of the views of teachers?

2   Can childhood be a time of innocence? What, in this context, is the opposite of 'innocence'?

3   Why might teaching about contraception sometimes delay sexual activity?

4   Should homosexuality be treated as a controversial issue or is this demeaning to some students – or is this too liberal a position?

5   What might be understood by 'responsible sexual behaviour'?

Further reading

For reviews of the effects of school sex education on sexual behaviour see:

- Grunseit, A. and Kippax, S. (1993) *Effects of Sex Education on Young People's Sexual Behaviour*, Geneva: Youth and General Public Unit Office of Intervention Development and Support Global Program on AIDS, World Health Organization.
- Kirby, D. (2001) *Emerging Answers: Research Finding on Programs to Reduce Teen Pregnancy*, Washington, DC: National Campaign to Prevent Teen Pregnancy.
- Wellings, K., Wadsworth, J., Johnson, A. M., Field, J., Whitaker, L. and Field, B. (1995) 'Provision of sex education and early sexual experience: the relation examined', *British Medical Journal* 311: 417–20.

The following books discuss different understandings of adolescent sexuality:

- Coleman, J. and Roker, D. (eds) (1998) *Teenage Sexuality: Health, Risk and Education*, Amsterdam: Harwood Academic.
- Holland, J., Ramazanoglu, C., Sharpe, S. and Thomson, R. (1998) *The Male in the Head: Young People, Heterosexuality and Power*, London: Tufnell Press.
- Mac an Ghaill, M. (ed.) (1996) *Understanding Masculinities: Social Relations and Cultural Arenas*, Buckingham: Open University Press.
- Moore, S. and Rosenthal, D. (1993) *Sexuality in Adolescence*, London: Routledge.

Part 4

Chapter 11

Sex education in the primary phase

The purpose and context of Chapters 11 and 12

We cannot in just two chapters provide an entire curriculum for school sex education. What we aim to do, rather, is to suggest what an approach to school sex education that takes values to heart might look like and why. We hope that those who have worked as sex educators will find much that is familiar, though perhaps with some different emphases and rationales, as there is rarely much to be gained from proposing a curriculum that departs entirely from its predecessors.

We have called this chapter 'Sex education in the primary phase' and Chapter 12 'Sex education in the secondary phase' using 'primary' and 'secondary' not rigidly to refer, respectively, to '5 to 11/12 years' and '11/12 to 16 years' but rather to the whole of life up to the age of 11 or 12 and the whole of life subsequently. Having said that, we do concentrate on school sex education between the ages of 5 and 16 years but, of course, much (arguably most) sex education takes place outside this age range; most of it certainly takes place out of school.

In this chapter, as well as dealing with a number of specific teaching topics – the human body, sexual abuse, families and friends, and puberty – we also address more general issues relevant to both Chapters 11 and 12: principles of school sex education, sex education before school, and teaching approaches and strategies.

Principles of school sex education

Our overriding principle is that school sex education should serve the needs of those who are being taught and those with whom they live and will live in society. In the light of the aims and frameworks for school sex education examined in Chapters 9 and 10, set within the context of the wider frameworks of values discussed in earlier chapters, we understand these needs to entail

- physical health
- the development of rational sexual autonomy
- consideration and respect for others.

This overriding principle leads to the following subsidiary principles:

- Schools need to take account of pupil/student wishes concerning the sex education they receive.
- Schools need to take account of parental wishes concerning the sex education their children receive.
- Schools provide sex education through formal teaching, informal teaching and the general ethos of the school.
- Teachers should consider carefully their own values and those embodied in the resources (materials, visitors, any places visited) they use for teaching about sex education.

Sex education before school

As Dilys Went points out, 'Sex education starts at birth, with parents' reactions to the sex of their child' (Went 1985: 50). Nowadays, with ultra-sonography being used to detect the sex of the unborn child, we might say that sex education starts months before birth. Each year millions of female fetuses are selectively aborted. Parents, other adults and other children communicate powerful messages to young children about their sexuality. Through both words and non-verbal communication, messages are sometimes still given – though in a number of countries this is less the case than used to be – that:

- it would have been better to have been born one sex, typically a boy, rather than the other
- there are certain things that girls shouldn't do that boys can (e.g. play football, go out without an accompanying adult, fight, play with mechanical toys) and certain things that boys shouldn't do that girls can (e.g. cry, play with dolls, enjoy ballet)
- there are parts of the body that we feel ashamed of, that should not be seen, that should not be touched or that should never be talked about.

Of course, such messages are almost always given unreflectively and often unintentionally. The growing influence of feminism means that more and more children now grow up in families where many of these messages are not given.

Teaching about the human body

By the time they are about 4 or 5 years old, many children ask questions of their parents about where babies come from, and a standard and appropriate aim for teaching in the earliest years at school is for pupils to know about their own bodies and to recognise similarities and differences between themselves and others. Classic research undertaken by Ronald and Juliette Goldman between 1979 and 1981 showed the extent to which 5–15 year olds in Australia, Canada, England, Sweden and the USA knew about sexual matters including the differences between girls and boys (Goldman and Goldman 1982). The Goldmans used careful one-to-one interviewing. Another useful technique, particularly in the primary phase, is to ask children to do drawings. Sandra Bourne (1995) got Year 3, Year 4, Year 5 and Year 6 pupils to draw and label a girl of their age with no clothes on and a boy of their age with no clothes on. One of her conclusions was that:

> The vast majority of pupils from Year 3 to Year 6 revert to stereotypes to explain differences, even when these are not actually apparent in real life, eg long/short hair; all females, regardless of age, with developed breasts.
>
> (Bourne 1995: 23)

In another study that used drawings, Reiss and Tunnicliffe (2001) looked at the drawings made by 158 people (ranging in age from 4 year olds to undergraduates) in England asked to draw what they thought was inside themselves. They found that at primary level:

- in Reception (4–5 years: 9 girls, 7 boys) and Year 2 (13 girls, 8 boys), none of the children drew or labelled any reproductive organs
- in Year 3 (18 girls, 15 boys), only 2 of the children – both of them boys – drew or labelled any reproductive organs
- in Year 6, 44 per cent (8 out of 18) of the boys drew and/or labelled reproductive organs, in every case male reproductive organs; 64 per cent (9 out of 14) of the girls drew and/or labelled reproductive organs, but strikingly 7 out of the 9 girls drew or labelled *male* reproductive organs.

Reiss and Tunnicliffe (2001) also found that on none of the 158 drawings was a clitoris either drawn or labelled whereas a penis was drawn on 13 of the drawings and labelled on 10 of them. A final observation was that females were much more likely to represent internal aspects of their reproductive system than were the males, suggesting that females, unlike males, are socialised into a discourse which sees their reproductive organs as sites simply of reproduction rather than of sexual pleasure.

As we discussed earlier (see pp. 140–2), an appropriate aim of school sex education is to reduce embarrassment, anxiety and inappropriate guilt. At the same time, privacy and modesty about oneself, particularly one's sexual self, are not just understandable, but appropriate. There is a fine line to be drawn by teachers of young children in helping them to understand their own bodies, and the bodies of those of the opposite sex, better without either embarrassing them or causing them to feel embarrassed, anxious or guilty about any feelings of modesty that they have.

Responding to children's needs

The whole issue of 'needs' is problematic, as we saw in Chapter 1. Here we take needs to be physical health, the development of rational sexual autonomy and consideration and respect for others. An effective, though partial, way of ensuring that one is responding to children's individual needs, whatever their ages, is to allow them to ask questions. Such questions may be oral and spoken in front of the whole class or written for the teacher's eyes and entered in some sort of question box. One advantage of the question box approach is that it gives a teacher time to decide how to answer the question and whether any questions are inappropriate. At the same time, a teacher should not be overly constrained by the questions that are asked. There are certain things that children need to know whether or not they ask them: some children are reluctant or not able to ask questions to which they need the answers.

Children should know the answers to such questions as 'Where do babies come from?' well before they leave their primary school. Tunnicliffe (1983, 2000) has written about the distinction between birth education and sex education, arguing that 'birth education' largely precedes 'sex education' and is concerned with 'learning about new life, its emergence and the development of the new organisms with or without parental care as is appropriate to the species' (Tunnicliffe 2000: 1). As far as learning about where human babies come from, one approach includes giving primary children unfettered access to some of the many excellent picture books available on the subject. Mayle ([1973] 1978), Stones ([1989] 1997) and Cole (1993) are UK classics and there are other more recent ones. Of course, books such as these work wonderfully well if read by parents with their children at home.

Whether at home or at school, much teaching is concerned with teaching about appropriate information at the appropriate time:

When she was three years old, my friend Ana challenged her nursery-school teacher, Jamie. Jamie had just told the children gathered around her, listening to her account of birth, that babies grow inside their mummies' tummies. 'No they don't,' countered Ana. Jamie patiently explained again. Ana was pleasant but firm. Finally, three repetitions later, Jamie asked Ana where she thought the baby was before birth. 'In the mommy's uterus,' she answered.

(Bernstein 1994: 62)

Such knowledge might be thought somewhat precocious. But Anne Bernstein, who talked with over 100 children aged from 3 to 12 years about their knowledge of how people get babies, details the confusion that can result for children who think that babies grow in the same place where the food one eats goes.

A complementary school approach, if feasible, to reading or talking with children about birth is for a parent with a baby to come into school – provided the parent is comfortable with the idea and doesn't mind being pestered with questions. Becky Francis observed that the secondary school boys she was studying were as fascinated as the girls by an 18-month-old baby brought in by a teacher of English when her childminder was ill, but 'to vocalize such interest would have been potentially damaging to their construction of masculinity' (Francis 2000: 48). Of course, in a planned activity of this sort intended as part of sex or birth education, a teacher would anticipate such gendered behaviour and behave accordingly. In our view this would mean proceeding so as to attempt to reduce such stereotypical behaviour, not in a crass way that would be likely only to exacerbate it but carefully, avoiding, for example, giving the impression that one sex would be more interested or vocal than the other and ensuring that all individuals had the opportunity to engage fully.

Detecting and responding to sexual abuse

In both primary and secondary schools, one important aim of sex education is for teachers and other adults in the school to be capable of detecting and responding to child abuse including sexual abuse. Teachers need appropriate education and training for many aspects of their work but rarely more so than here (e.g. Wonnacott 1995; Whitney 1996). For many teachers, dealing with sexual abuse is difficult simply because the notion of sexual abuse is emotionally painful; for a significant number of teachers, it is particularly so as they themselves will have been sexually abused. For a small minority of teachers, it is difficult because they themselves will have sexually abused or currently are sexually abusing children.

In its guide for teachers on child abuse, the National Society for the Prevention of Cruelty to Children (NSPCC) provide a definition of sexual abuse and go on succinctly to summarise its signs:

> When children are exploited sexually by adults who use them to meet their own sexual needs. It includes sexual intercourse, fondling, masturbation, oral sex and exposing children to pornographic materials. Children who have been sexually abused often become depressed and withdrawn, they display unusually aggressive behaviour, may have eating problems and relationships with adults that exclude others. They may display over-sexualised behaviour inappropriate for their age.
>
> (Barrett 1994: 20)

Sexual abuse may also be indicated in school by direct or indirect attempts by the child concerned to tell their teachers or friends. Children's writings and drawings may contain explicit or implicit efforts by sexually abused children to communicate this to others.

By failing to detect and respond appropriately to child abuse, a school fails to value, indeed betrays, its pupils. Precisely what constitutes an appropriate response differs from country to country. In England and Wales:

- All staff should be alert to signs of abuse and know to whom they should report any concerns or suspicions.
- All schools and colleges should have a designated member of staff responsible for co-ordinating action within the institution and liaising with other agencies, including the Area Child Protection Committee (ACPC).
- All schools and colleges should be aware of the child protection procedures established by the ACPC and, where appropriate, by the local education authority.
- All schools and colleges should have procedures (of which all staff should be aware) for handling suspected cases of abuse of pupils or students, including procedures to be followed if a member of staff is accused of abuse.
- Staff with designated responsibility for child protection should receive appropriate training.
- In every education authority a senior officer should be responsible for co-ordinating action on child protection across the Authority.

(DfEE 1995: 1)

This is to focus on the immediate response. Schools can also do a tremendous amount of good both by their general education and specifically through sex education to help children who have been abused (Smith 1995; Gillham and Thomson 1996). In general they can help abused children:

- develop self-esteem
- learn what is acceptable and what is unacceptable sexual behaviour (e.g. masturbating in public)
- clarify for themselves what they like and what they don't like
- develop age-appropriate relationships with peers and adults.

Teaching approaches and strategies

Much good school teaching in sex education is like good school teaching in any subject: taking account of prior knowledge and differences between pupils; being able to motivate pupils; using appropriate pacing; possessing – and knowing when to use to best effect – a variety of teaching methods; having a set of aims and objectives and the capacity to adapt these flexibly; creating a safe, welcoming, relaxed and purposeful environment; having the self-confidence to say 'I don't know but I'll find out' and 'I'm not sure, what do you think?' as appropriate; ensuring that there are consistent practices across the whole school; selecting and using appropriate resources – bearing in mind both the diversity of sexual knowledge that there may be in a class and the need to take account of the values reflected by existing resources.

In addition, there are (as we now go on to discuss under the subheadings below) some more specific approaches and strategies that are recommended either for sex education in particular (Dixon 1988; Clarity Collective 1989; Sanders and Swinden 1990; Massey 1991; Lenderyou 1993; Mellanby et al. 1995; Ray and Went 1995; Measor et al. 1996; Sex Education Forum 1996; Blake and Laxton 1998; Ray 1999; DfEE 2000a; Harrison 2000; Measor et al. 2000; Ray 2000; Milton et al. 2001; Sex Education Forum 2001; Forrest et al. 2002; Ofsted 2002; Ray and Jolly 2002; Baraitser et al. in press; Hilton in press; Strange et al. in press; see also pp. 50–2) or health education, citizenship education or values education more generally (Straughan 1988; National Curriculum Council 1990; Williams et al. 1990; Rowe and Newton 1994; Haydon 1997; DfEE 1999; Scottish Executive 1999; Halstead and Taylor 2000; Harden et al. 2001).

Ground rules and confidentiality

Ground rules are most likely to be accepted by a class if children have already come across the idea of deciding among themselves what is the best way of dealing with issues and have an appropriate trust in their teacher and in one another to keep promises. Ground rules usually establish such things as:

- nobody (pupils and teacher) should ask intimate questions of anybody else
- nobody has to speak if they don't want to
- everyone should try to respect others in the class: learning how to respect others, even if one disagrees with them, is a fundamental liberal value (see Chapter 4).

In a classroom, respect manifests itself in such actions as not sniggering, teasing or denigrating others. More positively, it entails listening to others, hearing them out, thinking about their feelings, trying to look at things from their point of view, and so on. It does not, of course, mean that one must necessarily come to agree with the views of others. Indeed, in a learning context, such as that which one hopes obtains in schools, it can be more respectful to disagree with someone – thus showing that one takes their view sufficiently seriously to mount an argument against it – than to say nothing and so avoid any debate with them.

As far as confidentiality goes, a school policy on this can be of value and include:

- assurance that teachers, parents and pupils know that teachers cannot give unconditional confidentiality to pupils
- ensuring that pupils are aware of sources of confidential help (e.g. school nurse, counsellor, family doctor, young person's advice service)
- details of the school's policy on child abuse and bullying.

Active learning and evaluation

Pupils often work well at sex and relationship education (SRE) activities when:

- Pupils work in groups chosen by themselves. Typically these will be single sex, and a combination of single-sex groups and single- or mixed-sex classes can work well, though some parents will require all sex education teaching to be single sex.
- Pupils can bring their own knowledge and experience to the task without feeling pressured to do so. This is especially important when, as is quite often the case, children in a class differ greatly in their sexual knowledge and/or values.
- Teachers are perceived as empathetic, non-judgemental, tolerant, non-evasive, skilled at handling discussions about sensitive issues, not embarrassed, able to keep control, and knowledgeable.

- A range of activities are used – e.g. games, simulations, role-plays, problem-solving exercises, questionnaires, surveys, creative writing, puppet making, music production and discussion using case studies, open-ended scenarios, videos, newspaper cuttings, magazine extracts and so on.
- Pupils can discuss issues, exploring their own and others' attitudes, beliefs and values and clarifying for themselves what they feel and think.
- The work is evaluated and the evaluation used to inform future teaching to the same group and teaching of the same (or similar) activities to future groups.

Using existing materials

Fictional books, unless short or used in language lessons, may not be ideal for use with a whole class in a school. However, they can be extremely valuable for individual pupils. Many classics of literature can be used and Simon Harris (1990) discusses how lesbian and gay issues can be addressed through the use of literature, *inter alia*. For many years, Judy Blume's numerous books about adolescence have been popular with girls. More recent fictional offerings about love, sex and young parenthood are often written to appeal to young teenagers of both sexes and include, in the English language, Morris Gleitzman's (1998) *Bumface*, Sandra Chick's (1999) *Don't Look Back*, Louise Rennison's (1999) *Angus, Thongs and Full-frontal Snogging* and Jean Ure's (1999) *Just Sixteen*. For painfully well-written autobiographical accounts of child abuse see Paddy Doyle's (1988) *The God Squad* and Andrea Ashworth's (1988) *Once in a House on Fire*.

There is a constant stream of well-meaning and carefully produced videos, television programmes and teaching packs about sex education. The best of them are outstanding though they can date quite quickly. The obvious thing to do before using one is to look through it and decide whether or not it is worth using and if so, how. As far as values are concerned, there is much to be said simply for using short video extracts from soap operas or the latest issue of a teenage magazine (see Chapter 3; Pinsent and Knight 1997). In such cases, pupils can learn by describing what is going on, by analysing how the affected individuals feel and by discussing what they themselves think.

Liaising with parents and the local community

Schools should work in partnership with parents, consulting them regularly on the content of sex and relationships education programmes, the values that underpin them and the methods used in the teaching. At the very least, parents should be able to see the materials that will be used and have the option to withdraw their children from timetabled sex education. Far better is for at least some parents to be involved in the preparation, and possibly the delivery too, of the sex programme.

Many schools work closely with health professionals in the development and teaching of a sex education programme. School nurses, other nurses and doctors can

- complement the role of teachers
- make valuable links between the school and other relevant professionals and services such as general practitioners, and family planning clinics
- tell pupils about health services available in the area
- provide confidential support and advice, e.g. through drop-in sessions
- provide expert knowledge about sexual health.

It is important that boys do not feel that such expertise and facilities are aimed only or principally at girls.

With any visitors to a school – e.g. a theatre group, a religious leader, a mother (young or not) and baby, a doctor, a social worker, a youth worker or someone from a commercial organisation (for example, from a sanitary protection company) – the golden rules are:

- meet with the person or group well in advance to discuss what their contribution will be to the school's overall programme
- ensure that they know about, agree to and have a copy of any relevant school policy documents
- be present with them throughout their time on school premises.

Peer education

Peer education, where teaching is done by students who are the same age or only a little older than those whom they are teaching, can be used alongside other teaching approaches. It can be very popular with young people.

A large-scale evaluation of peer-led sex education in English secondary schools found that a significantly greater proportion of students taught by peer educators rather than teachers felt that sex education was enjoyable, engaging and useful to them (Forrest *et al.* 2002). There seemed to be several reasons for this:

- Teacher-led lessons were more likely than peer-led ones to focus on puberty and reproduction. Peer-led lessons described STDs in some detail, provided opportunities to look at contraceptives and handle condoms, and had more discussions about relationships.

- In some schools students were highly critical of the didactic teaching style used by teachers. Peer-led lessons were more likely to be activity based.
- Peer educators were volunteers and trained by health promotion practitioners. However, teachers in the study received no additional training or support. As one girl said of teachers teaching sex and relationships education:

it's not their subject, is it PSE [personal and social education]? They've got to do it whether they're like PE [physical education] or geography . . . I mean with their subject they've obviously got compassion in it, because they're teaching it, but with PSE they're just like they've got to do it.

(Forrest *et al.* 2002: 203)

On the other hand, the study carried out by Forrest *et al.* (2002) students reported that peers were less good than teachers at controlling the sessions. It is also asking rather a lot of most peers to expect them consistently to teach sexual values in the way we are advocating.

Teaching about families and friends

Primary schools have often taught about families and friends. In the current guidance in England and Wales, sex and relationship education is said to have three main elements: attitudes and values; personal and social skills; knowledge and understanding. Attitudes and values are expanded as:

- learning the importance of values and individual conscience and moral considerations
- learning the value of family life, marriage, and stable and loving relationships for the nurture of children
- learning the value of respect, love and care
- exploring, considering and understanding moral dilemmas, and
- developing critical thinking as part of decision-making.

(DfEE 2000a: 5)

At the same time (as we discussed in Chapter 9) this official guidance strives to tread the narrow path between advocating marriage as the best context for sexual relationships and judging those in a sexual relationship, yet not married. Adrian Thatcher, while noting that 'this important document deserves a positive response' (Thatcher 2001: 234), also comments that it leaves much unsaid. Of course, there is much value in a teacher, even in the primary phase, getting children to talk about, draw or act out what they enjoy about their families, what is meant by a loving relationship, and who our friends are, and to consider whether marriage is a good idea or not. Many children will never have been to a wedding and a visit to a church, other place of worship where marriages are conducted or a registry office allows experiential learning.

In its review of teaching quality in sex and relationship lessons, Ofsted (2002) found from inspection evidence that in primary schools, teaching about relationships was the most effectively taught aspect of SRE:

> Creating a climate that encourages pupils to participate and to express their views and feelings is arguably the most difficult task that teachers of SRE face. It demands much confidence, a high level of empathy and very good skills in drawing pupils into discussion, which, while it needs to be serious, should not be without warmth and need not be without humour.

> At a London primary school, the teaching experimented with the use of 'flour babies' (babies made from bags of flour that had been decorated and dressed). Half the class had 'flour babies' for a week. The assortment of diversely dressed babies had been carried and cared for, or in some cases abandoned, by the pupils. Their parents had been alerted in advance that the exercise had serious objectives and would culminate in a mother bringing in a real baby and the whole class sharing in the experience of caring for a baby. This simple sequence was an effective way of providing pupils with an experience of a baby that they were able to discuss in terms of its impact on their feelings and behaviour.

> (Ofsted 2002: 24)

At the same time, it needs to be remembered that even young children are perfectly well aware of the differences between a real baby and a flour baby or a mechanical doll that 'wakes up' in the night. Teachers should never draw conclusions about how individual pupils might behave as mothers or fathers from the results of such exercises. It can also be the case that such exercises, and some of the resources we shall look at in Chapter 12 that are designed to reduce teenage conception rates, show only the negative aspects of parenthood. Babies are presented as inconveniences and nuisances rather than also as sources of wonder, love and personal enrichment.

In her educators' manual of methods, materials and additional resources for professionals who are providing sex education for people with learning difficulties, Hilary Dixon (1988) has a large section on relationships. For example, in 'Qualities of a friend' she suggests that learners could use the 'Field of words' (Figure 11.1) and circle qualities they think are important in a friendship. The group could then consider what has been done for them in the last day or week and what they have done for others.

Teaching about puberty

It might be supposed that teaching about puberty is simply a matter of teaching the biology, with little to do about values. However, while there is quite a bit of biology about female and male puberty that it is worth both girls and boys learning about, values are to the forefront too. For example, one teacher wrote in to the Sex Education Forum asking:

> The girls love having the 'tampon lady', think she's really funny and like the free samples. I am worried that some of her values are different from the school's. We try to respect all the individual pupils here so I feel uncomfortable when she says 'All modern women use tampons nowadays.' What shall I do?
>
> (Sex Education Forum 1996: 2)

The Sex Education Forum helpfully replied:

> You could explain to the visitor that the school sex education policy requires the session to cover all forms of sanitary protection in an objective way. You could use the checklist and clarify what values you want to encourage and foster, as described in the school's values framework, the equal opportunities policy and the sex education policy. Can she work within them? Is there a way you and she could work together on one or two sessions to test out a different approach? If you can't solve this problem by negotiating and working together, then you should consider not using the 'tampon lady' any more.
>
> (Sex Education Forum 1996: 2)

In a study of how menstruation was treated in 15 widely used school biology textbooks for 14–16 year olds, two main discourses were identified (Reiss 1998b). One can be called 'the physiological approach'. In this the emphasis is on the roles of the various hormones in providing a suitable internal environment for a fertilised egg to implant. The other main approach can be called 'the personal approach'. In this the emphasis is on the transition to adulthood, sanitary towels, tampons, pre-menstrual tension and period pains. All 15 books covered the physiological side to

Field of Words

Figure 11.1 'Field of Words' by Hilary Dixon

Source: Dixon (1988: 64)

menstruation; 6 of the 15 books also covered the personal side to varying degrees. One example of the personal approach was as follows:

> The hormones that control the menstrual cycle can affect different people in different ways. Some girls feel no change during a period. Others may notice that they have more spots than usual, or that they feel very 'bloated', or tearful and irritable, when a period is about to start. In fact, nearly all women show a gain in body mass just before a period and this is because more water than usual is retained in the body. Girls quite often have mild 'period pains' on the first day or two of a period – if these are very bad a doctor will usually prescribe medicine which will help to relieve them. But even though periods can be a nuisance, girls usually find that they do not interfere very much with their normal activities. Most girls now wear tampons (cottonwool cylinders which plug into the vagina), which means that even activities such as swimming are no problem during a period.
>
> (Monger 1988: 253)

While there may be a diversity of views as to the best ways to discuss personal aspects of menstruation, we would argue that an account such as Monger's, which covers both the personal and the physiological, whether the teaching is in the primary phase or the secondary phase, is preferable to one which focuses only on the physiological. Accounts which omit the personal side of menstruation give the impression that the personal does not exist, or that it is unimportant or that it is too embarrassing to talk about.

A good way for teachers to reflect on their values around puberty is to consider the following statements (developed from Alvarado and Power 1993):

- A girl's first period should be a time for celebration.
- It's better if women teach about menstruation to the girls and men teach about male aspects of puberty to the boys.
- Girls sometimes use the fact that they have a period to get out of doing things at school that they don't want to do.
- It's best if puberty is taught to pupils in single-sex groups.
- If a school's toilets are a mess, pupils are generally to blame.
- Picking up on boys if they express negative attitudes about menstruation just causes more problems for the girls.
- Boys need to know about sanitary wear as much as girls do.
- Women tend to be a bit moody at 'the wrong time of the month'.
- It's natural for boys to lark about more once they go through puberty.
- Masturbation is just one of those phases everyone goes through.
- Teachers responsible for puberty education need special training.

Summary

1   School sex education should serve the needs of those who are being taught and those with whom they live and will live in society. These needs entail physical health, the development of rational sexual autonomy and consideration and respect for others.

2   Sex education starts long before children go to school. Children need to know the answers to such questions as 'Where do babies come from?' well before they leave their primary school.

3   By failing to detect and respond appropriately to child abuse, including sexual abuse, a school fails to value its pupils.

4   Issues to be considered before embarking on a sex education programme include the ground rules to be used, confidentiality, the value of active learning, how the programme will be evaluated, liaison with parents and the local community, and the values that are reflected in materials used and teaching approaches adopted.

5   Teaching about families, friends and puberty in the primary phase allows a number of issues to do with values to be raised.

Issues for discussion

1   Should girls and boys be brought up in the same way or differently?

2   How can children be helped to understand their own bodies, and the bodies of those of the opposite sex, better without either embarrassing them or causing them to feel guilty about any feelings of modesty that they have?

3   How can sex education validly be evaluated?

4   Should children be taught that certain family structures are preferable to others?

5   What, if anything, should schools teach about masturbation?

Further reading

For practical resources on teaching sex education in the primary and secondary phases see:

- Clarity Collective (1989) *Taught not Caught: Strategies for Sex Education,* 2nd edn, Wisbech: LDA.
- Harrison, J. K. (2000) *Sex Education in Secondary Schools,* Buckingham: Open University Press.
- Lenderyou, G. (1993) *Primary School Workbook: Teaching Sex Education within the National Curriculum,* London: Family Planning Association.
- Ray, C. and Went, D. (1995) *Good Practice in Sex Education: A Sourcebook for Schools,* London: National Children's Bureau.
- Sanders, P. and Swinden, L. (1990) *Knowing Me, Knowing You: Strategies for Sex Education in the Primary School,* Wisbech: LDA.
- *Sex Education Matters,* the termly newsletter available from Sex Education Forum, 8 Wakley Street, London EC1V 7QE (tel +44 (0)207 843 6056/62).

Chapter 12

Sex education in the secondary phase

The purpose and context of Chapter 12

This chapter should be read after Chapter 11. In Chapter 11, in addition to considering sex education in the primary phase, we spell out the purpose and context of Chapters 11 and 12 and deal with a number of fundamental, generic issues such as:

- principles of school sex education
- teaching approaches and strategies
- ground rules and confidentiality
- liaising with parents and the local community
- using visitors to teach aspects of school sex education
- peer education.

In this chapter we concentrate on school sex education for 11/12 to 16 year olds, though we do say a little about sex education for 16–19 year olds and adults. As in Chapter 11, we focus on what an approach to school sex education that takes values to heart might look like and why.

Teaching about conception and contraception

In the secondary phase, teaching about conception is typically done in the context of biology lessons. The advantage of this is that biology (within science) is generally a privileged subject in the sense that it is of high status and is usually taught by specialists. There is a long and accepted tradition in biology of teaching about reproduction, so teaching about conception is likely to be factually accurate. At the same time, some biology teachers and authors of textbooks may not have reflected very deeply on the hidden assumptions of their teaching or authoring. In a study of 15 science textbooks widely used in England and Wales for teaching 14–16 year olds about human reproduction, Reiss (1988b) found that, for example, only 5 of the books referred to the clitoris, either in the text or on illustrations, whereas all 15 referred to the penis. Further, a typical example of how the clitoris was referred to when its presence was acknowledged was as follows:

> Close to the entrance to the urethra is a small 'lump', the clitoris. The clitoris is the female's equivalent of a penis and this can become erect during sexual intercourse when it is stimulated.
>
> (Michell 1987: 109)

It can be argued that to say that A is the equivalent of B is to belittle A. None of the textbooks described the penis as the male's equivalent of a clitoris.

There is a growing scholarship on how science teachers and textbooks often teach human reproduction in a way that simply reinforces unspoken and unconsidered essentialist notions of femininity and masculinity (Gilbert 1996; Scholer 2002). For example, the human egg is typically presented as a large, passive object that simply sits around awaiting active sperm. Another, biologically more accurate, way of picturing the events around fertilisation is either to say that the egg controls which sperm enters or that there is a partnership between egg and sperm.

That values are implicit in teaching about contraception is far more widely recognised. As we noted in Chapter 6, certain religions and religious denominations either forbid or have reservations about the use of contraception. In a school where all the pupils are Muslims or Roman Catholics, a consistent approach for teaching in the area can be agreed with parents, governors and (it is hoped) pupils. In a school where there is a wide range of pupils, finding a common position is more difficult. The practice in many schools has simply been to teach the bare minimum about contraception in the context of biology lessons, so attempting to eschew any controversy.

Such an approach is unfortunate for a number of reasons. First of all, it is not a very effective way of teaching about contraception if one hopes that a young person will be able to obtain and use it if and when (s)he wants to. As the superbly titled booklet, *'Don't Die of Ignorance' – I Nearly Died of Embarrassment: Condoms in Context* (Holland *et al.* 1990), indicates, condoms carry tremendous symbolic weight within a relationship. Negotiating their use in a sexual encounter is far from straightforward (see Figure 12.1). While the UK, along with a number of other countries, has seen a sustained increase in condom use at first intercourse during the 1990s (Wellings *et al.* 2001), it seems unlikely that the mere mention of condoms in school biology lessons as a suitable method of contraception can account for this. As we discuss in more detail in the final section of this chapter, adult education in an age of HIV and AIDS has

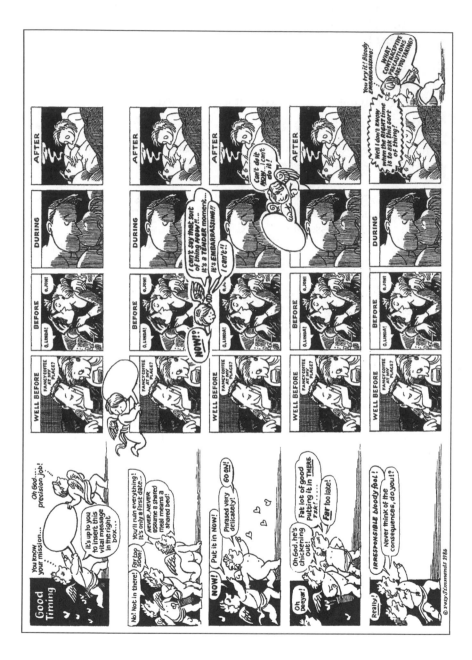

Figure 12.1 'Good Timing' by Posy Simmonds

Source: ©Posy Simmonds, from *Pure Posy* (London: Methuen, 1989)

led to significant changes in sexual practices, including condom usage, in some countries.

The most thorough review of what makes for effective sex and HIV education programmes comes from the USA. Here effectiveness is taken to mean 'reducing one or more sexual behaviors that lead to unintended pregnancy or HIV/STD infection' (Kirby 2001: 92). Kirby, from a large and rigorous meta-analysis concludes that effective programmes:

- focus on behavioural goals such as delaying the initiation of intercourse or using contraception
- are based on sound theoretical approaches, such as cognitive behavioural theory
- give clear messages and use group activities to change group norms
- provide basic, accurate information about the risks of teen sexual activity and about methods of avoiding intercourse or using protection against pregnancy and STIs
- include activities that address social pressures which influence sexual behaviour
- provide modelling of and practice with communication, negotiation and refusal skills
- employ a variety of teaching methods designed to involve participants and have them personalise the information
- incorporate goals, teaching methods and materials that are appropriate to the student body
- select teachers or peer leaders who believe in the programme and are provided with training.

Kirby's work has, deservedly, been extremely influential both in the USA and elsewhere. Other studies have emphasised the importance of national or regional cultures. For example, the very low rates of teenage conception in The Netherlands (see p. 146) have been attributed to:

> the combination of a relatively inclusive society with more open attitudes towards sex and sex education, including contraception. This has paved the way for sexual relationships to be discussed at an early age – before barriers of embarrassment can be raised and before sex education can be interpreted as sending a signal that the time has come to start having sex.
>
> (UNICEF 2001: 21)

The one additional point we would wish to emphasise here is the importance of how 'effectiveness' is construed. If the same amount of effort were to be put into researching what sorts of programmes led to less embarrassment or anxiety, greater sexual enjoyment, or more egalitarian relationships, the conclusions might be the same as Kirby's or they might be different (see Wight *et al.* 2002).

A second reason why teaching the bare minimum about contraception in the context of biology lessons is unfortunate connects with the point made in Chapter 2 that attempts to develop a value-free sex education run into a number of problems. Included among these are that such an approach renders children open to manipulation at the hands of those less concerned for their well-being than (one hopes) the school is. We suggest that there is much to be said for 14–16-year-old pupils reflecting on and discussing in school such contraception-related questions as:

- What does carrying condoms indicate about you to others?
- Is it more acceptable in a heterosexual relationship for the female or the male to suggest they use condoms? Why? Should this be the case?
- Why are couples less likely to use condoms the longer they remain in a sexual relationship?
- Are some forms of contraception (e.g. emergency contraception) ethically more problematic than others? If so, why?
- If not using contraception makes it more likely that a woman will have an abortion, is this a valid argument in favour of using contraception?
- Should schools provide contraception for 14–16 year olds?
- Should condoms be free or should you have to pay for them?

Conception may result in miscarriage or abortion. Abortion is obviously a value-laden subject that some schools teach well and others avoid. It raises major issues about whether there are moral absolutes, whether we become persons at a particular moment, such as conception, or whether we grow into personhood; the rights of women; the support available to parents who have children with disabilities; and what say, if any, a father should have over the fate of his unborn child (see Tabberer *et al.* 2000).

In the absence of a failure to implant, miscarriage, abortion or stillbirth, conception leads to parenthood. Schools vary greatly in what they teach about parenthood and in their aims for such teaching. Often, sex education and teaching about human reproduction end with conception or birth, or if the subsequent years are covered the emphasis may simply be on the biological facts of lactation, early growth and development.

Another approach, with the intention of reducing the number of teenage parents, is to try and convey what the reality of bringing young children up is like. We have already mentioned 'flour babies' (see p. 182). For older pupils, materials depicting the reality of parenthood may be used. For example, the video *Four Carrier Bags and a Buggy* (Red Rose Chain/Alpha Films n.d.) is a documentary about the lives of members of a Young Parents' Support Group and is divided into six uplifting sections described on the back of the video as follows:

1 **Having a Baby**: the physical and emotional effects of childbirth.
2 **Coping**: the everyday struggles of managing with young children.
3 **The Cost of Living**: the financial difficulties including finding accommodation and coping with everyday expenses.
4 **Relationships**: the strain that having a child can put on personal relationships.
5 **Depression**: how the situation can lead to severe mental stress.
6 **Looking Forward**: the positive effects of the support group and how the young parents view the future for themselves and their families.

Such resources face a difficult task in attempting to convey what it is like to have a child. As with so many things in life (sneezing, getting drunk, bungee jumping, a general anaesthetic, orgasm, losing a loved one), this is largely unimaginable until and unless one has. In addition, such resources, designed to reduce teenage conception or birth rates, may say little about the rewards of parenthood, which can be considerable for young mothers from economically challenging backgrounds as for all parents.

A rich resource for teaching about parenthood is provided by the Children's Society (1994). Impressively, unlike so many materials on sex and relationships education, they manage to inject an occasional element of humour. We particularly liked the last question of 'The Parenting Questionnaire':

Which of these skills is most important for a new father?

- being able to cope with looking after a crying baby in the night.
- being able to support your partner who is crying because she is so tired from looking after the baby.
- being able to cry when the emotion of realizing you're a father hits home.
- stopping yourself crying when you realize how much it costs to be a parent.

(Children's Society 1994: Unit 2: 7)

Teaching about sexual activity

As we noted in Chapter 10, few schools do much in any very direct sense to help students enjoy their sex lives. John Wilson considers whether school sex education 'should be "practical" in the sense of involving "hands-on" experience, rather than only the transmission of biological information and moral precepts' (Wilson in press). Wilson acknowledges that there are particular difficulties with this – in particular that we intuit that sexuality is essentially private so that practical education may be disruptive, invasive or otherwise inappropriate – but continues:

> The question 'How can I be a good lover?', or 'How can I do justice to myself and my partner in bed?' does not have to wait for an answer until such time as I actually fall in love with somebody and go to bed with him/her: any more than the question 'How can I be a good soldier?' has to wait for an answer until I actually go to war, or 'How can I be a good parent?' until I actually have children of my own. Until then the learning involved may be preparatory, in a certain sense theoretical or academic, because it has no immediate practical application; but that does nothing to diminish its importance.
>
> (Wilson in press)

Wilson concludes that while individual privacy must be respected, much more should nevertheless be done by way of examples, role-playing and the use of visual and literary material which is:

> (a) aesthetically meritorious in its own right, (b) educational rather than just designed to titillate, and (c) shows the range of physical expression in full detail with no holds barred and without shame or prurience.
>
> (Wilson in press)

There is a certain delicacy or coyness here in Wilson's language which leaves the reader unclear as to precisely what is intended – is video material of full sexual intercourse envisaged, for example? – but provided such materials are approved by both parents and pupils (a significant proviso) we would welcome them, though as we have already mentioned, there is much to be said for the argument that authentic loving entails findings certain things out for oneself *in situ* (see p. 163). There is a rather good bit in Monty Python's *The Meaning of Life* which parodies the notion that schoolchildren can (or even want to) learn about sexual intercourse through watching it in reality.

That having been said, appropriate materials would help to address the concerns of Louisa Allen's (2001) interviewees which we cited in Chapter 10 and which others have noted. Indeed, back in 1988 Fine wrote about 'the missing discourse of desire' (Fine 1988: 29), pointing out that US school sex education programmes were silent about the subject of female desire. In the UK, Lynda Measor and her colleagues interviewed 17-year-old school students who looked back on their earlier school sex education and concluded that they had 'needed more information about the actual feelings of desire and lust' (Measor *et al.* 2000: 125), and love too, we would add. They were critical of their sex education's silence over the powerful feelings that accompanied sexual activity. A number of other pupils commented on how sex education concentrated only on the dangers of sex. As one 14-year-old boy put it:

> All they ever do is talk about the dangers of sex and that, and nothing about the pleasure.
>
> (Measor *et al.* 2000: 126)

Teaching about sexual orientation

In few countries is teaching about sexual orientation undertaken in any depth. In a survey of 105 schools, mainly English comprehensives, Lawrence *et al.* (2000) identified 17 topics in sex education and found that of these, homosexuality was covered in least detail. Just 23 per cent of the schools managed 'considerable coverage' defined as 'in good detail with good opportunity for reflection and/or practice of skills' (Lawrence *et al.* 2000: 6). By comparison, 'Puberty, difference in growth and development' came top of the list with 83 per cent, and even '"Love-making"', i.e. arousal, foreplay, intercourse' in twelfth place scored 45 per cent.

Part of the reason for the rare appearance of detailed teaching about homosexuality, as we have discussed (see p. 156), is that it does not command as much parental support as do other topics in sex education. In England and Wales an additional reason is undoubtedly the infamous 'Section 28'. This is a very long-running saga. Section 28 was introduced by a Conservative government in the Local Government Act (50/1) 1988 and states:

> A local authority shall not – (a) intentionally promote homosexuality or publish material with the intention of promoting homosexuality; (b) promote the teaching in any maintained school of the acceptability of homosexuality as a pretended family relationship by the publication of such material or otherwise.

Many teachers became concerned that they might fall foul of the law simply by referring to issues of sexual orientation; other teachers reacted with fury both at the perceived injustice and prejudice and at the crude assumptions implicit in phraseologies about 'a pretended family relationship'; a minority of teachers welcomed the clause. However, it then transpired that this part of the Local Government Act did not apply to schools as Section 18 of the Education Act (No. 2) 1986 – which gave school governors responsibility for decisions on sex education in schools – took precedence. Despite this, Section 28 has continued to deter a considerable proportion of teachers from teaching in this area (Douglas *et al.* 1997) and at the time of writing remains on the statute books despite more than one attempt to repeal it.

Many of the arguments from those against the repeal of Section 28 have centred on the belief that boys need to be protected from older, predatory gay men (e.g. Moran 2001). In our opinion children, whether girls or boys, do indeed sometimes need to be protected from the sexual advances of adults, whether heterosexual or homosexual – hence our argument that schools should detect and respond to sexual abuse (see pp. 139–40) and help young people develop rational sexual autonomy (see pp. 158–9). However, what is at issue in teaching about homosexuality is how the issue is to be handled by a teacher. We have already argued first that schools should teach about homosexuality; second that they should treat it as a controversial issue (see pp. 161–2). How then should they teach about it?

For a start, it is important that teaching in this area neither problematises nor stigmatises either homosexuality or heterosexuality. In most cases, of course, it is more likely that homosexuality will be discriminated against. A teacher may unwittingly use 'them' to refer to homosexuals and 'us' to refer to heterosexuals when a more neutral approach is to use phrases such as 'someone who is homosexual' and 'someone who is heterosexual'. Such an approach may strike some as long-winded and unnecessarily 'politically correct'. However, a generation or more of familiarity with non-sexist and non-racist language, now regarded as *de rigeur* in classrooms, has helped sensitise teachers and students to the advantages of non-prejudicial language. Equally, the point of view that 'homosexuality is a phase through which many heterosexuals pass' is acceptable, but needs to be examined alongside the complementary point of view that 'heterosexuality is a phase through which many homosexuals pass'. Notable publications which theorise heterosexuality in a way analogous to the way in which homosexuality has been theorised include Kitzinger *et al.* (1992) and Richardson (1996).

That being said, we envisage two principal and parallel aims when teaching about sexual orientation:

- to help pupils clarify for themselves what they think about heterosexuality and homosexuality and why they think this (e.g. whether one form of sexual orientation is better than another; whether sexual orientation is a given or open to individual choice; the extent to which our attitudes towards sexual orientation come from our families, our cultures and the media)
- to enable students to understand what it might be like to feel very differently about these issues (which can help pupils to become more tolerant of those who differ from themselves).

As we have already indicated (see p. 162), such aims may not be easy to realise. However, there are some aspects connected with sexual orientation that are not controversial. For example, bullying in schools, including homophobic bullying, is simply unacceptable and teachers need to take steps to prevent it:

> in too many secondary schools homophobic attitudes among pupils often go unchallenged. The problem is compounded when derogatory terms about homosexuality are used in everyday language in school and their use passes unchallenged by staff. Where problems arise, staff have often had insufficient guidance on the interpretation of school values and what constitutes unacceptable language or behaviour.
>
> (Ofsted 2002: 10)

There is now a large literature, inside and out of school, on sexual bullying and discrimination and on the accompanying abuses of power (e.g. Mac an Ghaill 1994; Dunne 1997; Valentine 1998; Duncan 1999; Fineran and Bennett 1999; Rivers 2001; Warwick and Douglas n.d.; Sharpe 2002). Much sexual bullying at school manifests itself in girls endlessly being the objects either of unwanted sexual advances or of sexual disparagement. Homophobia in schools seems often to have more to do with pupils, particularly boys, policing overstrict gender identities than it has to do with sexuality (e.g. Sharpe 2002). In school, boys, in particular, often insult other boys by referring to them as girls or as gay. For example, Neil Duncan recorded the following conversation with Year 7 boys:

ND:	What is the worst thing they could call you?
Brian:	Gay.
Alan:	Gay.
Brian:	Pervert, or poof.
ND:	And would that upset you?
Brian:	No.
Colin:	A bit.
Alan:	No.
Brian:	We'd know that we'd get them back.
ND:	But do you think there are some lads it would upset?
Brian:	Yeah.
ND [to Colin]:	You said you wouldn't like it.
Colin:	Some lads can't take it but if they said it to us . . .
Brian:	If they said it to us four, well, we'd just ignore them, but there is some lads that would start hitting them.

(Duncan 1999: 18)

Many societies in general, and schools in particular, do nothing to discuss, let alone counteract, hidden assumptions that the only good sexuality is heterosexuality. A culture of heteronormativity (i.e. unquestioned heterosexuality) develops in which any other sexualities – notably homosexualities and celibacy – are effectively silenced. Holland, Ramazanoglu, Sharpe and Thomson provide a collective, feminist analysis of how institutionalised heterosexuality results (Holland *et al.* 1998). They title their book *The Male in the Head*, indicating how young men and women jointly and largely unwittingly engage in constituting a single standard of heterosexuality and then being surveyed and regulated by it. Other sociological accounts have also looked at how we all learn our interpersonal and intrapsychic sexual scripts, in school and elsewhere (e.g. Parker and Gagnon 1995; M. F. Rogers 1999; Mirembe and Davies 2001).

Good teaching about sexual bullying can do a considerable amount to reduce its incidence and impact. It should not be assumed that only heterosexual boys can bully or harass sexually – all categories of pupils can, though the techniques differ. The key is for schools both to provide an environment where all the adults respect all the pupils, and to help pupils to see one another as individuals deserving of respect. This is easy to say but can be difficult to develop in a school that hasn't had such a history: hence our earlier emphasis on the importance of school ethos (Chapter 3). We end this section by providing an account from an 18-year-old young woman who indicates how she felt her school sex education had provided a classroom environment in which she and others could discuss what they needed to:

> We were told everything, and our teacher was very good, she told us about her experiences. She told us all about orgasms and things like that . . . There was two of them. One was I should say she was thirty, and the other was near enough retirement age. The younger one would talk about it freely and the older one would turn round and say 'before I met Mrs Barker I didn't even know what an orgasm was, and I thought crabs were things that walked sideways over the beach'. It used to be dead informal, and we used to have discussions about mixed race marriages and things like that. I remember a discussion about abortion . . . I did a role play with this lad and we had an almighty row because he said that abortions should not be allowed, even if the girl had been raped. I was stood there nearly in tears shouting at him. I could have killed him I was so annoyed . . . We talked about homosexuality, we did loads, and it was really good. Because say a lad was sat there that was homosexual and we were just going by heterosexual relationships all the time, they would feel alienated . . . It was brilliant, we used to love it.
>
> (quoted in Thomson and Scott 1991: 14)

Pregnant and still at school

In most countries there has long been, and often still is, a tradition in which young mothers, but not young fathers, leave school before the official school-leaving age. In a recent review of the situation in England and Wales, the Office of Her Majesty's Chief Inspector of Schools found a wide range of practice. Some pregnant young mothers benefited from leaving conventional schooling and attending specialist pupil referral units. Others did equally well by remaining in school. For example:

> When one of the Year 11 girls at a Midlands school informed the head of year that she was pregnant, the head of year discussed the matter with her before bringing family and staff together to discuss how best to offer support.
>
> The parents were initially concerned that their daughter would be asked to leave the school. This was not the case and the girl, her parents, the father's family and the school worked together to plan how best to provide support during and after the pregnancy.
>
> During the pregnancy, with minor adjustments, she continued to follow the Year 11 curriculum. In the final weeks of the pregnancy she received tuition at home. The appointed tutor worked with her in school before her home leave. This helped to ensure that the tutor could provide a curriculum similar to that in the school.
>
> After the birth, she returned to school. Her parents, and those of the father, provided good support for her and her baby. This enabled her to continue her studies through to GCSE examinations.
>
> (Ofsted 2002: 31–2)

On the other hand, a certain amount of sensitivity, not to mention common sense, is needed when expectant mothers are in school sex education classes. As one pregnant young woman recalled:

> I had to put a condom on a cucumber. They made me do it and, like, everybody already knew I were pregnant and there were like about forty people there and they were there . . . all watching me.
>
> (Hirst and Selmes 1997: 12)

In her study of teenage mothers in Canada and the USA, Kelly (2000) notes that such mothers are scapegoats for social anxieties. They are portrayed in the media and elsewhere as stupid sluts, as children having children, as teen rebels who flaunt their non-conformity and treat their babies as objects, as vulnerable girls whom nobody loved, as victims of child abuse, as welfare moms, as dropouts and as neglectful mothers. Kelly studied two schools in depth. Not surprisingly, she found that school-age mothers need flexibility from their schools with regard to such things as attendance and workload expectations. Interestingly, she noted that in both schools the young mothers weren't alone in needing such flexibility:

> Some students were living independently, either with social assistance or away from their reserve [reservation]. Still others were working long hours, either to supplement their family's income or to care for younger siblings. Still others were sometimes needed by immigrant parents to serve as translators in important matters affecting the family. Some school staff members, although relatively materially advantaged, also found it a struggle to meet family and work obligations around the rigid school timetable.
>
> (Kelly 2000: 117)

In other words, a flexible policy about teen mothers would also have benefited many others in the schools' communities.

In a study of pregnancy policies in the education systems of sub-Saharan African countries, Chilisa (2002) found that in many countries the practice of expelling pregnant girls from schools continues to this day. In some places the practice is enshrined in law; in others it is main-tained by informal custom. Only a small proportion of girls who drop out of school due to pregnancy re-enter the school system. Indeed, given the competition for school places in a number of countries, Chilisa concluded that 'expulsion of girl mothers becomes a way of creating spaces for boys' (Chilisa 2002: 32).

Teaching about sex in society

By the time pupils leave school, they have formed many of their opinions. We have already discussed above how schools typically enforce a dis-course of heteronormativity. Of course, it is not just gay and lesbian pupils who are policed in this way. Just as frequently, boys make dispara-ging comments about the physical appearance of girls. As Measor and her colleagues noted in their ethnographic study of secondary school sex education in the south-east of England:

> In our classroom observations we recorded a number of jokes which involved male pupils commenting on girls' bodies and appearance. They showed some of the implications that male views of female bodies have for girls. The girls found the teasing unpleasant and deni-grating; we observed girls looking very uncomfortable in response to it, and in interviews they complained about it. As we spent time in the schools we heard frequent male commentary on bodily matters, such

as breast size. Boys would walk through school corridors admiring 'the size of her knockers' or disparaging 'her little tits'. They also discussed 'the size of her arse', commented about whether a particular girl had 'good legs' or spoke in judgement about a 'pig-ugly' face. Girls could be placed into the categories of 'fit bird' or 'fly bird'; they could be 'tasty', a 'dog' or a 'log'.

(Measor *et al.* 2000: 85)

Nor (as we discuss in Chapter 3) can it be assumed that such attitudes and language appear only once pupils reach secondary school. Schools should not only help pupils appreciate what is appropriate and what inappropriate language and behaviour in schools. They should also help their pupils live in the outside world and once they have left school by considering in the classroom such issues as the legal and moral aspects of sexual harassment, indecent assault, obscene telephone calls, the age of consent, abortion and rape.

To concentrate on one of these issues, pupils aged 14 to 16 might profitably consider moral and legal aspects of rape. For example:

- What precisely is meant by rape? Does rape require physical force or other coercion? Or is it enough for it to be non-consensual (see Bogart [1991] 1995)? Does rape require sexual penetration?
- How are rape trials reported in the media? What comments are made about the clothing and lifestyle of defendants (see Lees 1997)?
- Why is most rape conducted by men on women?
- What is meant by 'date rape' (see Hollway and Jefferson 1998)? How common is it?

Sex education after school

As we have already noted (see p. 23), most sex education takes place out of school. Although in many countries, there is little formal sex education for 16–19 year olds, this age range is an appropriate one, in many ways, for teaching in more depth about contraception and respectful behaviour in sexual relationships. The arrival of HIV and AIDS has meant that this age range is now more often targeted for sex education in schools, youth groups and colleges.

Some of the best data on the effectiveness of sex education come from programmes to tackle STIs with adults who have many sexual partners. In a number of western countries, gay men in the late 1980s markedly changed their sexual behaviour (notably the number of partners per year with whom they had unprotected sexual intercourse). Such changes in the early days were not the result of externally imposed sex education campaigns but of rapid responses by gay communities to a new threat.

In Zambia, a country with high levels of HIV infection since the early 1990s, AIDS prevention campaigns have made a difference (Bloom *et al.* 2000). In urban Lusaka, the first half of the 1990s saw a decline in pre-marital sexual activity and a decrease in the number of women and men who had extramarital partners – though findings from more recent years indicate that further change has stagnated. In Thailand, a major preventive intervention that addressed condom use and brothel patronage, improved negotiation and condom skills in the Royal Thai Army and proved to reduce STD incidence by a factor of seven relative to controls (Celantano *et al.* 2000).

The above studies focus on sex education for the purpose of benefiting physical health. We conclude by noting that there has, of course, never been an age with more materials tackling other aspects of sex education for adults. There are books, magazines, films, television programmes, newspaper articles and organisations about sexual techniques, contraception, pregnancy and parenthood. Goldman and Bradley (2001) review the mass of material available for sexuality education on the Internet. They carefully chart the diversity of sites available for every age group from 6–10 year olds to the over-sixties and conclude optimistically that:

> On a personal level, the growth of people's sexual understanding will enhance their personal development, self-esteem, maturity, and decision-making skills. Socially, people will benefit by becoming more knowledgeable, more aware and more self-confident about both themselves and their enhanced social relationships, and develop greater personal self-management. Economically, it will cost the community less in terms of lowered STD rates, fewer unplanned and unwanted pregnancies, sexual abuse and rape litigation health costs, personal depression and other sexually related health problems. Finally, overall, accessibility to web sexuality education for all people will enhance their lifelong learning, in helping to develop well-adjusted teenagers into well-rounded adults, and well-rounded adults into well-adjusted seniors.
>
> (Goldman and Bradley 2001: 215)

A more pessimistic analysis is provided by Hart and Wellings (2002) who argue that our sexual behaviour is being increasingly medicalised so that the demand today is for medicine to provide more and better ways of sexual gratification, where gratification is measured in such units as number of orgasms per month. The pharmaceutical industry and cosmetic surgeons once concerned themselves with clear-cut diseases and facial deformities but Viagra (sildenafil citrate) now earns Pfizer more than the gross national product of some countries and women can have their vagina completely resculpted and rejuvinated with a one-hour laser procedure.

Whether Goldman and Bradley's or Hart and Wellings' vision is the more accurate remains to be seen. In either event, a values-informed sex education will have much to contribute. Unless we can help young people to understand human values in relation to sexuality, people may increasingly attempt to measure sexual fulfilment in terms of quantifiable experiences rather than in terms of fundamental and mutual human enrichment.

Summary

1 There are values implicit in teaching about both conception and contraception. A considerable amount is now known about how to design and implement sex education programmes to reduce teenage pregnancy or STI rates. Less is known about how to design and implement sex education programmes to meet other aims.

2 Schools do little to teach pupils about sexual pleasure but it is unclear to what extent they should.

3 Teaching about sexual orientation can help pupils clarify for themselves what they think about the issue and why. It can also help students to understand what it might be like to feel very differently about these issues.

4 Schools should address bullying, including sexual and homophobic bullying.

5 The actions taken by schools in regard of any parents or parents-to-be among their pupils send out powerful messages about how schools regard sexual behaviour and the rights of pupils.

6 Sex education continues throughout our lives. A values-informed sex education has much to contribute.

Issues for discussion

1   Should schools promote contraception or be neutral about it?
2   List arguments for and against schools teaching about sexual pleasure.
3   What amount of diversity among the teachers in a school is acceptable with regard to their attitudes towards heterosexuality and homosexuality?
4   Should schools look at the causes of different categories of bullying or simply deem all bullying unacceptable and try to reduce its occurrence?
5   Is it always best for pregnant schoolgirls to remain at school?
6   Should we welcome or decry the increasing medicalisation of our sexual behaviour and the increasing accessibility of information about sex?

Further reading

For books about sexual desire see:

- Buss, D. M. (1994) *The Evolution of Desire: Strategies of Human Mating*, New York: Basic Books.
- Regan, P. C. and Berscheid, E. (1999) *Lust: What We Know about Human Sexual Desire*, Thousand Oaks, CA: Sage.
- Stoller, R. J. ([1979] 1986) *Sexual Excitement: Dynamics of Erotic Life*, London: Karnac.

For materials and suggestions about how to deal with sexual bullying and discrimination in schools and colleges see:

- Duncan, N. (1999) *Sexual Bullying: Gender Conflict and Pupil Culture in Secondary Schools*, London: Routledge.
- Epstein, D. (ed.) (1994) *Challenging Lesbian and Gay Inequalities in Education*, Buckingham: Open University Press.
- Epstein, D. and Sears, J. T. (eds) (1999) *A Dangerous Knowing: Sexuality, Pedagogy and Popular Culture*, London: Cassell.
- Forrest, S., Biddle, G. and Clift, S. (1997) *Talking about Homosexuality in the Secondary School*, Horsham, Sussex: AVERT.
- Garber, L. (ed.) (1994) *Tilting the Tower: Lesbians Teaching Queer Subjects*, New York: Routledge.

References

Abbott, E. (2001) *A History of Celibacy*, Cambridge: Lutterworth Press.

Abrams, M., Gerard, D. and Timms, N. (1985) *Values and Social Change in Britain*, London: Macmillan.

Aggleton, P. (1999) *Men Who Sell Sex: International Perspectives on Male Prostitution and AIDS*, London: UCL Press.

Alderson, P. (2000) *Young Children's Rights: Exploring Beliefs, Principles and Practice*, London: Jessica Kingsley.

Allen, I. (1987) *Education in Sex and Personal Relationships*, London: Policy Studies Institute.

Allen, L. (2001) 'Closing sex education's knowledge/practice gap: the reconceptualisation of young people's sexual knowledge', *Sex Education* 1: 109–22.

Alternative Service Book (1980) *Service authorized for use in the Church of England in conjunction with The Book of Common Prayer*, Beccles: William Clowes (and others).

Alvarado, S. and Power, P. (1993) *The Inside Story: Menstruation Education for Young Men and Women*, Wisbech: LDA.

Anon (2002) 'Teen birth rates decline', *Campaign Update* summer: 8. See www.teenagepregnancy.org/america

Archard, D. (1998) 'How should we teach sex?', *Journal of Philosophy of Education* 32: 437–48.

Archard, D. (2000) *Sex Education (Impact Series no. 7)*, London: Philosophy of Education Society of Great Britain.

Arcus, M. E., Schvaneveldt, J. D. and Moss, J. J. (1993) *Handbook of Family Life Education* (Vols 1 and 2), Newbury Park, CA: Sage.

Arnot, M. (1996) 'Education for citizenship: the concerns of student teachers in England and Wales', seminar discussion paper presented at the National Symposium *Education for Adult Life*, School Curriculum and Assessment Authority, London, 15 January.

Aronowitz, S. and Giroux, H. A. (1991) *Postmodern Education: Politics, Culture and Social Criticism*, Minneapolis, MN: University of Minneapolis Press.

Ashraf, S. A. (1998) 'The concept of sex in Islam and sex education', in M. J. Reiss and S. A. Mabud (eds) *Sex Education and Religion*, Cambridge: Islamic Academy.

Ashworth, A. (1998) *Once in a House on Fire*, London: Picador.

Atkinson, E. (2002) 'Education for diversity in a multisexual society: negotiating the contradictions of contemporary discourse', *Sex Education* 2: 119–32.

Bagley, C. and Tremblay, P. (1997) 'Suicidal behaviors in homosexual and bisexual males', *Crisis* 18: 24–34.

Bailey, C. (1984) *Beyond the Present and the Particular: A Theory of Liberal Education*, London: Routledge and Kegan Paul.

Bailey, J. (2002) *Conversations in a Brothel: Men Tell Why They Do It*, Sydney: Hodder.

Bain, P., Gale, W. and Taylor, R. (1989) *HIV and AIDS Training Pack for Young People: 16–19 years*, 2nd edn, Liverpool: Liverpool Health Authority.

Baker, C. and Davies, B. (1989) 'A lesson on sex roles', *Gender and Education* 1: 59–76.

Balswick, J. O. and Balswick, J. K. (1995) 'Gender relations and marital power', in B. B. Ingoldsby and S. Smith (eds) *Families in Multicultural Perspective*, New York: Guilford.

Bantock, G. (1965) *Education and Values*, London: Faber and Faber.

Baraitser, P., Dolan, F. and Cowley, S. (in press) 'Developing relationships between sexual health clinics and schools: more than clinic nurses doing sex education sessions?', *Sex Education*.

Barker, D., Halman, L. and Vloet, A. (1992) *The European Values Study 1981–1990*, Aberdeen: Gordon Cook Foundation for European Values Group.

Barr, J. (1984) *Escaping from Fundamentalism*, London: SCM (Student Christian Movement) Press.

Barrett, K. (1994) *Protecting Children: A Guide for Teachers on Child Abuse*, revised edn, London: NSPCC.

Barry, S. M. K. (1979) 'Sex education in its curricular context: The evaluation of a sex education programme in Boreham schools with a view to assessing its contribution to the development of "social maturity"', PhD thesis, Brunel University.

Baxter, J. (2002) 'A juggling act: a feminist, post-structuralist analysis of girls' and boys' talk in the secondary classroom', *Gender and Education* 14: 5–19.

Beck, C. (1990) *Better Schools: AValues Perspective*, London: Falmer Press.

Beck, J. (1999) 'Should homosexuality be taught as an acceptable alternative lifestyle? A Muslim perspective: a response to Halstead and Lewicka', *Cambridge Journal of Education* 29: 121–30.

Beck, J. (2001) '"Moral democratic education and homosexuality: censoring morality" by John Petrovic: a rejoinder', *Sex Education* 1: 235–45.

Berg, J. (1993) 'How could ethics depend on religion?', in P. Singer (ed.) *A Companion to Ethics*, Oxford: Blackwell.

Berlin, I. (1969) *Four Essays on Liberty*, London: Oxford University Press.

Bernardes, J. (1997) *Family Studies: An Introduction*, London: Routledge.

Bernstein, A. C. (1994) *Flight of the Stork: What Children Think (and When) about Sex and Family Building*, revised edn, Indianapolis, IN: Perspectives Press.

Berwick, D. (2002) '"We all have AIDS": case for reducing the cost of HIV drugs to zero', *British Medical Journal* 324: 214–16.

Blackburn, S. (2001) *Being Good: A Short Introduction to Ethics*, Oxford: Oxford University Press.

Blake, S. and Frances, G. (2001) *Just Say No! to Abstinence Education: Lessons Learnt from a Sex Education Study Tour to the United States*, London: National Children's Bureau.

Blake, S. and Katrak, Z. (2002) *Faith, Values and Sex and Relationships Education*, London: National Children's Bureau.

Blake, S. and Laxton, J. (1998) *Strides: A Practical Guide to Sex and Relationships Education with Young Men*, London: Family Planning Authority.

Bloom, S. S., Banda, C., Songolo, G., Mulendema, S., Cunningham, A. E. and Boerma, J. T. (2000) 'Looking for change in response to the AIDS epidemic: trends in AIDS knowledge and sexual behavior in Zambia, 1990 through 1998', *Journal of Acquired Immune Deficiency Syndromes* 25: 77–85.

Bodi, F. (1994) 'The nature of sex education', *Q News* 3, 2–9 December: 6.

Bogart, J. H. ([1991] 1995) 'On the nature of rape', in R. M. Stewart (ed.) *Philosophical Perspectives on Sex and Love*, New York: Oxford University Press.

Bosacki, S. and Ota, C. (2000) 'Preadolescents' voices: a consideration of British and Canadian children's reflections on religion, spirituality, and their sense of self', *International Journal of Children's Spirituality* 5: 203–19.

Boswell, J. (1980) *Christianity, Social Tolerance and Homosexuality*, Chicago: University of Chicago Press.

Bouhdiba, A. (1985) *Sexuality in Islam*, London: Routledge and Kegan Paul.

Bourne, S. (1995) *Girls Have Long Hair: What do Key Stage 2 Pupils Know about Sex?*, Cambridge: Daniels.

Braun, D. (1988) *Responding to Child Abuse: Action and Planning for Teachers and Other Professionals*, London: Bedford Square Press.

Brehm, S. S. (1992) *Intimate Relationships*, 2nd edn, New York: McGraw-Hill.

Bridges, D. (1986) 'Dealing with controversy in the curriculum: a philosophical perspective', in J. J. Wellington (ed.) *Controversial Issues in the Curriculum*, Oxford: Basil Blackwell.

British Medical Association (1987) *AIDS and You*, London: British Medical Association.

British Medical Association Board of Science and Education (1997) *School Sex Education: Good Practice and Policy*, London: British Medical Association.

British Medical Association Board of Science and Education (2002) *Sexually Transmitted Infections*, London: British Medical Association. Available at www.bma.org.uk

Brown, A. (1993) *Sex Education: Guidelines for Church School Governors*, London: National Society (Church of England) for Promoting Religious Education.

Brown, J. C. (1990) 'The focus on single mothers', in C. Murray (ed.) *The Emerging British Underclass*, London: IEA Health and Welfare Unit.

Brown, J., Comber, M., Gibson, K. and Howard, S. (1985) 'Marriage and the family', in M. Abrams, D. Gerard and N. Timms (eds) *Values and Social Change in Britain*, London: Macmillan.

Burstall, E. (1994) 'Cheers and tears over candid nurse', *The Times Educational Supplement* 1 April: 5.

Buss, D. M. (1994) *The Evolution of Desire: Strategies of Human Mating*, New York: Basic Books.

Buston, K. and Wight, D. (2002) 'The salience and utility of school sex education to young women', *Sex Education* 2: 233–50.

Cancian, F. (1987) *Love in America*, Cambridge, MA: Cambridge University Press.

Carr, W. (1995) *For Education: Towards Critical Educational Enquiry*, Buckingham: Open University Press.

Carter, S. and Clift, S. (2000) 'Tourism, international travel and sex: themes and research', in S. Clift and S. Carter (eds) *Tourism and Sex: Culture, Commerce and Coercion*, London: Pinter.

Cash, K., Hashima-E-Nasreen, A., Bhuiya, A., Chowdhury, A. M. R. and Chowdhury, S. (2001) 'Without sex education: exploring the social and sexual vulnerabilities of rural Bangladeshi girls and boys', *Sex Education* 1: 219–33.

Castro-Vázquez, G. and Kishi, I. (2002) '"If you say to them that they have to use condoms, some of them might use them. It is like drinking alcohol or smoking": an educational intervention with Japanese senior high school students', *Sex Education* 2: 105–17.

Catholic Education Service (n.d.) [1994] *Education in Sexuality: Some Guidelines for Teachers and Governors in Catholic Schools*, London: Catholic Education Service.

Celentano, D. D., Bond, K. C., Lyles, C. M., Eiumtrakul, S., Go, V. F.-L., Beyrer, C., na Chiangmai, C., Nelson, K. E., Khamboonruang, C. and Vaddhanaphuti, C. (2000) 'Preventive intervention to reduce sexually transmitted infections', *Archives of Internal Medicine* 160: 535–40.

Chen, Y-H. (1988) 'The strengths of Chinese immigrant families' (unpublished manuscript), Lincoln, NE: University of Nebraska-Lincoln Department of Human Development and the Family.

Cherlin, A. J. (1996) *Public and Private Families: An Introduction*, New York: McGraw-Hill.

Chick, S. (1999) *Don't Look Back*, London: Livewire Books.

Children's Society (1994) *Education for Parenthood: A Resource Pack for Young People*, London: Children's Society.

Chilisa, B. (2002) 'National policies on pregnancy in education systems in sub-Saharan Africa: the case of Botswana', *Gender and Education* 14: 21–35.

Clarity Collective (1989) *Taught not Caught: Strategies for Sex Education*, 2nd edn, Wisbech: LDA.

Clark, A. (1998) 'The Catholic perspective on sex education: the contribution of one counter-cultural challenge', in M. J. Reiss and S. A. Mabud (eds) *Sex Education and Religion*, Cambridge: Islamic Academy.

Clark, J. A. (2001) 'Sex education in the New Zealand primary school: a tangled skein of morality, religion, politics and the law', *Sex Education* 1: 23–30.

Clift, S. and Carter, S. (eds) (2000) *Tourism and Sex: Culture, Commerce and Coercion*, London: Pinter.

Cole, B. (1993) *Mummy Laid an Egg!*, London: Jonathan Cape.

Coleman, J. and Roker, D. (eds) (1998) *Teenage Sexuality: Health, Risk and Education*, Amsterdam: Harwood Academic.

Coleman, L. and Ingham, R. (1999) 'Contrasting strategies used by young people to ensure condom use: some findings from a qualitative research project', *AIDS Care* 11: 473–9.

Coleman, P. (1989) *Gay Christians: A Moral Dilemma*, London: SCM Press.

Collyer, J. (1995) *Sex Education in Primary Schools: A Guide to Policy Development in Primary Schools*, London: Forbes.

Comfort, A. (1993) *The New Joy of Sex*, London: Mitchell Beazley.

Commission on the Christian Doctrine of Marriage (1971) *Marriage, Divorce and the Church: The Report of a Commission appointed by the Archbishop of Canterbury to Prepare a Statement on the Christian Doctrine of Marriage*, London: SPCK.

Connell, R. W. (1987) *Gender and Power: Society, the Person and Sexual Politics*, Cambridge: Polity Press.

Connolly, M. (1994) 'Parents win apology over sex act words', *Guardian* 25 March: 3.

Countryman, L. W. (1988) *Dirt, Greed and Sex: Sexual Ethics in the New Testament and their Implications for Today*, Philadelphia, PA: Fortress Press.

Cram, R. H. (1996) 'Knowing God: children, play and paradox', *Religious Education* 91. 55–73.

Crittenden, B. (1999) 'Moral education in a pluralist liberal democracy', in J. M. Halstead and T. H. McLaughlin (eds) *Education in Morality*, London: Routledge.

Davidson, N. (1990) *Boys Will Be . . . ? Sex Education and Young Men*, London: Bedford Square Press.

Davie, G. (1994) *Religion in Britain since 1945: Believing without Belonging*, Oxford: Blackwell.

Davies, J. (ed.) (1993) *The Family: Is It Just Another Lifestyle Choice?* London: IEA Health and Welfare Unit.

Davis, K. E. and Todd, M. J. (1985) 'Assessing friendship: prototypes, paradigm cases and relationship description', in S. Duck and D. Perlman (eds) *Understanding Personal Relationships: An Interdisciplinary Approach*, London: Sage.

Dearden, R. F. (1966) '"Needs" in education', *British Journal of Educational Studies* 14(3): 5–17.

Dearden, R. F. (1984) *Theory and Practice in Education*, London: Routledge and Kegan Paul.

Deigh, J. (1995) 'Ethics', in R. Audi (ed.) *The Cambridge Dictionary of Philosophy*, Cambridge: Cambridge University Press.

Delphy, C. and Leonard, D. (1992) *Familiar Exploitation: A New Analysis of Marriage in Contemporary Western Societies*, Cambridge: Polity Press.

Dennis, N. and Erdos, G. (1992) *Families without Fatherhood*, London: IEA Health and Welfare Unit.

Department for Education (DfE) (1994) *Sex Education in Schools (Circular 5/94)*, London: DfE.

Department for Education and Employment (DfEE) (1995) *Protecting Children from Abuse: The Role of the Education Service (Circular 10/95)*, London: DfEE.

Department for Education and Employment (1999) *National Health School Standard: Getting Started – A Guide for Schools*, Nottingham: DfEE Publications. Available at www.wiredforhealth.gov.uk

Department for Education and Employment (2000a) *Sex and Relationship Education Guidance, DfEE 0116/2000*, London: DfEE.

Department for Education and Employment (2000b) *Sex and Relationship Education Guidance: Draft for Consultation 16 March 2000*, London: DfEE.

Dickenson, D. L. (2002) *Ethical Issues in Maternal-Fetal Medicine,* Cambridge: Cambridge University Press.

Dion, K. K. and Dion, K. L. (1985) 'Personality, gender and the phenomenology of romantic love', in P. Shaver (ed.) *Review of Personality and Social Psychology: Vol 6. Self, Situations and Social Behaviour,* Beverly Hills, CA: Sage.

Dion, K. K. and Dion, K. L. (1996) 'Cultural perspectives on romantic love', *Personal Relationships* 3: 5–17.

Dion, K. L. and Dion, K. K. (1988) 'Romantic love: individual and cultural perspectives', in R. J. Sternberg and M. L. Barnes (eds) *The Psychology of Love,* Newhaven, CT: Yale University Press.

Dixon, H. (1988) *Sexuality and Mental Handicap: An Educator's Resource Book,* Wisbech: LDA.

Doherty, L., Fenton, K. A., Jones, J., Paine, T. C., Higgins, S. P., Williams, D. and Palfreeman, A. (2002) 'Syphilis: old problem, new strategy', *British Medical Journal* 325: 153–6.

Donnellan, C. (ed.) (1994) *Family Values,* Cambridge: Independence.

Douglas, N., Warwick, I., Kemp, S. and Whitty, G. (1997) *Playing it Safe: Responses of Secondary School Teachers to Lesbian, Gay and Bisexual Pupils, Bullying, HIV and AIDS Education and Section 28,* London: Institute of Education, University of London.

Dowell, S. (1990) *They Two Shall Be One: Monogamy in History and Religion,* London: Collins Flame.

D'Oyen, F. M. (1996) *The Miracle of Life: A Guide on Islamic Family Life and Sex Education for Young People,* Markfield, Leicester: Islamic Foundation.

Doyle, P. (1988) *The God Squad,* London: Corgi.

Duin, J. (1988) *Sex and the Single Christian,* London: Marshal Pickering.

Duncan, B., Hart, G., Scoular, A. and Bigrigg, A. (2001) 'Qualitative analysis of psychosocial impact of diagnosis of *Chlamydia trachomatis*: implications for screening', *British Medical Journal* 322: 195–9.

Duncan, N. (1999) *Sexual Bullying: Gender Conflict and Pupil Culture in Secondary Schools,* London: Routledge.

Dunlop, F. (1996) 'Democratic values and the foundations of political education', in J. M. Halstead and M. J. Taylor (eds) *Values in Education and Education in Values,* London: Falmer Press.

Dunne, G.A. (1997) *Lesbian Lifestyles: Women's Work and the Politics of Sexuality,* London: Macmillan.

Dworkin, R. (1978) 'Liberalism', in S. Hampshire (ed.) *Public and Private Morality,* Cambridge: Cambridge University Press.

Dyson, S. (1993) *The Option of Parenthood,* London: Sheldon Press.

Elam, S. M., Rose, L. C. and Gallup, A. M. (1996) 'Poll of the public's attitudes towards the public schools', *Phi Delta Kappa* 78: 41–59.

Elliston, F. ([1975] 1995) 'In defence of promiscuity', in R. M. Stewart (ed.) *Philosophical Perspectives on Sex and Love,* New York: Oxford University Press.

Epstein, D. (ed.) (1994) *Challenging Lesbian and Gay Inequalities in Education,* Buckingham: Open University Press.

Epstein, D. (ed.) (2000) 'Special issue: sexualities and education', *Sexualities* 3: 387–511.

Epstein, D. and Sears, J. T. (eds) (1999) *A Dangerous Knowing: Sexuality, Pedagogy and Popular Culture*, London: Cassell.

Erooga, M. and Masson, H. (eds) (1999) *Children and Young People Who Sexually Abuse Others: Challenges and Responses*, London: Routledge.

Evans, M. J. (1983) *Woman in the Bible*, Exeter: Paternoster Press.

Farrell, C. (1978) *My Mother Said . . . The Way Young People Learned about Sex and Birth Control*, London: Routledge and Kegan Paul.

Fine, M. (1988) 'Sexuality, schooling, and adolescent females: the missing discourse of desire', *Harvard Educational Review* 58: 29–51.

Fineran, S. and Bennett, L. (1999) 'Gender and power issues of peer sexual harassment among teenagers', *Journal of Interpersonal Violence* 14: 626–41.

Fisher, N. (1994) *Your Pocket Guide to Sex*, Harmondsworth: Penguin.

Flandrin, J-L. (1985) 'Sex in married life in the Early Middle Ages: the church's teaching and behavioural reality', in P. Ariès and A. Bejin (eds) *Western Sexuality: Practice and Precept in Past and Present Times*, Oxford: Basil Blackwell.

Fletcher, A. and Hussey, S. (eds) (1999) *Childhood in Question: Children, Parents and the State*, Manchester: Manchester University Press.

Ford, N. (1991) *The Socio-Sexual Lifestyles of Young People in South West England*, Bristol: South Western Regional Health Authority.

Forrest, S., Biddle, G. and Clift, S. (1997) *Talking about Homosexuality in the Secondary School*, Horsham, Sussex: AVERT.

Forrest, S., Strange, V., Oakley, A. and the RIPPLE study team (2002) 'A comparison of students' evaluations on a peer-delivered sex education programme and teacher-led provision', *Sex Education* 2: 195–214.

Foucault, M. (1990) *The History of Sexuality: An Introduction* (translated from the French by Robert Hurley), Harmondsworth: Penguin.

Francis, B. (2000) *Boys, Girls and Achievement: Addressing the Classroom Issues*, London: RoutledgeFalmer.

Francis, B. and Skelton, C. (2001) 'Men teachers and the construction of heterosexual masculinity in the classroom', *Sex Education* 1: 9–21.

Francis, L. J. and Kay, W. K. (1995) *Teenage Religion and Values*, Leominster: Gracewing/Fowler Wright.

Francis, R. (1997) 'Power plays: children's constructions of gender and power in role plays', *Gender and Education* 9: 179–91.

Fromm, E. (1956) *The Art of Loving*, New York: Harper and Row.

Gallagher, C. A., Maloney, G. A., Rousseau, M. F. and Wilczak, P. F. (1983) *Embodied in Love: Sacramental Spirituality and Sexual Intimacy*, New York: Crossroad.

Garber, L. (ed.) (1994) *Tilting the Tower: Lesbians Teaching Queer Subjects*, New York: Routledge.

Gaus, G. (1983) *The Modern Liberal Theory of Man*, London: Croom Helm.

Gelles, R. J. (1995) *Contemporary Families: A Sociological View*, Thousand Oaks, CA: Sage.

General Synod Board of Social Responsibility (1979) *Homosexual Relationships: A Contribution to Discussion*, London: Church Information Office.

General Synod of the Church of England (1991) *Issues in Human Sexuality: A Statement by the House of Bishops of the General Synod of the Church of England, December 1991*, London: Church House Publishing.

Giddens, A. (1992) *The Transformation of Intimacy: Sexuality, Love and Eroticism in Modern Societies*, Cambridge: Polity Press.

Gilbert, J. (1996) 'The sex education component of school science programmes as a "micro-technology" of power', *Women's Studies Journal* 12(2): 35–57.

Gillham, B. and Thomson, J. A. (eds) (1996) *Child Protection: Problem and Prevention from Preschool to Adolescence – A Handbook for Professionals*, London: Routledge.

Gilligan, C. (1982) *In a Different Voice: Psychological Theory and Women's Moral Development*, Cambridge, MA: Harvard University Press.

Gittins, D. (1985) *The Family in Question: Changing Households and Familiar Ideologies*, London: Macmillan Education.

Gleitzman, M. (1998) *Bumface*, Ringwood, Victoria: Puffin.

Goldman, J. D. G. and Bradley, G. L. (2001) 'Sexuality education across the life-cycle in the new millennium', *Sex Education* 1: 197–217.

Goldman, R. and Goldman, J. (1982) *Children's Sexual Thinking*, London: Routledge and Kegan Paul.

Goldman, R. and Goldman, J. (1988) *Show Me Yours: Children Talking about Sex*, Harmondsworth: Penguin.

Goody, J. (1983) *The Development of the Family and Marriage in Europe*, Cambridge: Cambridge University Press.

Gordon, G. and Klouda, T. (1988) *Talking AIDS: A Guide for Community Workers*, London: International Planned Parenthood Federation.

Graham, G. (1994) 'Liberal vs radical feminism revisited', *Journal of Applied Philosophy*, 11(2): 155–70.

Greenberg, J. S. (1989) 'Preparing teachers for sexuality education', *Theory into Practice* 28: 227–32.

Grunseit, A. and Kippax, S. (1993) *Effects of Sex Education on Young People's Sexual Behaviour*, Geneva: Youth and General Public Unit Office of Intervention Development and Support Global Program on AIDS, World Health Organization.

Gutmann, A. (1980) *Liberal Equality*, Cambridge: Cambridge University Press.

Gutmann, A. (1987) *Democratic Education*, Princeton, NJ: Princeton University Press.

Halstead, J. M. (1986) *The Case for Muslim Voluntary-aided Schools: Some Philosophical Reflections*, Cambridge: Islamic Academy.

Halstead, J. M. (1992) 'Ethical dimensions of controversial events in multicultural education', in M. Leicester and M. Taylor (eds) *Ethics, Ethnicity and Education*, London: Kogan Page.

Halstead, J. M. (1996a) 'Values and values education in schools', in J. M. Halstead and M. J. Taylor (eds) *Values in Education and Education in Values*, London: Falmer Press.

Halstead, J. M. (1996b) 'Liberal values and liberal education', in J. M. Halstead and M. J. Taylor (eds) *Values in Education and Education in Values*, London: Falmer Press.

Halstead, J. M. (1996c) 'Liberalism, multiculturalism and toleration: a review article', *Journal of Philosophy of Education* 30: 257–72.

Halstead, J. M. (1997) 'Muslims and sex education', *Journal of Moral Education* 26: 317–30.

Halstead, J. M. (1998) 'Values and sex education in a multicultural society', in M. J. Reiss and S. A. Mabud (eds) *Sex Education and Religion*, Cambridge: Islamic Academy.

Halstead, J. M. (1999a) 'Moral education in family life: the effects of diversity', *Journal of Moral Education* 28: 265–81.

Halstead, J. M. (1999b) 'Teaching about homosexuality: a response to John Beck', *Cambridge Journal of Education* 29: 131–6.

Halstead, J. M. (2000a) 'Developing a values framework for sex education in a pluralist society', in M. Leicester, C. Modgil and S. Modgil (eds) *Moral Education and Pluralism*, London: Falmer Press.

Halstead, J. M. (2000b) 'High spirits in the playground: the contribution of playground songs to children's spiritual and moral growth', paper presented at the First International Conference on Children's Spirituality, Chichester, 9–12 July.

Halstead, J. M. (ed.) (2001a) Special issue: Sexuality and Spirituality, *International Journal of Children's Spirituality* 6(2).

Halstead, J. M. (2001b) Editorial, *International Journal of Children's Spirituality* 6: 141–5.

Halstead, J. M. and Lewicka, K. (1998) 'Should homosexuality be taught as an acceptable alternative lifestyle? A Muslim perspective', *Cambridge Journal of Education* 28: 49–64.

Halstead, J. M. and McLaughlin, T. H. (eds) (1999) *Education in Morality*, London: Routledge.

Halstead, J. M. and Taylor, M. J. (eds) (1996) *Values in Education and Education in Values*, London: Falmer Press.

Halstead, J. M. and Taylor, M. J. (2000) *The Development of Values, Attitudes and Personal Qualities: A Review of Recent Research*, Slough: NFER.

Halstead, J. M. and Waite, S. (2001a) '"Living in different worlds": gender differences in the developing sexual values and attitudes of primary school children', *Sex Education* 1: 59–76.

Halstead, J. M. and Waite, S. (2001b) 'Nurturing the spiritual in children's sexual development', *International Journal of Children's Spirituality* 6: 185–206.

Hampshire Education (n.d.) *Guidelines: Sex Education in Hampshire Schools*, Winchester: Winchester Health Promotion Department.

Harden, A., Oakley, A. and Oliver, S. (2001) 'Peer-delivered health promotion for young people: a systematic review of different study designs', *Health Education Journal* 60: 339–53.

Hardwick, D. and Patychuk, D. (1999) 'Geographic mapping demonstrates the association between social inequality, teen births and STDs among youth', *Canadian Journal of Human Sexuality* 8. 77–90.

Harris, A. (1971) 'What does "sex education" mean?', *Journal of Moral Education* 1: 7–11.

Harris, R. H. (1997) *Let's Talk about Sex: Growing Up, Changing Bodies, Sex and Sexual Health*, London: Walker.

Harris, S. (1990) *Lesbian and Gay Issues in the English Classroom*, Buckingham: Open University Press.

Harrison, D. M. (2002) 'Rethinking circumcision and sexuality in the United States', *Sexualities* 5: 300–16.

Harrison, J. K. (2000) *Sex Education in Secondary Schools*, Buckingham: Open University Press.

Hart, G. and Wellings, K. (2002) 'Sexual behaviour and its medicalisation: in sickness and in health', *British Medical Journal* 324: 896–900.

Hart, H. L. A. (1963) *Law, Liberty and Morality*, Oxford: Oxford University Press.

Hart, H. L. A. (1984) 'Are there any natural rights?', in J. Waldron (ed.) *Theories of Rights*, Oxford: Oxford University Press.

Harvey, I. (ed.) (1993) *Condoms across the Curriculum*, Cambridge: Daniels.

Harvey, I. and Reiss, M. J. (1987) *AIDSFACTS: Educational Material on AIDS for Teachers and Students*, Cambridge: Cambridge Science Books.

Haworth, L. (1986) *Autonomy: An Essay in Philosophical Psychology and Ethics*, New Haven, CT: Yale University Press.

Haydon, G. (1995) 'Thick or thin? The cognitive content of moral education in a plural democracy', *Journal of Moral Education* 24: 53–64.

Haydon, G. (1997) *Teaching about Values: A New Approach*, London: Cassell.

Hayek, F. A. (1960) *The Constitution of Liberty*, London: Routledge and Kegan Paul.

Health Education Authority (1995) *Parents, Schools and Sex Education: A Compelling Case for Partnership*, London: Health Education Authority.

Health Promotion Agency for Northern Ireland (1996) *Sex Education in Northern Ireland: Views from Parents and Schools*, Belfast: Health Promotion Agency for Northern Ireland.

Herbert, C. (1992) *Sexual Harassment in Schools: A Guide for Teachers*, London: David Fulton.

Heron, A. (ed.) (1994) *Two Teenagers in Twenty: Writings by Gay and Lesbian Youth*, Boston, MA: Alyson.

Higonnet, A. (1998) *Pictures of Innocence: The History and Crisis of Ideal Childhood*, London: Thames and Hudson.

Hilton, G. L. S. (2001) 'Sex education – the issues when working with boys', *Sex Education* 1: 31–41.

Hilton, G. S. L. (in press) 'Listening to the boys: English boys' views on the desirable characteristics of teachers of sex education', *Sex Education*.

Hinnells, J. R. (ed.) ([1984] 1991) *A Handbook of Living Religions*, London: Penguin.

Hirst, J. and Selmes, S. (1997) *'How Was It for You?' Young People's Evaluation of School Sex Education in Southern Derbyshire: A Research Report*, Sheffield: Health Research Institute, Sheffield Hallam University.

Hirst, P. H. (1974) *Moral Education in a Secular Society*, London: Hodder and Stoughton.

Hirst, P. H. (1999) 'The demands of moral education: reasons, virtues, practices', in J. M. Halstead and T. H. McLaughlin (eds) *Education in Morality*, London: Routledge.

Hirst, P. H. and Peters, R. S. (1970) *The Logic of Education*, London: Routledge and Kegan Paul.

Hite, S. (1994) *The Hite Report on the Family: Growing up under Patriarchy*, London: Bloomsbury.

Holland, J., Ramazanoglu, C., Scott, S., Sharpe, S. and Thomson, R. (1990) *'Don't Die of Ignorance' – I Nearly Died of Embarrassment: Condoms in Context*, London: Tufnell Press.

Holland, J., Ramazanoglu, C., Sharpe, S. and Thomson, R. (1998) *The Male in the Head: Young People, Heterosexuality and Power*, London: Tufnell Press.

Hollway, W. and Jefferson, T. (1998) '"A kiss is just a kiss": date rape, gender and subjectivity', *Sexualities* 1: 405–23.

Holly, L. (eds) (1989) *Girls and Sexuality: Teaching and Learning*, Milton Keynes: Open University Press.

Home Office (1998) *Supporting Families: A Consultation Document*, London: The Stationery Office.

Home Office Communications Directorate (2000) *A Choice by Right: The Report of the Working Group on Forced Marriages*, London: Home Office.

Hopson, B. and Scally, M. (1980) *Lifeskills Teaching Programme No. 1*, Leeds: Lifeskills Associates.

Hubbard, P. (1999) *Sex and the City: Geographies of Prostitution in the Urban West*, Aldershot: Ashgate.

Human Rights Watch (2001) *Scared at School: Sexual Violence against Girls in South African Schools*, New York: Human Rights Watch.

Humphries, S. (1988) *A Secret World of Sex*, London: Sidgwick and Jackson.

Isherwood, L. (ed.) (2000) *The Good News of the Body: Sexual Theology and Feminism*, Sheffield: Sheffield Academic Press.

Islamic Academy (1991) *Sex Education in the School Curriculum: The Religious Perspective – An Agreed Statement*, Cambridge: Islamic Academy.

Jackson, S. (1982) *Childhood Sexuality*, Oxford: Basil Blackwell.

John, M. (ed.) (1996) *Children in Charge: The Child's Right to a Fair Hearing*, London: Jessica Kingsley.

Johnson, A. M., Wadsworth, J., Wellings, K. and Field, J. (1994) *Sexual Attitudes and Lifestyles*, Oxford: Blackwell Scientific.

Johnson, A. M., Mercer, C. H., Erens, B., Copas, A. J., McManus, S., Wellings, K., Fenton, K. A., Korovessis, C., Macdowell, W., Nanchahal, K., Purdon, S. and Field, J. (2001) 'Sexual behaviour in Britain: partnerships, practices, and HIV risk behaviours', *The Lancet* 358: 1835–42.

Jones, R. (1989) 'Sex education in personal and social education', in P. White (ed.) *Personal and Social Education: Philosophical Perspectives*, London: Kogan Page.

Kajan, C. and Lewis, S. (1996) 'Families with parents who have multiple commitments', in M. Moore, J. Sixsmith and K. Knowles (eds) *Children's Reflection on Family Life*, London: Falmer Press.

Kakavoulis, A. (2001) 'Family and sex education: a survey of parental attitudes', *Sex Education* 1: 163–74.

Katrak, Z. and Scott, I. (in press) *Diverse Communities: Identity and Teenage Pregnancy – A Resource Exploring Issues of Sexual Health Concerning Faith and Minority Ethnic Communities*, London: Teenage Pregnancy Unit.

Kehily, M. J. and Nayak, A. (1997) '"Lads and laughter": humour and the production of heterosexual hierarchies', *Gender and Education* 9: 69–87.

Kelly, D. M. (2000) *Pregnant with Meaning: Teen Mothers and the Politics of Inclusive Schooling*, New York: Peter Lang.

Khan, F., Ditton, J., Elliott, L., Short, E., Morrison, A., Farrall, S. and Gruer, L. (2000) 'EscapEs: what sort of ecstasy do package tour ravers seek?', in S. Clift and S. Carter (eds) *Tourism and Sex: Culture, Commerce and Coercion*, London: Pinter.

Khayatt, D. (1994) 'Surviving school as a lesbian student', *Gender and Education* 6: 47–61.

Kirby, D. (2001) *Emerging Answers: Research Finding on Programs to Reduce Teen Pregnancy*, Washington, DC: National Campaign to Prevent Teen Pregnancy.

Kitzinger, C., Wilkinson, S. and Perkins, R. (1992) Special issue: Heterosexuality, *Feminism and Psychology* 2: 293–509.

Kitzinger, S. and Kitzinger, C. (1989) *Talking with Children*, London: Pandora.

Kohlberg, L. (1969) 'Stage and sequence: the cognitive-developmental approach to socialisation', in D. Goslin (ed.) *Handbook of Socialisation, Theory and Research*, Chicago: Rand McNally.

Laffey, A. L. (1988) *An Introduction to the Old Testament: A Feminist Perspective*, Philadelphia, PA: Fortress Press.

Lamb, M. E. (1999) *Parenting and Child Development in 'Nontraditional' Families*, Mahwah, NJ: Lawrence Erlbaum.

Lamb, S. (1996) *The Trouble with Blame: Victims, Perpetrators, and Responsibility*, Cambridge, MA: Harvard University Press.

Lamptey, P. R. (2002) 'Reducing heterosexual transmission of HIV in poor countries', *British Medical Journal* 324: 207–11.

Landry, D., Kaeser, L. and Richards, C. (1999) 'Abstinence promotion and the provision of information about contraception in public school district sexuality education policies', *Family Planning Perspectives* 31: 280–6.

Langille, D., MacKinnon, D., Marshall, E. and Graham, J. (2001) 'So many bricks in the wall: young women in Nova Scotia speak about barriers to school-based sexual health education', *Sex Education* 1: 245–57.

Laumann, E. O., Michael, R. T., Gagnon, J. H. and Michaels, S. (1994) *The Social Organization of Sexuality: Sexual Practices in the United States*, Chicago: University of Chicago Press.

Lawrence, J., Kanabus, A. and Regis, D. (2000) *A Survey of Sex Education Provision in Secondary Schools*, Horsham, Sussex: AVERT.

Lee, C. (1983) *The Ostrich Position: Sex, Schooling and Mystification*, London: Writers and Readers Publishing Cooperative.

Lee, J. A. (1988) 'Love-styles', in R. J. Sternberg and M. L. Barnes (eds) *The Psychology of Love*, Newhaven, CT: Yale University Press.

Lees, S. (1994) 'Talking about sex in sex education', *Gender and Education*, 6: 281–92.

Lees, S. (1997) *Ruling Passions: Sexual Violence, Reputation and the Law*, Buckingham: Open University Press.

Leicester, M., Modgil, C. and Modgil, S. (eds) (2000) *Education, Culture and Values* (Vols I–VI), London: Falmer Press.

Leichter, H. J. (1974) 'Some perspectives on the family as educator', in H. J. Leichter (ed.) *The Family as Educator*, New York: Teachers College Press.

Lenderyou, G. (1993) *Primary School Workbook: Teaching Sex Education within the National Curriculum*, London: Family Planning Association.

Lenderyou, G. (1995) 'School sex education, faith and values', in D. E. Massey (ed.) *Sex Education Source Book: Current Issues and Debates*, London: Family Planning Association.

Lenderyou, G. and Porter, M. (eds) (1994) *Sex Education, Values and Morality*, London: Health Education Authority.

Levine, L. and Barbach, L. (1983) *The Intimate Male*, New York: Signet.

Levine, R. V. (1993) 'Is love a luxury?', *American Demographies* February: 27–9.

Levinson, M. (2000) *The Demands of Liberal Education*, Oxford: Oxford University Press.

Lickona, T. (1991) *Educating for Character: How our Schools can Teach Respect and Responsibility*, New York: Bantam.

Mabray, D. and Labauve, B. J. (2002) 'A multidimensional approach to sexual education', *Sex Education* 2: 31–44.

Mabud, S. A. (1998) 'An Islamic view of sex education', in M. J. Reiss and S. A. Mabud (eds) *Sex Education and Religion*, Cambridge: Islamic Academy.

McAdams, D. P. (1993) *Stories We Live By*, New York: William Morrow.

Mac an Ghaill, M. (1994) *The Making of Men: Masculinities, Sexualities and Schooling*, Buckingham: Open University Press.

Mac an Ghaill, M. (ed.) (1996) *Understanding Masculinities: Social Relations and Cultural Arenas*, Buckingham: Open University Press.

McGrellis, S., Henderson, S., Holland, J., Sharpe, S. and Thomson, R. (2000) *Through the Moral Maze: A Quantitative Study of Young People's Values*, London: Tufnell Press.

McKay, A. (1997) 'Accommodating ideological pluralism in sexuality education', *Journal of Moral Education* 26: 285–300.

McKeganey, N. and Barnard, M. (1996) *Sex Work on the Streets: Prostitutes and their Clients*, Buckingham: Open University Press.

Mackie, J. L. (1977) *Ethics: Inventing Right and Wrong*, Harmondsworth: Penguin.

McLaughlin, T. H. (1995) 'Liberalism, education and the common school', *Journal of Philosophy of Education* 29: 239–55.

McLaughlin, T. H. and Halstead, J. M. (2000) 'John Wilson on moral education', *Journal of Moral Education* 29: 247–68.

McMahon, K. (1990) 'The *Cosmopolitan* Ideology and the management of desire', *Journal of Sex Research* 27: 381–96.

Mason, A. and Palmer, A. (1996) *Queerbashing: A National Survey of Hate Crimes against Lesbians and Gay Men*, London: Stonewall.

Massey, D. E. (1988) *Teaching about HIV and AIDS*, London: Health Education Authority.

Massey, D. E. (1990) 'School sex education: knitting without a pattern?', *Health Education Journal* 49: 134–42.

Massey, D. E. (1991) *School Sex Education. Why, What and How – A Guide for Teachers*, 2nd edn, London: Family Planning Association.

Massey, D. E. (ed.) (1995) *Sex Education Source Book: Current Issues and Debates*, London: Family Planning Association.

Masson, H. (1995) 'Children and adolescents who sexually abuse other children: responses to an emerging problem', *Journal of Social Welfare and Family Law* 17: 325–36.

Masters, R. (1992) 'Sexual overload: the effects of graphic sex education on innocent minds', *Family Matters* November.

Masters, W. H. and Johnson, V. E. (1966) *Human Sexual Response*, Boston, MA: Little, Brown.

Masters, W. H., Johnson, V. E. and Kolodny, R. C. (1994) *Heterosexuality*, London: Thorsons.

Matthews, M. (1980) *The Marxist Theory of Schooling*, London: Routledge and Kegan Paul.

Mayle, P. ([1973] 1978) *'Where Did I Come From?': The Facts of Life without any Nonsense and with Illustrations*, London: Macmillan.

Mayle, P. (1978) *'What's Happening to Me': The Answers to Some of the World's Most Embarrassing Questions*, London: Macmillan.

Measor, L., Tiffin, C. and Fry, K. (1996) 'Gender and sex education: a study of adolescent responses', *Gender and Education* 8: 275–88.

Measor, L., with Tiffin, C. and Miller, K. (2000) *Young People's Views on Sex Education: Education, Attitudes and Behaviour*, London: RoutledgeFalmer.

Meikle, J. (1994) 'Mars bar lesson revives sex debate', *Guardian* 24 March: 2.

Mellanby, A. R., Phelps, F. A., Crichton, N. J. and Tripp, J. H. (1995) 'School sex education: an experimental programme with educational and medical benefits', *British Medical Journal* 311: 414–17.

Mellman, M., Lazarus, E. and Rivlin, A. (1990) 'Family ties, family values', in D. Blankenhorn, S. Bayme and J. B. Elshtain (eds.) *Rebuilding the Nest: A New Commitment to the American Family*, Milwaukee, WI: Family Service America.

Michael, R. T., Gagnon, J. H., Laumann, E. O. and Kolata, G. (1994) *Sex in America: A Definitive Survey*, London: Little, Brown.

Michell, M. (ed.) (1987) *Macmillan Integrated Science Book 2*, London: Macmillan Education.

Mill, J. S. ([1859] 1972) *On Liberty*, London: Dent.

Miller, G. P. (2000) 'Female genital mutilation: a cultural-legal analysis', New York University Public Law and Legal Theory Working Paper.

Miller, G. P. (in press) 'Circumcision: a cultural-legal analysis', *Virginia Journal of Social Policy and the Law*.

Milton, J., Berne, L., Peppard, J., Patton, W., Hunt, L. and Wright, S. (2001) 'Teaching sexuality education in high schools: what qualities do Australian teachers value?', *Sex Education* 1: 175–86.

Ministry of National Health and Welfare (1995) *Canadian Guidelines for Sexual Health Education*, Ottawa: Division of STD Control and Health Service Systems Division.

Mirembe, R. and Davies, L. (2001) 'Is schooling a risk? Gender, power relations and school culture in Uganda', *Gender and Education* 13: 401–16.

Monger, G. (1988) *Nuffield Co-ordinated Sciences: Biology*, London: Longman.

Moore, M., Sixsmith, J. and Knowles, K. (1996) *Children's Reflections on Family Life*, London: Falmer Press.

Moore, S. and Rosenthal, D. (1993) *Sexuality in Adolescence*, London: Routledge.

Moran, J. (2001) 'Childhood sexuality and education: the case of Section 28', *Sexualities* 4: 73–89.

Morgan, D. (1992) *Discovering Men*, London: Routledge.

Morgan, K. P. (1996) 'The moral politics of sex education', in K. P. Morgan and M. Ayim (eds) *The Gender Question in Educational Theory, Pedagogy and Politics*, Boulder, CO: Westview Press.

MORI (1991) *Young Adults: Health and Lifestyle Report*, London: Health Education Authority.

Morris, R. W. (1994) *Values in Sexuality Education: A Philosophical Study*, Lanham, MD: University Press of America.

Motluk, A. (2002) 'Boys to men', *New Scientist* 22 September: 16.

Mulhall, S. and Swift, A. (1992) *Liberals and Communitarians*, Oxford: Blackwell.

Muncie, J. and Sapsford, R. (1995) 'Issues in the study of "the Family"', in J. Muncie, M. Wetherell, R. Dallas and A. Cochrane (eds) *Understanding the Family*, London: Sage.

Murray, C. (1990) *The Emerging British Underclass*, London: IEA Health and Welfare Unit.

Nash, R. (2002) 'Sex and schooling: the sexual activity of young people and its implications for education', *Gender and Education* 14: 149–65.

National Curriculum Council (1990) *Curriculum Guidance 5: Health Education*, York: National Curriculum Council.

Nelson, J. B. (1988) *The Intimate Connection: Male Sexuality, Masculine Spirituality*, Philadelphia, PA: Westminster Press.

Newman, D. M. (1999) *Sociology of Families*, Thousand Oaks, CA: Pine Forge Press.

Ng, M. N. and Haeberle, E. J. (1997) *Sexual Behavior in Modern China: Report on the Nationwide Survey of 20,000 Men and Women by Liu, D., Ng, M. N., Zhou, L. P. and Haeberle, E. J. – English-Language Edition*, New York: Continuum.

Nicoll, A. and Hamers, F. F. (2002) 'Are trends in HIV, gonorrhoea, and syphilis worsening in western Europe?', *British Medical Journal* 324: 1324–7.

Noibi, D. (1993) 'An Islamic perspective', in R. Thomson (ed.) (1993) *Religion, Ethnicity and Sex Education: Exploring the Issues – A Resource for Teachers and Others Working with Young People*, London: National Children's Bureau.

Noibi, D. O. S. (1998) 'The Islamic concept of sex, sexuality and "sex education": a theological perspective', in M. J. Reiss and S. A. Mabud (eds) (1998) *Sex Education and Religion*, Cambridge: Islamic Academy.

Noller, P. (1996) 'What is this thing called love? Defining the love that supports marriage and family', *Personal Relationships* 3: 97–115.

Nussbaum, M. (1999) *Sex and Social Justice*, New York: Oxford University Press.

Office for Standards in Education (Ofsted) (2002) *Sex and Relationships HMI 433*, London: Ofsted. Available at www.ofsted.gov.uk

Oldham, M. (ed.) (1997) *Blackstone's Statutes on Family Law*, London: Blackstone.

Olson, D. H. and DeFrain, J. (1994) *Marriage and the Family: Diversity and Strengths*, Mountain View, CA: Mayfield.

Opie, I. and Opie, P. (1985) *The Singing Game*, Oxford: Oxford University Press.

Orenstein, P. (1995) *Schoolgirls: Young Women, Self-esteem and the Confidence Gap*, New York: Anchor.

Park, J. (1999) 'Emotional literacy: education for meaning', *International Journal of Children's Spirituality* 4: 19–28.

Parker, R. G. and Gagnon, J. H. (eds) (1995) *Conceiving Sexuality: Approaches to Sex Research in a Postmodern World*, New York: Routledge.

Pasko, L. (2002) 'Naked power: the practice of stripping as a confidence game', *Sexualities* 5: 49–66.

Passy, R. (2003) 'Children and family values: a critical appraisal of "family" in schools', unpublished PhD thesis, University of Plymouth.

Peck, M. S. (1985) *The Road Less Travelled*, London: Rider.

Peters, R. S. (1966) *Ethics and Education*, London: Allen and Unwin.

Petrovic, J. E. (1999) 'Moral democratic education and homosexuality: censoring morality', *Journal of Moral Education* 28: 201–9.

Petrovic, J. E. (2002) 'Promoting democracy and overcoming heterosexism: and never the twain shall meet?', *Sex Education* 2: 133–44.

Phasha, T. (2002) 'Child sexual abuse: its impact on school functioning', PhD thesis, University of Cambridge.

Phoenix, A. (1991) *Young Mothers?* Cambridge: Polity Press.

Pinsent, P. and Knight, B. (n.d.) [1997] *Teenage Girls and their Magazines*, London: Roehampton Institute.

Pope John Paul II (1993) *Veritatis Splendor: Encyclical Letter addressed by the Supreme Pontiff Pope John Paul II to all the Bishops of the Catholic Church regarding certain fundamental Questions of the Church's Moral Teaching*, London: Catholic Truth Society.

Porter, R. and Hall, L. (1995) *The Facts of Life: The Creation of Sexual Knowledge in Britain, 1650–1950*, New Haven, CT: Yale University Press.

Postman, N. (1983) *The Disappearance of Childhood*, London: W. H. Allen.

Potts, A. (2000) 'Coming, coming, gone: a feminist deconstruction of heterosexual orgasm', *Sexualities* 3: 55–76.

Prendergast, S. (1992) *Girls' Experience of Menstruation in School*, Cambridge: Health Promotion Research Trust.

Primoratz, I. (1999) *Ethics and Sex*, London: Routledge.

Qualifications and Curriculum Authority (QCA) (1999) *The National Curriculum: Handbook for Secondary Teachers in England*, London: Department for Education and Employment and QCA. Available at www.nc.uk.net

Qualifications and Curriculum Authority (QCA) (2000) *Personal, Social and Health Education and Citizenship at Key Stages 1 and 2*, London: QCA.

Raths, L. E., Harmin, M. and Simon, S. B. (1966) *Values and Teaching: Working with Values in the Classroom*, Columbus, OH: Charles E. Merrill.

Ray, C. (1999) 'Read all about it! Using children's books in sex and relationship education', *Sex Education Matters* 18: 9–11.

Ray, C. (2000) 'Saying it with puppets in sex and relationships education', *Sex Education Matters* 22: 6–7.

Ray, C. (2001) '"They did this really cool lesson . . ."': a guide to condom demonstrations', *Sex Education Matters* 24: 7–8.

Ray, C. (2002) 'Home page', *Sex Education Matters* 27: 2.

Ray, C. and Jolly, J. (2002) *Forum Factsheet: Sex and Relationships Education for Primary Age Children*, London: National Children's Bureau.

Ray, C. and Went, D. (1995) *Good Practice in Sex Education: A Sourcebook for Schools*, London: National Children's Bureau.

Reavey, P. and Gough, B. (2000) 'Dis/locating blame: survivors' constructions of self and sexual abuse', *Sexualities* 3: 325–46.

Red Rose Chain/Alpha Films (n.d.) *Four Carrier Bags and a Buggy*, Ipswich: Red Rose Chain.

Regan, P. C. and Berscheid, E. (1999) *Lust: What We Know about Human Sexual Desire*, Thousand Oaks, CA: Sage.

Reiss, M. (1990) 'Homosexuality: sense and sensibility', *Crucible* 29: 66–74.

Reiss, M. (1990 [1991]) 'Theological questions raised by current vocational training', *British Journal of Theological Education* 4(1): 27–38.

Reiss, M. (1993a) 'AIDS and syphilis: sexually transmitted diseases in history', *Hindsight* 3(3): 22–4.

Reiss, M. (1993b) 'What are the aims of school sex education?', *Cambridge Journal of Education* 23: 125–36.

Reiss, M. J. (1995) 'Conflicting philosophies of school sex education', *Journal of Moral Education* 24: 371–82.

Reiss, M. J. (1996) 'Food, smoking and sex: values in health education', in J. M. Halstead and M. J. Taylor (eds) *Values in Education and Education in Values*, London: Falmer Press.

Reiss, M. J. (ed.) (1997a) Special issue: Moral Values and Sex Education, *Journal of Moral Education* 26(3).

Reiss, M. J. (1997b) 'Teaching about homosexuality and heterosexuality', *Journal of Moral Education* 26: 343–52.

Reiss, M. J. (1998a) 'Christian views of sex and sex education', in M. J. Reiss and S. A. Mabud (eds) *Sex Education and Religion*, Cambridge: Islamic Academy.

Reiss, M. J. (1998b) 'The representation of human sexuality in some science textbooks for 14–16 year-olds', *Research in Science and Technological Education* 16: 137–49.

Reiss, M. J. (1999) 'How should we teach in schools about sexual orientation? A rejoinder to Petrovic', *Journal of Moral Education* 28: 211–14.

Reiss, M. J. (2001) 'Loves that have a quiet voice', *International Journal of Children's Spirituality* 6: 243–5.

Reiss, M. J. and Mabud, S. A. (eds) (1998) *Sex Education and Religion*, Cambridge: Islamic Academy.

Reiss, M. J. and Tunnicliffe, S. D. (2001) 'Students' understandings of human organs and organ systems', *Research in Science Education* 31: 383–99.

Rennison, L. (1999) *Angus, Thongs and Full-frontal Snogging: Confessions of Georgia Nicolson*, London: Piccadilly.

Richardson, D. (1996) *Theorising Heterosexuality: Telling it Straight*, Buckingham: Open University Press.

Riches, V. (1998) 'Shortcomings of present-day practice in school sex education', in M. J. Reiss and S. A. Mabud (eds) *Sex Education and Religion*, Cambridge: Islamic Academy.

Rivers, I. (1995) 'The victimization of gay teenagers in schools: homophobia in education', *Pastoral Care* 13: 35–41.

Rivers, I. (2001) 'The bullying of sexual minorities at school: its nature and long-term correlates', *Educational and Child Psychology* 18: 32–46.

Rogers, E. F. Jr (1999) *Sexuality and the Christian Body: Their Way into the Triune God*, Oxford: Blackwell.

Rogers, M. F. (1999) *Barbie Culture*, London: Sage.

Rogers, W. S. and Rogers, R. S. (1999) 'What is good and bad sex for children?' in M. King (ed.) *Moral Agendas for Children's Welfare*, London: Routledge.

Rout, U., Sixsmith, J. and Moore, M. (1996) 'Asian family life', in M. Moore, J. Sixsmith and K. Knowles (eds) *Children's Reflection on Family Life*, London: Falmer Press.

Rowe, D. and Newton, J. (eds) (1994) *You, Me, Us! Social and Moral Responsibility for Primary Schools*, London: Citizenship Foundation.

Royal College of Obstetricians and Gynaecologists (RCOG) (1991) *Report of the RCOG Working Party on Unplanned Pregnancy*, London: RCOG.

Ruse, M. (1988) *Homosexuality: A Philosophical Inquiry*, Oxford: Basil Blackwell.

Russell, D. E. H. (1995) *Incestuous Abuse: Its Long-term Effects*, Pretoria: Human Sciences Research Council.

Salisbury, J. and Jackson, D. (1996) *Challenging Macho Values: Practical Ways of Working with Adolescent Boys*, London: Falmer Press.

Sanders, P. and Swinden, L. (1990) *Knowing Me, Knowing You: Strategies for Sex Education in the Primary School*, Wisbech: LDA.

Sarwar, G. (1989) *Sex Education: The Muslim Perspective*, London: Muslim Educational Trust.

Saul, R. (1999) 'Teen pregnancy: progress meet politics', *The Guttmacher Report on Public Policy* 2(3): 6–9.

Schmitt, A. and Sofer, J. (eds) (1992) *Sexuality and Eroticism among Males in Moslem Societies*, New York: Harrington Park Press.

Scholer, A-M. (2002) 'Sexuality in the science classroom: one teacher's methods in a college biology course', *Sex Education* 2: 75–86.

Scott, L. with Hood, J. and Jenks, J. (1994) *Sexwise II: Sex Education in Schools*, London: Borough of Hammersmith and Fulham.

Scottish Executive (1999) *Health Promotion: Issue for Councils and Schools – A Report by HM Inspectors of Schools*, Edinburgh: HM Inspectors of Schools. Available at www.scotland.gov.uk

Scroggs, R. (1983) *The New Testament and Homosexuality: Contextual Background for Contemporary Debate*, Philadelphia, PA: Fortress Press.

Scruton, R. (1986) *Sexual Desire: A Philosophical Investigation*, London: Weidenfeld and Nicolson.

Secretary of State for Health (1992) *The Health of the Nation: A Strategy for Health in England*, London: HMSO.

Segal, L. (1990) *Slow Motion: Changing Masculinities, Changing Men*, London: Virago.

Selman, P. and Glendinning, C. (1996) 'Teenage pregnancy: do social policies make a difference?', in J. Brannen and M. O'Brien (eds) *Children in Families: Research and Policy*, London: Falmer Press.

Sex Education Forum (1992) *A Framework for School Sex Education*, London: National Children's Bureau.

Sex Education Forum (1996) *Forum Factsheet 8: Guidelines on the Effective Use of Outside Visitors in School Sex Education*, London: National Children's Bureau.

Sex Education Forum (2001) *Forum Factsheet 24: PSHE and Citizenship – Ensuring Effective Sex and Relationships Education*, London: National Children's Bureau.

Shah-Kazei, S. N. (2001) *Untying the Knot: Muslim Women, Divorce and the Shariah*, London: Nuffield Foundation.

Shalit, W. (1999) *A Return to Modesty: Discovering the Lost Virtue*, New York: The Free Press.

Shapiro, B. Y. (2001) 'School-based sex education in Russia: the current reality and prospects', *Sex Education* 1: 87–96.

Sharpe, S. (2001) *More than Just a Piece of Paper? Young People's Views on Marriage and Relationships*, London: National Children's Bureau.

Sharpe, S. (2002) '"It's just really hard to come to terms with": young people's views on homosexuality', *Sex Education* 2: 263–77.

Shaver, J. P. and Strong, W. (1976) *Facing Value Decisions: Rationale-building for Teachers*, Belmont, CA: Wadsworth.

Shaver, P. R., Morgan, H. J. and Wu, S. (1996) 'Is love a "basic" emotion?', *Personal Relationships* 3: 81–96.

Sheldon, S. and Wilkinson, S. (1998) 'Female genital mutilation and cosmetic surgery: regulating non-therapeutic body modification', *Bioethics* 12: 263–85.

Shumba, A. (2002) '"Who guards the guards in schools?" A study of reported cases of child abuse by teachers in Zimbabwean secondary schools', *Sex Education* 1: 77–86.

Siegel, H. (1988) *Educating Reason: Rationality, Critical Thinking and Education*, London: Routledge.

Silva, E. B. and Smart, C. (eds) (1999) *The New Family?* London: Sage.

Singer, P. (1993) *Practical Ethics*, 2nd edn, Cambridge: Cambridge University Press.

Singh, B. R. (1989) 'Neutrality and commitment in teaching moral and social issues in a multicultural society', *Educational Review* 41: 227–42.

Sketchley, J. (1986) *Teaching AIDS: Educational Materials about AIDS for School Teachers*, London: BLAT Centre for Health and Medical Education.

Smart, N. (1989) *The World's Religions: Old Traditions and Modern Transformations*, Cambridge: Cambridge University Press.

Smith, C. (2002) 'Shiny chests and heaving G-strings: a night out with the Chippendales', *Sexualities* 5: 67–89.

Smith, G. (1995) *The Protectors' Handbook: Reducing the Risk of Child Sexual Abuse and Helping Children Recover*, London: Women's Press.

Social Exclusion Unit (1999) *Teenage Pregnancy*, London: The Stationery Office.

Solomon, R. C. ([1988] 1995) 'The virtue of (erotic) love', in R. M. Stewart (ed.) *Philosophical Perspectives on Sex and Love*, New York: Oxford University Press.

Spencer, L., Faulkner, A. and Keegan, J. (1988) *Talking about Sex: Asking the Public about Sexual Behaviour and Attitudes*, London: Health Education Authority.

Spong, J. S. (1988) *Living in Sin? A Bishop Rethinks Human Sexuality*, San Francisco, CA: Harper and Row.

Stafford, J. M. (1988) 'In defence of gay lessons', *Journal of Moral Education* 17: 11–20.

Steiner, C. and Paul, P. (1997) *Achieving Emotional Literacy*, London: Bloomsbury.

Sternberg, R. (1996) 'Love stories', *Personal Relationships* 3: 59–79.

Sternberg, R. J. and Barnes, M. L. (eds) (1988) *The Psychology of Love*, Newhaven, CT: Yale University Press.

Stewart, R. M. (ed.) (1995) *Philosophical Perspectives on Sex and Love*, New York: Oxford University Press.

Stoller, R. J. ([1979] 1986) *Sexual Excitement: Dynamics of Erotic Life*, London: Karnac.

Stone, C. M. (1990) 'Autonomy, emotions and desires: some problems concerning R. F. Dearden's account of autonomy', *Journal of Philosophy of Education* 24: 271–83.

Stone, N. and Ingham, R. (1998) *Exploration of the Factors that Affect the Delivery of Sex and Sexuality Education and Support in Schools: Final Report*, Southampton: Centre for Sexual Health Research, Faculty of Social Sciences, University of Southampton.

Stones, R. ([1989] 1997) *Where Babies Come From*, London: Puffin.

Stradling, R., Noctor, M. and Baines, B. (eds) (1984) *Teaching Controversial Issues*, London: Edward Arnold.

Strange, V., Forrest, S., Oakley, A. and the RIPPLE study team (in press) 'Mixed or single sex sex education: how would young people like their sex education and why?', *Gender and Education*.

Straughan, R. (1988) *Can We Teach Children to be Good? Basic Issues in Moral, Personal and Social Education*, new edn, Milton Keynes: Open University Press.

Strong, B., DeVault, C. and Sayad, B. W. (1996) *Core Concepts in Human Sexuality*, Mountain View, CA: Mayfield.

Surrey Inspectorate (1987) *Curriculum Guidelines: Sex Education – Primary and Secondary*, Woking: Surrey County Council.

Szirom, T. (1988) *Teaching Gender? Sex Education and Sexual Stereotyping*, London: Allen and Unwin.

Tabberer, S., Hall, C., Prendergast, S. and Webster, A. (2000) *Teenage Pregnancy and Choice: Abortion or Motherhood: Influences on the Decision*, York: Joseph Rowntree Foundation.

Thatcher, A. (1993) *Liberating Sex: A Christian Sexual Theology*, London: SPCK.

Thatcher, A. (2001) 'Sex education "after Modernity"', *International Journal of Children's Spirituality* 6: 233–41.

Thatcher, A. (2002) *Living Together and Christian Ethics*, Cambridge: Cambridge University Press.

Thomson, R. (ed.) (1993) *Religion, Ethnicity and Sex Education: Exploring the Issues – A Resource for Teachers and Others Working with Young People*, London: National Children's Bureau.

Thomson, R. (1997) 'Diversity, values and social change: renegotiating a consensus on sex education', *Journal of Moral Education* 26: 257–71.

Thomson, R. and Scott, S. (1991) *Learning about Sex: Young Women and the Social Construction of Sexual Identity*, London: Tufnell Press.

Townend, A. (1985) *Assertion Training: A Handbook for those Involved in Training*, London: Family Planning Education Unit.

Trenchard, L. and Warren, H. (1984) *Something to Tell You*, London: Gay Teenagers' Group.

Tunnicliffe, S. D. (1983) *Guide to Running a Birth Workshop: Content, Materials, Different Approaches*, London: National Childbirth Trust.

Tunnicliffe, S. D. (2000) 'Boys and girls asking questions about pregnancy and birth in primary school', paper presented at British Educational Research Association Conference, Cardiff, 7–10 September. Available at www.leeds.ac.uk/educol

UNICEF (2001) 'A league table of teenage births in rich nations', *Innocenti Report Card* 3, Florence: Innocenti Research Centre. Available at www.unicef-icdc.org

Unks, G. (ed.) (1995) *The Gay Teen: Educational Practice and Theory for Lesbian, Gay, and Bisexual Adolescents*, New York: Routledge.

Ure, J. (1999) *Just Sixteen*, London: Orchard.

Valentine, G. (1998) '"Sticks and stones may break my bones": a personal geography of harassment', *Antipode* 30: 305–32.

van den Berghe, P. (1979) *Human Family Systems*, New York: Elsevier.

Vasey, M. (1995) *Strangers and Friends: A New Exploration of Homosexuality and the Bible*, London: Hodder and Stoughton.

Vickerman, S. (1992) *Christianity and Homosexuality: A Resource for Students*, London: Lesbian and Gay Christian Movement.

Ward, I. M. (1995) 'Talking about sex: common themes about sexuality in the prime-time television programs children and adolescents view most', *Journal of Youth and Adolescence* 24: 595–615.

Warnock, M. (1979) *Education: The Way Ahead*, Oxford: Blackwell.

Warnock, M. (1996) 'Moral values', in J. M. Halstead and M. J. Taylor (eds) *Values in Education and Education in Values*, London: Falmer Press.

Warwick, I. and Douglas, N. (n.d.) *A Best Practice Guide to Prevent Homophobic Bullying in Secondary Schools*, London: Citizenship 21.

Weatherill, R. (2000) 'The seduction of therapy', *British Journal of Psychotherapy* 16: 263–73.

Webb, R. and Vulliamy, G. (2001) 'The primary teacher's role in child protection', *British Educational Research Journal* 27: 59–77.

Webster, A. R. (1995) *Found Wanting: Women, Christianity and Sexuality*, London: Cassell.

Weeks, J. (1995) *Invented Moralities: Sexual Values in an Age of Uncertainty*, Cambridge: Polity Press.

Welbourne-Moglia, A. and Moglia, R. J. (1989) 'Sexuality education in the United States: what it is; what it is meant to be', *Theory into Practice* 28: 159–64.

Wellings, K., Wadsworth, J., Johnson, A. M., Field, J., Whitaker, L. and Field, B. (1995) 'Provision of sex education and early sexual experience: the relation examined', *British Medical Journal* 311: 417–20.

Wellings, K., Nanchahal, K., Macdowall, W., McManus, S., Erens, B., Mercer, C. H., Johnson, A. M., Copas, A. J., Korovessis, C., Fenton, K. A. and Field, J. (2001) 'Sexual behaviour in Britain: early heterosexual experience', *Lancet* 358: 1843–50.

Welwood, J. (1985) 'Dancing on the razor's edge', in J. Welwood (ed.) *Challenge of the Heart: Love, Sex and Intimacy in Changing Times*, Boston, MA: Shambhala.

Went, D. (1985) *Sex Education: Some Guidelines for Teachers*, London: Bell and Hyman.

Westphal, S. P. (2002) 'Lost innocence', *New Scientist* 6 April: 6–7.

Whelan, R. (1995) *Teaching Sex in Schools: Does It Work?* Oxford: Family Education Trust.

Whinchup, P. H., Gilg, J. A., Odoki, K., Taylor, S. J. C. and Cook, D. G. (2001) 'Age of menarche in contemporary British teenagers: survey of girls born between 1982 and 1986', *British Medical Journal* 322: 1095–6.

White, C. (1994) 'Tackling the sex education class barrier', *Telegraph and Argus* 14 April: 32.

White, J. (1990) *Education and the Good Life: Beyond the National Curriculum*, London: Kogan Page.

White, M. (n.d.) [1994] *Children and Contraception – A Time to Change? A Critical Appraisal of Government Policy on Teenage Sexual Activity*, London: Order of Christian Unity.

White, M. (1998) *The Safe Sex Hoax*, London: Family Welfare Project.

White, P. (1991) 'Parents' rights, homosexuality and education', *British Journal of Educational Studies* 39: 398–408.

White, R. (2001) *Love's Philosophy*, Lanham, MD: Rowman and Littlefield.

Whitehead, B. D. (1994) 'The failure of sex education', *Atlantic Monthly* October: 55–80.

Whitehead, B. D., Wilcox, B. and Rostosky, S. S. (2001) *Keeping the Faith: The Role of Religion and Faith Communities in Teen Pregnancy Prevention*, Washington, DC: National Campaign to Prevent Teen Pregnancy.

Whitney, B. (1996) *Child Protection for Teachers and Schools: A Guide to Good Practice*, London: Kogan Page.

Whyld, J. (1986) *Anti-sexist Teaching with Boys*, Caistor, Lincs: Whyld Publishing Co-op.

Whyld, J., Pickersgill, D. and Jackson, D. (eds) (1990) *Anti-sexist Work with Boys and Young Men*, Caistor, Lincs: Whyld Publishing Co-op.

Wight, D., Raab, G. M., Henderson, M., Abraham, C., Buston, K., Hart, G. and Scott, S. (2002) 'Limits of teacher delivered sex education: interim behavioural outcomes from randomised trial', *British Medical Journal* 324: 1430–3.

Williams, T., Roberts, J. and Hyde, H. (1990) *Exploring Health Education: Material for Teacher Education*, London: Macmillan.

Wilson, J. (1965) *Logic and Sexual Morality*, Harmondsworth: Penguin.

Wilson, J. (1990) *A New Introduction to Moral Education*, London: Cassell.

Wilson, J. (1995) *Love between Equals*, London: Macmillan.

Wilson, J. (in press) 'Can sex education be practical?', *Sex Education*.

Wolf, N. (1997) *Promiscuities: A Secret History of Female Desire*, London: Chatto and Windus.

Wolpe, A-M. (1987) 'Sex in schools: back to the future', *Feminist Review* 27: 37–47.

Wonnacott, J. (1995) *Protecting Children in School: A Handbook for Delivering Child Protection Training in Schools*, London: National Children's Bureau.

Woodcock, A., Stenner, K. and Ingram, R. (1992) '"All these contraceptives and videos and that . . .": young people talking about school sex education', *Health Education Research* 7: 517–31.

Working Party of the Board for Social Responsibility (1995) *Something to Celebrate: Valuing Families in Church and Society*, London: Church House Publishing.

Wringe, C. (1994) 'Family values and the value of the family', *Journal of Philosophy of Education* 28: 77–88.

Zirkel, P. A. (1996) 'Hot, sexy – and safer?', *Phi Delta Kappan* 78(1): 93–4.

Index

Page numbers for illustrations *in italics*